The Cow in the Doorway

GINO B. BARDI

me believe that if I quit he would kill me. Without my dear friend David, this would be just one more story I pull out at cocktail parties just before people's eyes glaze over and they look at their watches.

Claudia Handler was the first to see the completed draft. She is one of the most astute, perceptive and generous people an individual can be lucky enough to know. I got lucky in 1967; she sat across from me in my high school Latin class. She became a poet, writer, musician, songwriter, and counselor. After reading *The Cow in the Doorway*, cover to cover , she gave me 300 pages of question marks, stars, red X's, big circles and cryptic notes, like 'WTF??' That guided me through draft number two...

Which landed in the lap of Kit Duncan, an incredibly well-read and generous editor, who, over a period of three weeks revealed wonderful truths about it that convinced me that I had to see the project to the end. At least I think they were truths. They were, weren't they? Kit? Kit?

Draft three (or was it six?) received the attention of two friends who are far more detail oriented than I am, and have brains that work differently from mine. Neither had the time to read it, but somehow, they did. Mimi Ansbro, a Cornell alumna from that vintage, pointed out inconsistencies that she could remember... then, to my horror, she *researched* even more, finding so many flaws in details that I jumped into action by actively ignoring most of them. I hope no one will notice.

My good friend Peter Kassan, a novelist and software designer, showed me just how unreliable and marginally useful spell-and-grammar-checking programs are. If people still used red pencils, I'd owe him a few boxes. I find it astonishing that the same mind that can proofread at that level can also create plot and characters. My friends Bill Wilson, Ken Powell, Eileen Parlow and Jean Gogolin pitched in to chase down and slay the sneakiest typos.

My lovely wife, Pat Donohoo, was incredibly helpful to me by leaving me alone. She has not actually read this book, although I have made it available to her, putting it under her pillow, hiding her toothbrush on page twenty-five and in general dropping little hints, like "PLEASE, PLEASE read my book!" which I tape to a five dollar bill and hang from her mirror. She says she knows all the stories; that she was there for them. She is wrong, of course. I made most of it up, as I said. Now that I know she won't read it, I can be much more graphic— and interesting—when I write the sequel.

I owe a debt of gratitude to all the members of my writing group, who, nearly every week from May 2014 through August of 2015 were subjected to (some say flogged by) a dramatic reading as the story unfolded. Many of their comments helped steer the direction the plot took. Unpopular characters met their demise before the final draft. Popular characters got more lines and had to get their union cards. We had a spirited disagreement (see *Tarpon Fiction Writers Vs. G. Bardi, Author*) regarding the title *The Cow in the Doorway*, which I won by a decision (my own).

This is my first full-length novel, and I am glad it is completed. As much as I like the protagonist Tony Vitelli, I fear that the other guy, Gino Bardi, has had adventures I might have missed in the last year or so. If I have appeared to be in a fog or otherwise inattentive, like, maybe I have not recognized you as a close friend or family member, please forgive me.

Chapter 1

My father's finger rapped the letter in front of me, right above the drawing of a clock tower and the words *Cornell University*. "Sign it. Tony. What are you waiting for? For God's sake, *you were held back in first grade!* Now they want to give you a seat in the Class of 1972! At an *Ivy League school!* What's to think about?"

He reminded me at least once a week that I had to repeat first frigging grade. I guess that's something you never outgrow. I knew that arguing with Lou—everyone but me called him Lou—was a waste of time. He only called me Tony when he was getting pissed off. If things were good, I was 'son' or even 'Sarge.' I guess he missed the army. When he inspected my room every Saturday morning I had to snap to attention and salute. That was fun, when I was eight. But not at nineteen! My mom usually sided with me. But she always caved as soon as she felt my dad's steel resolve.

Cornell was about the last place I wanted to go, for several reasons. Each one, all by itself, would be enough to set him off. So I lied to him.

"But, Dad, Cornell is so expensive." This was Tony-speak for "I'll have to work too hard."

"I'll find the money," he said, which, of course, meant, "You'll get a job."

"It's so far away."

"It's closer than Plattsburgh. You were all set to go there. What's the difference?"

"Plattsburgh has a great English department," I replied, which we both understood to mean "Plattsburgh is easy."

"The only reason why you like Plattsburgh is because it's the biggest party school in New York State. Forget it. Why the hell do you want to be an English major, anyway? How can you make a living with a degree in English? Or do you think you're going to support yourself playing poker?" I gave my mom the puppy dog's eyes.

"What about Kurt Vonnegut, Lou? I think he's doing pretty well for himself. He went to Cornell."

I nodded. As if I had another "Cat's Cradle" welling up within me, ready to burst out on the page. Maybe not... "Also," I said, "you can make a lot of money playing poker."

"Yeah, maybe," said my dad. "But you're a terrible poker player, Tony. Even your mother can beat you."

What? I turned to look at my mom. She looked down at the table. "That's true," she said quietly. "I always let you win."

My dad changed the subject. "One thing is for sure: Cornell has the most beautiful campus in the state. Maybe the whole country."

No argument there. I had toured seven colleges. I had been to Ithaca. I had seen the famous clock tower, heard the chimes, hiked the trails through the gorges. I had walked the suspension bridge high over a rushing waterfall. I had sampled coffee with cinnamon and whipped cream in dark coffee houses where aspiring poets wailed and moaned. It was, absolutely, the best school I had seen. But...

"Is it the girls?" asked my dad. "You weren't impressed, were you? Yeah, I saw them too. They all look like they spend every night studying and eating donuts, right?"

"The place is, like, three quarters guys."

"That's because a girl needs to be twice as smart as a boy to get into that school," said my mom. "But that's changing. By the time you graduate, there will be more girls than boys. You watch."

By the time I graduate? That's the problem right there. What if I didn't? I had one card left to play. *The truth* was always a dangerous, last chance move.

"What if I can't do the work?" The fear in my voice was genuine. "What if I flunk out? I'll get drafted in a heartbeat. Did you see the casualties in Vietnam now? They'll send me home in a box, Dad. Don't you think maybe an easier school would be—"

"What's the matter, crybaby? Afraid of a challenge? Afraid of being left back again? That's the best reason in the world to go to a tough college. Maybe you'll knuckle down and work for once in your life. Maybe you'll get some ambition and learn to stand up for yourself. Maybe you'll grow some *cogliones*. Some balls."

"I know what cogliones are, Dad."

"Well, you could do with a pair, son. I'm just saying."

He called me "son." That meant that as far as he was concerned the discussion was closed. I had lost.

My mom tried to make me feel better. "They wouldn't have accepted you if they thought you couldn't do the work, Tony." She almost sounded like she meant it. "Don't worry so much. You'll be fine. And if you do meet a girl, at least she'll be smart! Maybe she'll help you with your French homework!"

My old man tapped the paper again. "Sign it. Get on with your life."

"You'll be fine, Tony," my mom said again.

That made three times. Who was she trying to convince?

It seemed like forever before I got my room assignment. In the intervening weeks I was introduced by my parents to everyone—friends, family and complete strangers—as "Our son, the Cornellian," as if I wore a cap and gown and clutched a rolled-up diploma. "I got in," I said under my breath. "I haven't gotten out." No matter. There was no turning back. It didn't matter what I wanted. Hell, it was only my life. Why should I get a vote?

I sat down at the kitchen table and dumped the envelope from the Housing Department. My roommate's name was Clarence Carter, from South Michigan Avenue in Chicago. "Unfortunately," the letter said, "because of an unusually large incoming class, you will be sharing a small single in one of the university's historic buildings. Space will be extremely limited."

My father dug into the letter as soon as he returned that evening. His face told me that something had gone horribly wrong. His eyebrows rose as he read the letter aloud. "South Michigan Avenue, Chicago? He's a ghetto—" He stopped abruptly.

"Lou!" My mother jumped all over him. I thought she might smack him. It would have been a big first for her. I had no idea what this was about.

3

"What's wrong with South Michigan Avenue?" I asked. How could my father know anything about anybody who lived in Chicago? We lived on Long Island, a thousand miles away.

"That street is the toughest part of town. It's the ghetto. One big slum. The kids there are all in gangs. Your roommate is going to be a tough black kid." And I was a very untough, short white kid. I got that…Clang! I was out of my corner. Round two had started.

"You don't know that. Anyway, so what?" I sounded defiant, arrogant, even passionate about something I had barely thought about. "Why should a white kid from Long Island get to go to a good school but not a black kid from Chicago?"

"Think, Tony." His expression suggested that if he didn't tell me to think, I would simply forget to do it. "He's a ghetto kid. Don't you get it? An angry kid with a chip on his shoulder, with something to prove." My father leaned into it, his breath coming hard, surprising the hell out of me. I had always thought his occasional racist comments were just a product of his upbringing, his military service, his boyhood on the streets of Manhattan. He had always been careful about that stuff around my sister and me.

"I thought you had to be smart to get into that school," I said in my best snot-nosed way. "Don't smart black kids deserve to go to college?"

His face turned red. I must have said something stupid. "You don't get it. The goddamned government is making the colleges accept minorities. They call it 'affirmative action.' They accept any dumb-ass if his skin is dark while the white kids like you have to work their butt off to get in. Who do you think pays for that?"

"But," I began, with no idea what to say next.

"The hell with that. You're going to ask for a different roommate."

"I'm the guy who's going to college, Dad, not you. I get a say in this. I'll take what they give me. I haven't even met him yet. I'm not starting college already hating people I don't know." I sounded pompous and arrogant. Where did this come from all of a sudden? My usual strategy was to choose whichever path had the fewest obstacles. I had a real talent for sliding through my life the easiest way possible. Was I going to make a stand for this, for a kid I had never met, in a place I didn't want to be? "You sound like a racist, Dad."

He answered me slowly. "I am not a racist. Don't be such a naïve idiot. This is your *life* we're talking about."

"You're right. It *is* my life. I'll make my own decisions. *If you don't mind.*"

"Fine. Have it your way. But don't come crawling to me when you see what a goddamned mistake you just made."

I looked at my mother. She would support me, she would agree that this was the only choice. But she looked away. I realized I had no idea what I was in for. What kind of hell was South Michigan Avenue, Chicago?

It was mid-September when my dad loaded my small pile of luggage into the station wagon. My precious twelve-string guitar and my 1938 Underwood typewriter—tools of the trade for an English major and aspiring folksinger—were piled in the back along with a box of school supplies that my mom had bought for, apparently, a seventh grader. Inside a wooden cigar box secured with rubber bands were four decks of cards and two stacks each of red, blue, and black poker chips. All my clothes fit easily in my dad's green duffel bag stenciled *Louis Vitelli, U.S. Army*. I sat quietly in the back seat, thinking—without even being told to—about what waited for me at the end of the five hour drive from the south shore of Long Island to the middle of upstate New York.

I wasn't worried. Who calls their kid "Clarence" anyway? I had never met a kid with that name. I hoped he had an edgy-sounding nickname, like Spike or Rico. I just couldn't imagine me ever saying something like, "This is my bro, Clarence."

"What are you giggling at?" asked my mom as Lou pointed the wagon north on Highway 17.

"Nothing," I said as I smiled at the image in my mind of some guy named Clarence Carter. He would probably be a bookworm or a nerd, with thick glasses that made his eyes look like blurry marbles, his hair in cornrows, and maybe even braces on his teeth.

Chapter 2

Clarence Carter, my new roommate, had already moved in and unpacked by the time we arrived. The bottom bunk, the large desk, and the unbroken chair had been claimed as clearly as if he had planted a flag. The tiny room was barely ten feet on a side, stuffed with a bunk bed and two desks and dressers. The bare floor was cold stone terrazzo, the walls were ancient plaster the color of old newspaper. A single window let in a pale light through glass too high to be washed by anything other than the bleak Ithaca weather.

Clarence didn't make an appearance until after my parents had left. The Clarence of my imagination—the guy with the thick glasses and the cornrows—it wasn't him.

He didn't look anything like that. Compared to me, Clarence was a giant, well over six feet tall, slender and wiry. His skin was black, not brown, and his hair was a dense mat, closely cropped, just long enough to support the thick plastic comb that stuck out of the back like the feather on an Indian brave. The only similarity between Clarence Carter and my imaginary Clarence was the glasses. His had black frames that made him look like a journalist or an angry scholar. He was organized, meticulous and disciplined.

He was also completely terrifying.

"Hi, Clarence," I said. "I'm Tony."

"Pleased to meet you," came the reply, in a voice as flat as his smile

6

was fake. I had to tilt my head back to look him in the eye. I thrust my hand out to shake his in a manly grip like my dad had taught me. His hand slid past mine, barely touching mine. I disliked him instantly. His expression would have been right at home on a robot that distrusted humans and was secretly planning to revolt and rule the world. The idea that I had once imagined introducing him as "This is my bro, Clarence," soon became ridiculous.

"I'm going to be an English major," I said. "What are you studying?" He didn't reply. He continued to unpack his suitcase and milk crates. He didn't have much stuff other than a clothes suitcase. No stereo or sports equipment. Just a small electric typewriter and books. Tons of books. "Clarence?" I asked again.

"Government." That was it for the small talk. I might be in for a long, and quiet, semester.

I had at least three times as much stuff as my roommate and it was time to unpack. Where should I put it? I looked around the room, it was only a little bigger than a prison cell and about as attractive. The few items of furniture that were left for me could have been hand-me-downs from kids who fought in the First World War. The only place to keep my expensive guitar was on my bunk. Each night I'd have to put it on my desk, and each morning I'd put it back on my bed. Clarence would probably put his foot through the case and crush the thing if I left it out during the day. He probably would not even notice. I should have played the harmonica.

Trying to sleep that first night made me appreciate my old bedroom. The narrow top bunk posed a challenge just to get into it. I had to stand on my chair, then step on my desk. The mattress was lumpy and pushed up against the wall. I couldn't find a position that felt comfortable without dangling my arm over the side like a freshly caught fish, still on the hook. I squirmed and twisted so much that Clarence banged on the bottom of my bunk.

"Cut that crap out," he growled. "I'm trying to sleep."

He can talk, I thought. *We'll take this one day at a time.*

I didn't spend a lot of time in the room. The room was so small. The room was hot. I needed to work in the library… I had dozens of excuses. Each time I returned, Clarence made me feel like an unwelcome guest, who had personally done something terrible to him or his family.

I had never met anyone like him. I had a few black friends in high school, but they were so popular I doubt they would even remember me. The Long Island neighborhood where I lived was nearly all white and the few black kids were all high school heroes. The star basketball player, the football quarterback, the lead saxophone in the dance band—kids like that. They were friendly and hip and had an easy style that made us white kids envious. The black kids were…they were cool. There were three black kids in my high school graduating class of four hundred.

One night Clarence and I worked quietly at our desks. By 'quietly' I mean in complete silence. Ours was the quietest room in the dorm, maybe the whole college. We weren't roommates, we were 'tomb mates' and I was tired of it. I sat at my desk and stared at him. Eventually he looked up and said one word. "What?"

"It's not my fault," I said.

"What's not your fault?" he asked, but the way he said it sounded a lot like "Oh yes it is, and you know it."

"It's not my fault. *I* didn't own slaves."

He took off his glasses and studied me as if searching for the exact right words. Finally he nodded. "Good." He put his glasses back on and went back to his reading.

"I didn't do anything to you. Why are you treating me like this?"

"Please elucidate," he said. "Like what, exactly?"

"Why won't you talk to me?"

"I am talking to you right now. What is the problem?"

"*You* are the problem," I said.

"Fine," he said. "I am the problem. I'm going back to work now. I am glad we were able to clear the air of this pressing issue." And that was pretty much the beginning, middle and end of our conversation. I had a space alien for a roommate. A mysterious creature no more like me than a giant squid or a Tasmanian devil. Maybe my dad was right. Maybe I had made a huge mistake and I had sentenced myself to a year of hard time.

But my father was wrong about one thing. Clarence wasn't a tough kid in a gang. He didn't wear gang colors or tattoos or even a ball cap. Instead, every day, he wore clean khaki pants, a white-button down shirt and a narrow black tie—a real one, not a clip on. Each morning he would set up his ironing board and bring the iron out of hiding and press his slacks and shirt until the creases were sharp as the blade on a stiletto. The Mexican woman who brought us new sheets every week could have reported him for the contraband electric iron, but I think she was scared of him. I know I was.

His desk had carefully stacked file folders full of leaflets from political groups like the Afro American League and Students for Peace and other radical organizations. If I had brought that crap home to my dad, he would have ranted for hours about the 'crazy, commie pinko faggot revolutionaries.' My own desk was a rat's nest of books, papers, and Cliffs Notes. Freshman English majors got socked with a reading list that would have killed Evelyn Wood. I couldn't even see the top of my desk after the third day of classes.

One morning, Clarence finished his fifty one-handed pushups. Instead of dressing in slacks, white shirt and black tie, he unwrapped a brand new shirt, one with a deep V neck. It went nearly to his knees and was so brightly colored it was tough to look at it at six-thirty in the morning when he woke me up with his grunting.

"What the hell is that?" I groaned from under my pile of blankets.

"A dashiki," he said with no further explanation. Along with loose, baggy jeans, sandals, and mirrored aviator sunglasses, Clarence now resembled an African prince. The only part of his wardrobe that remained the same was the outrageous comb which stayed firmly jammed into the back of his head like a weapon he planned to use in a fight.

Chapter 3

I soon realized my place on campus, and in the scheme of college life: the bottom of the hill, and not because of the location of the freshman dorm. I was just a run-of-the-mill first year student, a dime-a-dozen English major, which I had wrongly assumed would be a piece of cake. *Hell,* I reasoned, *I could already speak English, so how hard could it be?* Biology 101, Psych 101, Government 101...all my courses were entry level 101s. I was going to "college for beginners."

By the time I crawled out of bed and carefully lowered myself to the floor, Clarence had been gone at least an hour. My first class started at eight, and incredibly, it was pool. Not pool as in eight ball, but pool as in swimming. I had learned to swim when I was four years old, but I had to take swimming lessons all over again. Three times a week I trudged to the aquatic center to swim—naked!—with a bunch of other guys. With just fifteen minutes to get dressed and hustle across campus to my second period class, I had no time to dry my hair. When the weather turned cold, which happened almost immediately, my hair had frozen solid by the time I got to Bailey Hall for my Psych 101 lecture, along with a thousand other kids. When my hair melted, I left a trail of water everywhere I went, like an undiscovered missing link, a species that was half human and half fish.

I wasn't particularly good at anything and I didn't have any idea what I wanted to study. I didn't want to be there. I didn't want a roommate and I didn't know what I wanted to be when I grew up. There was just one thing that I absolutely knew I wanted, and in the first few weeks at Cornell it looked to be a long shot: A girlfriend.

The entry-level course that I really needed, Co-eds 101, wasn't offered. I had barely had a conversation with a girl since I had arrived. There weren't too many of them on campus, and none seemed to have time for anything other than studying. The girls lived on one side of the campus, the guys on the other, a half mile away. The best opportunity to meet a girl outside of class was during dinner, when we were all crowded into the big dining halls.

One cold Thursday night, in late October, I grabbed my guitar and parka and headed up the hill to the Straight cafeteria. It was "Ithacating" outside, which is what we called the ever-present sleet and rain combination which covered everything in frost. It instantly melted and drenched me with cold water when I entered the building.

I balanced my tray with two hot dogs, fried cheese sticks, and tater tots with one hand while I carried the guitar case in the other. I sat down and leaned the case against the big oak table. Although it had not yet happened, maybe a girl, carrying a tray of yogurt and bean sprouts would sit at the table, and make the mistake of asking me, "Do you play?"

There was an unwritten rule about who sat where in the dining hall. The black kids had their own tables at the far end of the room. No one made them do this. The room was as segregated as if the Ku Klux Klan had drawn up the seating arrangements. I had seen Clarence at those tables before. He sat there tonight, right in the middle, laughing and doing some kind of secret handshake with his friends.

So it's just me he doesn't talk to. I stood up, working up the nerve to wander over there and sit down and say hi, like we were best buddies, but I stopped myself. Why bother? We had seen each other. He had made no attempt to invite me to his table. I ate, alone, in silence. I was getting used to that.

I grabbed the guitar and carried the tray to the dish window. Then I was off. There was only one place I wanted to be.

Every kid on campus who sang or played an instrument that you could carry around knew about it. The entrance to Anabel Taylor Hall had marble floors and walls with a vaulted ceiling like a cathedral. We called it the Echo Chamber. The room had a rich, sweet reverberation, which made lousy singers and players—people like me—sound good enough to listen to.

At the end of the long hallway was a coffeehouse called The Commons, and just outside its door was the office of Father Dan, a Catholic priest who was rumored to be on the FBI's Most Wanted list for sabotaging draft records. Father Dan was legendary. Kids claimed to have met him or even worked for him. To me, he was just one more big Cornell mystery, it had nothing to do with me. All I wanted was to sit in the Echo Chamber, play my guitar, and hope a lonely single girl would wander in. Maybe tonight would be the night. Maybe I'd finally get lucky.

The huge door to the Echo Chamber was made of solid oak. It was more like the entrance to an ancient castle than the door to a university building. A stone monument surrounded by steps provided a dry place to sit and play. I knocked the slush off my boots, settled down on the marble steps, and unsnapped the guitar case. I listened to the long decay of the *clack*. Even that sounded good. The room probably wouldn't be too busy on a Thursday night, not like Friday and Saturday when it would quickly fill with kids carrying guitars and banjos.

This education thing was not working out. The lousy weather, loneliness, crappy food and cranky roommate were ganging up on me. My *Blonde on Blonde* songbook rested beneath the big twelve-string. What should I play? What was the perfect song? The picture of Bob Dylan on the cover looked just like I felt. I turned the pages to *Visions of Johanna*, a song with about a hundred verses. Okay, it has five verses—but five *long* ones, about pain and loneliness and awkward silences—it matched my mood perfectly. There are only three chords, which you can learn to play the same day you get a guitar. I didn't know anyone who could remember all the words. That's why I had a songbook.

The twelve-string was a little out of tune, which was normal. It was impossible to tune perfectly. I got it close, then began to play, carefully fingerpicking each note, working myself up to a genuine plaintive Dylan wail. "Ain't it just like the night?" I asked the ghosts in the empty room, "To play tricks when you're trying to be so quiet?" My voice bounced back from the stone walls.

The oak door opened with an ancient creak followed by a blast of cold air sweeping in behind a girl I hadn't seen before. She carried a guitar case. I stopped playing but she nodded and smiled as if she wanted me to keep going. She slipped off her fur coat, sat on the steps and took out her guitar, a well-worn Gibson, a vintage six string with an orange macramé guitar strap. She didn't look anything like the hippie folksinger types who filled the Echo Chamber on a weekend. Small and compact, she had long, straight brown hair, the color of roasted chestnuts, perfectly brushed, flowing to the middle of her back. Dark eyes. Big silver hoop earrings, tailored store-bought bell bottoms, not homemade from an old pair of dungarees. A beige turtle neck sweater just the right amount too big. She put her ear against her guitar and tuned it to mine, so quickly and quietly I didn't believe it would be in tune, but it was. Then, she watched my hand form a chord and she began to play, her long fingernails striking the strings more clearly than any finger picks, hitting each note precisely. She played with me note for note, then strayed off the melody and played new ones, like little songs, melodies that worked like they were written for it. As if she had discovered the only copy of an unpublished Bob Dylan songbook. Then she began to sing. And I stopped.

My hand felt paralyzed. I couldn't force a sound from my throat.

"What's the matter?" she asked.

"You sing like an angel. I can't sing with you. I'll ruin it."

"That's silly. You sound fine. Keep playing. Please." So I did.

She started to sing again, in a soaring voice that filled the room, a voice that didn't need the echo. She never looked at the songbook. She knew all the words, the lyrics to all the verses, complicated obtuse poetry, that seemed to make perfect sense in her voice. Then a shudder went through me…for the first time, the lyrics made sense to me also, though I don't think I could explain why. Somewhere deep in the song, I sang too, and we harmonized. I felt like I was auditioning for the Queen. Somehow it all worked.

I realized something, something big. I knew right away that everything had just changed: God had put me on this earth just to sing and play with this girl whose name I didn't know—not yet. We rolled into the last verse. On the last line, she bent the note and her voiced sailed up the scale to land a full octave above mine…a full octave! The song ended and an icy chill ran down my back as if someone had dumped a bucket of Ithaca slush on me.

The echo took forever to fade. She sat, hugging the guitar across her knees and smiling, waiting for me to say something. I realized I was suddenly, desperately in love with her. I had never felt this way before. Not with anyone, not ever.

13

"What's your name?" I finally managed.

"Melissa." For the first time since leaving home I knew exactly what I wanted.

Chapter 4

Clarence and I had barely spoken since we met the first week. But when I returned from the Echo Chamber I was in too good a mood to keep my mouth shut. I had just met the most beautiful girl— no, *woman*—I had ever seen. No girl in my high school even came close. A musician, a fabulous singer, she could speak three languages fluently. She wore new tailored jeans and a fur coat and earrings on a campus where it was unusual to see someone in clean clothes. And perfume and lipstick! I didn't give a damn what kind of bug Clarence had jammed up his ass, or what his opinion of his honky roommate was, I was going to tell him all about Melissa. If he walked out on me, I didn't care. He was the only person in earshot and I had to talk to someone.

I entered the room like a conquering hero. I threw the guitar case onto the top bunk and stood there grinning, as if I knew a secret that all the world wanted to hear. Clarence sat at his desk, at ten o'clock on Thursday night, typing on his portable electric typewriter, the hum and whir rattling against the stone floor and ceiling. I said nothing, just stood in the tiny room, grinning. He looked up. He had to.

"What the hell happened to you tonight?" he asked. It worked. He talked to me!

"I met a girl!" I took a breath, preparing to launch into a half-crazed description of a creature who could only exist in the imagination of a love-struck nineteen-year-old. He held up his hand to stop me.

"Good for you." Then he looked down at the typewriter keyboard and resumed typing. He didn't raise his eyes again. I had been dismissed.

"Maybe you know her," I babbled on. "She's in all the government and sociology courses like you are. She's really political. And gorgeous. Boy, is she gorgeous. She can sing. She sings like a frigging angel."

I paused. Was there even a flicker of recognition on his face, the slightest hint of interest? Meeting Melissa was the most noteworthy thing I had done in my entire life. Did he give even a tiny little shit?

"Is she black?"

"Of course not…" I started to back pedal. Why did I say, "Of course not?"

"Oh. Excuse me. How silly of me. Of course not." He looked up. "What's her name?" he added, as if he was actually curious.

"Melissa. Melissa Kolaski. I think that's Polish."

"Bring her around. I'd like to meet her." Then his eyes fell back on the typewriter and the conversation was over.

Bring her around? Fat frigging chance.

Chapter 5

Friday morning I practically sprang out of bed. It's a good thing I didn't actually do that because I would have cracked my head on the ceiling, about twenty inches over my face. Clarence, as usual, had already left for class, so I took the opportunity to thumb through his copy of the *Pig Book*, which was neatly slipped into a stack of textbooks on his perfectly organized desk. The *Pig Book* looked as if it had been copied and stapled together by hand. The cover said it was the "Class of 1972 Freshman Register." Inside were the pictures, names and majors of every new freshman. I quickly found Melissa's picture. In fact, the book opened right to that page. Had Clarence checked her out?

The photo of Melissa Kolaski looked exactly like Melissa Kolaski should: gorgeous. Long hair, dazzling smile, sparkling eyes...these were obvious even in the blurry, black and white, thumbnail-sized picture. Melissa *Louise* Kolaski, to be exact. Valedictorian of the class of 1968, Olympia, Washington. That was just about as far away as you could get from Ithaca and still be in the United States. School of Arts and Sciences, just like me. Triple major: (*Triple? Do they have that?*) Political Science, Music, French.

The photo, like all of them, was her high school yearbook picture. My yearbook picture had been heavily airbrushed to vaporize my acne until I was barely recognizable. I doubted they had to do any work to Melissa's. She was pretty much perfect right out of the box. But that's all I could find. No favorite food or sport or useful information about what turned her on. But this wasn't *Playboy* magazine. The *Pig Book* didn't reveal any secrets about how she liked "long walks on the beach" and "sharing a cup of hot chocolate by a roaring fire." I'd have to find that stuff out for myself. I couldn't wait. But I did know one important fact about her. She had given me her dorm phone number.

After eight tries—all busy signals—a tired-sounding girl's voice finally answered. It wasn't Melissa. She seemed irritated by the task of finding her, whose room was at the other side of the dorm. I could hear footsteps echoing through the dorm hallway long before I heard a familiar voice say, "Hello?"

"Melissa!" I said, delighted to hear her voice again.

"Tony!" She barely knew me but she recognized my voice! I charged ahead, thrilled.

"I'm so glad to get you on the phone, I've been trying like for an hour or something. Are you, you know, busy tonight? Or, uh, you know, maybe, um…"

"Of course I'm busy. But I think I can make a little space in my schedule…for you." That was all it took to blow my frigging mind. She said yes. It was just that easy.

We met at the Echo Chamber again, carrying our guitars. Melissa wore long, black slacks which flared at the bottoms, and a huge knit fisherman's sweater. She looked like a model on the cover of a magazine about clothes you will never, ever see on college kids. I had on the best stuff in my half of the tiny closet—clean blue jeans, a black turtleneck. A medallion hung around my neck on a thin chain. It was some sort of Egyptian symbol. I didn't know what it meant, but I was pretty sure it was either peace or fertility. Either one worked fine.

It was Friday night, and that meant no classes the next day, so there were a dozen hippies with musical instruments—guitars, banjos, dulcimers, even a washtub bass. Everyone but us looked like they had been "rode hard and put away wet," which is how my mom usually described me.

We sat together on the floor, our backs to the stone wall, not touching. People didn't pay much attention to us—not to me, anyway— until someone played *Blowin' in the Wind* and everyone began to sing, including Melissa. One by one, all the other voices dropped out until

Melissa sang alone. Their faces looked like mine must have when I first heard her.

We left the Echo Chamber and walked across the bridge to a coffeehouse in Collegetown called the Unmuzzled Ox. My right hand was free, just hanging there, and Melissa's left hand was dangling…until I reached over and took it. She didn't protest. She smiled when I did that. The campus was busy on a Friday night, with kids walking across the bridge into Collegetown in search of food or music or each other.

Some of them stared at us. I knew why. I had seen this before…in Las Vegas. My Uncle Eddie had taken me there for my eighteenth birthday, so he could sneak me into a casino and teach me to play craps. I couldn't stop staring at one particular couple, just like people were staring at us now. He was an overweight bald guy in a wrinkled suit that didn't fit. On his arm was an absolutely gorgeous chick, tall, slender, and with big boobs in a shiny, white satin dress, "Holy crap, Uncle Eddie," I had said. "How does a guy like that get a bombshell like her?" He didn't answer me. He just laughed, as if that was something I'd have to figure out myself.

Melissa surprised me with, "What would you say to a little vino?"

"I'd rather get some wine," I said. Come on, laugh. Please God, make her laugh. She giggled and squeezed my hand. It sounded like the tinkling of—of—who cares? It sounded frigging great. But it wasn't enough, like throwing a starving man a potato chip. I wanted more. I needed to hear her *laugh*.

It was no use pretending I knew anything about wine. I'd drink anything that was available. I still got a kick out of the fact that anyone older than eighteen could actually walk into a liquor store and buy a bottle in New York. We stopped at Collegetown Liquors and I asked the guy to recommend a good wine. He looked at Melissa, then at me, then down at the counter. He got it. I put my right hand next to the register and opened my fingers to reveal the three bucks hidden inside. He found us something called *Mateus,* in a classy-looking bottle with a label that I couldn't read. Perfect.

The girl at the Unmuzzled Ox offered to lend us two coffee mugs. Then she smiled and asked, "Would you like me to open the bottle for you?" I could hardly believe it. I almost floated away. College life was looking better and better.

"Let's sit in the back," said Melissa. "Where it's dark."

I couldn't agree fast enough. We sat down at a tiny well-worn table lit by a single flickering candle. As soon as my rear end touched the chair, every thought in my head left by the back door. My brain went blank, like a TV set stuck between channels, all white noise and static. What would we talk about? Then Melissa spoke.

"Do you like Ithaca? What do you think?" Thank God. Then, more: "What's your favorite course?" followed by "What's your favorite place to eat?" and a dozen other questions. I answered everything with just half a brain. The other half was busy. *What will make this girl laugh? What's it gonna take?*

"I have a question for you," I said. It was time to throw the dice. Melissa was brilliant. A joke that would crack up another girl might not budge her. Plus, all the jokes I knew were dirty; I didn't know her well enough for that. If I told her a joke and she didn't get it, I'd spend the evening trying to explain something that would get beaten and bloody. This was insanely difficult and I'd only get one chance. I bet my wad on what I said next.

"How do know when you're an insomniac, agnostic, dyslexic?"

She tilted her head and wrinkled her brow as if squeezing out the answer. *Stay with me here, God,* I thought. *Don't tell her.*

"Say that again?"

"How do you know you're an insomniac…agnostic…dyslexic ?" I said each word separately and distinctly. "Give up?"

She grinned. "Okay. I give up. How do you know?"

"You stay up all night, wondering…if there really is…a dog." I held very still and didn't change my expression. Melissa's face scrunched up even more. Then her eyes opened wide, and finally, she burst out in a laugh that made people up by the espresso machine turn to look at us. Score! I did it! I hit it out of the park!

That was all it took. I was hooked. I knew that I would rather hear her laugh than any other sound in the world. I had just become addicted, as completely as if I had a needle full of smack hanging out of my arm.

She put her hand on mine and tilted her head toward the bottle of wine. "So, are we going to drink this or just admire the pretty label?"

"Ah, *bien sur,*" I said, and poured her a generous portion, then filled my own mug. The wine looked like mud in the dim candle light.

"Is that French? That's the worst accent I've ever heard." She giggled again.

"Ah, *Je sais,*" I said, and hoped that meant "I know." My accent was awful, but I knew she would think it was French if I started every sentence with "Ah." She wouldn't be surprised when I asked for help with my French homework.

"Why don't you just speak English, Tony? That way we'll be able to understand each other. Tell me, *monsieur sommalier,* how do you pronounce the name of this wine? Is it *Matoose* or *Ma-tay-us?*"

How the hell did I know? That was really far down on my list of things I was responsible for. But I don't let an invitation like that slip past me. It was an opportunity to take a solo.

"That would be pronounced *Matoose,* which is Spanish for 'grown on the south side of the hill.' They use only the grapes that face the sun. In fact, the grape pickers take only the grapes on the south side of the vines. Then the *sliciers* cut each one in half lengthwise and they use only the south side of the grape. It's one of the best wines made in Spain."

"Fascinating," said Melissa. "There's just *un petite problem.* This stuff was made in Portugal." She pointed to the word "Portugal" on the bottom of the label. "Tell me, do you do this a lot, this extemporaneous, free style, stream of consciousness, bullshitting thing that you are so good at?"

"Yes," I said. "All of the time, actually. That's how I got through high school."

"You must eat up essay tests."

"Like candy."

"What was your verbal SAT score?"

Terrific question! I had never met anyone with a higher score than mine. "Seven hundred ninety."

"I beat you."

What? She *beat* me? I stared at her with my mouth open.

With an angelic smile, she said, "Eight hundred. This is going to be fun, Tony." It already was.

Chapter 6

A few days later I still had a terrible hangover. Not from drinking, not this time. I had a Melissa hangover. I couldn't stop thinking about her. We couldn't get together. She was busy every minute of the day, and so far, almost impossible to get on the phone. But I needed to see her again like I needed to breathe.

I filled my cup from the coffee urn in the main dining room of Willard Straight Hall. The Straight was another building that resembled a medieval castle, and the vaulted ceilings and the huge fireplace made you feel like you should be gnawing on a beef joint with a flagon of ale in front of you instead of biting into an undersized crappy hamburger. The coffee was weak but that was okay. I was just developing a taste for coffee. I never drank it in high school. I was taking my time getting used to my new life as a sophisticated intellectual at a prestigious Northeast Ivy League school.

When I was with Melissa, I made a pretty passable intellectual. By myself, not so much. I felt like a fraud in my recent thrift shop purchase: a brown corduroy sports coat with leather covered buttons and patches on the elbows. I completed this outfit with the same black turtleneck shirt that I had worn with Melissa, but now I had artistically faded blue jeans. I had washed them in the dorm sink at least ten times before wearing them. The Egyptian medallion turned out to be something about a bountiful wheat harvest, so I had ditched that in favor of a simple but classic metal peace symbol, which dangled from my neck. A meerschaum pipe poked out of my jacket pocket. I had actually bought a meerschaum pipe. I still couldn't believe it.

I looked like the host of *Poet's Corner* on public television. Everyone would know I was a phony. But the vast dining room was sprinkled with kids and faculty that represented every conceivable fashion trend and style. No one person stuck out from the rest. Some wore shorts and sandals even though it was forty degrees outside. Law students and some grad students wore suits and ties. Some kids dressed like their clothes came from yard sales and military surplus stores. Foreign kids wore saris and robes. There was no agreement about a dress code on a college campus. Nobody seemed to give a damn about what I looked like.

Many of the kids could be loosely described as radicals, a cross between a hippie and a guerrilla soldier. The kids at Cornell took their politics very seriously. T-shirts and jeans or overalls combined with worn army jackets and fatigues. Head bands, knapsacks, clothes made out of, or patched, with American flags. These kids were in the SDS— the Students for a Democratic Society, and were sort of entry-level communists. My dad called them pinkos, or traitors, or usually just assholes. I felt better seeing that I wasn't the only idiot in a jacket with leather patches on the elbows but I would have been more comfortable sitting with the pinkos. I had already learned to stay out of political arguments. Neither side really made a lot of sense to me, and I was tired of the constant haranguing. But the pinkos had a better sense of humor.

I didn't know how long I could keep up the hip, intellectual thing. I was really nothing like that. The pipe in my pocket was as alien to me as a ray gun. Also, I didn't smoke...not really, just maybe a cigarette every now and then. I never bought a pack, because...I didn't smoke.

A kid I recognized from my Psych 101 class sat down at the table. His name was CJ, which stood for Charles Joseph, which was what the teaching assistant called him. CJ wore a long sleeve tie-dyed sweatshirt under a denim jacket. His hair fell down his neck in a five month old pony tail. I think he started on it the day he graduated high school. CJ was in the SDS. He, too, held a cup in his hand.

"Hey, Tony. Is that coffee? You're better off drinking it here and not down the hill. Whatever you do, don't drink the crap they serve by the freshman dorms."

"Why is that?"

"Because they pump the freshmen's coffee full of saltpeter so the guys can't get hard-ons. That's what I've heard, anyway."

"What crap. I've been drinking it for weeks. Believe me, that's not my problem."

"Speaking of boners, I heard you had a date with one Melissa Kolaski."

"How do you know that?"

He put his cup down and laughed.

"Are you kidding? Dig it! She's famous! She's the classiest girl on campus and this is just her first year. I can't wait to see her when she's a senior. If I make it that long, anyway. What a babe. She's pure dynamite, Tony. How did you do it, my man?"

I ignored the question. "How do you know Melissa?" I asked.

"She's in my third year French class."

"You just got here!" Not CJ too! Damn! Was I the only kid at Cornell taking first year courses? "How come you're in third year French already?"

"*C'est simple!*" he said, sounding just like a waiter in a frigging French restaurant. I was getting mighty sick of people speaking French at me. "My dad was stationed in Paris when I was a kid. I speak *Francais* better than I speak English. It's a pure gut for me."

"Then why didn't you take French Four?"

"I'm saving it for my gut class next semester. So tell me. Did you get any?"

An innocent question, one asked by every guy to every other guy after a date. I shouldn't have been offended, but I couldn't help it. Hearing it in reference to *Melissa*...was just outrageous. It was disgusting. "That's none of your business, CJ."

"So *non*, then, huh? Too bad. She's attracting a lot of attention, buddy. Better move fast. Hey, Tony. News flash: She just walked in. In the fur coat already! She's in line for coffee. Check it out!"

"How about you take off? Do me a favor and make yourself scarce. This is tough enough as it is."

He stood up. "You owe me, buddy. *Bon chance, mon ami.* But first tell me—you didn't get any, did you?"

"Scram, CJ." I smiled at him but there wasn't much smile in my voice.

The truth was I didn't get anything...not what he was talking about.

But what I got on our date, I would not have traded for anything in the world. I got a whole evening of undivided attention from the classiest, most intelligent, most beautiful girl imaginable. Two hours of conversation and laughter. I had walked her home from the little coffeehouse on the edge of campus, to her dorm. I kissed her. I didn't even have to try. It was her idea. It was nothing like kissing the girls I had made out with at high school parties, in dark basements while the parents watched TV and got plastered in the upstairs living room. It was just a good night kiss.

That's all it took for me to know this was a whole different deal. *Melissa* was a whole different deal. I had to take it slow and be thankful for every inch of ground gained. Whatever this was, it was fragile.

Chapter 7

Melissa paid for her coffee, holding it in one hand and a massive pile of textbooks in the other. A big leather handbag hung from her arm. She turned from the cash register to face the dining room. I stood up and waved with a huge smile—probably too huge—until I caught her eye.

She smiled back and headed in my direction. I stood at attention as she approached. *A queen,* I thought. *I have met a queen.*

Melissa dropped her bundle on the table and slipped the fur coat off her shoulders as gracefully as if she had been practicing for weeks. I almost fell over the table trying to help her. I got a whiff of her perfume, and the evening we spent together came slamming back to me in a rush. I sat down again, and looking at her, studying her, in her sleeveless white blouse, white boots and scarf, I stopped feeling like a fraud. I had just been transported to a Fifth Avenue cafe; the Straight cafeteria became a famous fancy restaurant, and my silly jacket with the patches on the elbows was the attire of the moment, the minimum that could meet the dress code when you dined with Melissa.

"Hi, Tony," she said. "Long time no see, huh?"

"Yeah. No kidding," I told her. "A couple of days without seeing you is a real long time."

"You're sweet. You're a sweet kid." No one had ever called me sweet, except my mom. "Is the coffee safe to drink here?" she asked.

"You mean the saltpeter thing? That's baloney."

"Good. Because we don't want that. Do we?"

Did she just say what I think she said? "No, we sure don't." I said, and I meant every word. I started to breathe a little faster. I faked a cough to cover it up.

"I had fun the other night. I enjoyed it. Thank you," she said.

"Me too. I hope we can do it again."

She began to shuffle and reorganize her books, finding the stuff she needed for her one o'clock class. A familiar looking textbook, one like I had seen on Clarence's desk, got pushed to the side. *Political Evolution of the Disenfranchised and Marginalized.* What a mouthful. If I had to read that book I'd be sound asleep in ten minutes. It must have weighed fifteen pounds. I'd have to think twice before offering to carry her books. I pointed to it.

"I know that book. That's for Gov 102, right? Did you skip 101?"

"Of course. Almost everyone skips 101 classes." Oh, of course they do. Everybody but me.

"My instructor is a serious radical." She talked quickly. "He's a PhD candidate. He does most of the teaching. I've only seen the professor on the first day of class. Anyway, I'm kind of liberal but this guy's a nut case. He's exciting to be around. He lives and breathes conflict. He absolutely loves arguments. I think he's a socialist!" I had no idea she was that intense about politics.

"What's the instructor's name?" I asked, just to slow her down.

"Gary Borack. How do you know about that book?"

"My roommate is in your class. I've seen it before."

"What's his name?"

"Clarence. Clarence Carter."

"Clarence. There aren't too many kids named Clarence here. I may have met him. Is he a black man?"

"That's him."

"Clarence..." she said. Her voice drifted off. "The beautiful black man..."

What? I jumped in. "Beautiful? What makes him beautiful?"

"It's no secret...he's beautiful. He looks like he was carved from a piece of ebony and polished by the hand of God." *Holy crap. Did she just say that?* "He's so serious. He argues with the instructor. He's the only one with enough nerve. He almost always wins. At least, I think he does. He has a beautiful mind. He thinks so clearly. Of course he's beautiful. You don't think so?"

"No, I don't think so... at all." That came out a little hard. She backed away from me. There was no stopping me. "He's the most unfriendly guy I ever met. He won't even talk to me. He pays no attention to me. It's like I don't exist."

"Really? I think he's very perceptive. Maybe it's something you've said that you're not aware of. Or maybe the way you look at him. He can probably pick up on stuff like that. Prejudice isn't always obvious, you know. Sometimes we do things without knowing what we do. You can be a racist and not even know it."

"I am not a racist!" *Boy, does that sound familiar.* "I'm not even a little prejudiced. I tried to like the guy!"

"Maybe he thought you're trying too hard. He's very sensitive to that, I think. It's easy to come across as condescending, maybe even obsequious. Pandering to him."

"You sound like a vocabulary test. The answer is D, none of the above. It has nothing to do with me. The guy is angry all the time."

"You're the one who sounds angry, Tony. Can you hear the tone of your voice?" She began to assemble her books and pack up, sliding farther from the table. Her smile had vanished. "Let's not make a word game out of this, okay?"

"I am not a racist!" Damn it! I said it again! "Unless just being white makes you one."

"Maybe it does," she said. Her voice sounded tired.

"Then by that definition you're a racist too."

She looked away. The hint of a smile tried to brighten her face but it couldn't overcome the far-away look in her eyes. "Maybe I am."

She was slipping away, I had to move fast. I reached out and took her hand and squeezed it. "You're not a racist, Melissa. You know that as well as I do. Stop thinking that."

"And you're not either," she said. But she wouldn't look at me. She didn't sell it. I wasn't convinced. Then she pulled her hand away.

"He's a jerk, Melissa." I just had to say that. No way could I have let that go by. That makes two of us.

"Okay," she said. "He's a jerk. A beautiful jerk."

What had I done? Had I screwed this up so quickly, so completely? Melissa began to fade right in front of my eyes. My face flushed, my heart pounded. What could I do?

She stood up and gathered her pile in her arms.

"Anyway," she said. "Will I see you this weekend?"

Thank God. I had dodged a well-deserved bullet.

Chapter 8

That evening I needed to find a quiet place to hide where no one, not even Melissa, would find me. I needed to think. I didn't need to eat. I wasn't hungry. I had lost my appetite which only happened when I was very sick. My stomach churned as if some giant parasitic snake had crawled in there. I sought refuge in the one place I knew no one would look for me: the college library.

I watched the sun go down over the campus. The grounds and buildings seemed to go on forever. I had found a study carrel way up in the stacks, on the fourth floor, next to a huge window. As far as I could see, in all directions, were campus buildings: the Arts Quad in one direction, the Engineering Quad to the right, the law school across from it. On the distant horizon stood the enormous towers of the agriculture school and beyond that hundreds of acres of experimental farms, and livestock barns. This place was huge, bigger than any town I had lived in. I felt very small. My problems should have shrunk with the rest of me, but they didn't. My existence at school to date, three months, had been lonely and...awful. Then I met Melissa. Now it was all at risk.

Melissa had noticed Clarence? How could she miss him? There were a total of 125 black kids on the whole campus. Clarence was probably one of the taller, and certainly the darkest, of the African American students. He stuck out from the crowd in the first few months in his ironed slacks and white shirt. Now, six foot two in a blazing yellow, orange and purple dashiki; even the blind kids could see him coming. *Melissa must think I'm the Grand Wizard of the Ku Klux Klan, in a white robe and hood, waving the battle flag.* This was the exact opposite of how I viewed myself.

The two hours in the library lost in thought were a complete waste. I might as well have been studying. I trudged down the hill through gently falling snow—just a different version of the sleet and slush that never seemed to quit—back to my room and climbed another four flights of stairs.

Clarence had rearranged the room so that he now had a typewriter table separate from his desk. This made it almost impossible to wedge a chair next to my own. When I entered the room, he looked up at me, surprising me by actually making eye contact. He spoke first.

"So when do I get to meet your girlfriend?"

I had spent my entire high school career learning to avoid the quick response that gets the crap beaten out of you. I did *not* say, "Never, asshole." I was certain that Clarence could rip my head off before my hand got to the doorknob. Instead I said, "She's not my girlfriend. We've only had one date. It wasn't even really a date. Anyway, you don't know her."

"Oh, I know her, all right. We all know her." He pronounced each word crisply and carefully, like he was reading lines in a play.

"Who is 'we', Clarence?"

He looked down at the keyboard and didn't reply. Then he said, "Why don't you just come out and say it? It is not healthy to keep your feelings under such careful control. You will feel better if you just say what is on...your...mind."

"What the hell are you talking about?"

"That you do not want to see a Negro man take up with a white woman."

I had seen lots of black guys with white girls. I had noticed them, of course. I mean, how could you miss them? But then a picture of Melissa in Clarence's arms flashed in my head and a strange ripple ran through me. I answered him quickly. "Oh, bullshit. That has nothing to do with it. You're the one who is prejudiced, not me."

"You are the *product*," he began (and somehow he made that word click like a pistol being cocked) "of your white, middle class upbringing and your bigoted parents. You are the result of what you think and what you have been told and what you have been taught." *I have to stand here and listen to this crap?* "You know nothing about the black experience. You know nothing of my people. You see everything through the narrow eyes of a white man who is afraid of his own shadow. You are the very definition of a *honky.*"

It was my turn. "Are you done making speeches? So tell me this: it's okay for you to call me a honky but I can't call you a…" I stopped. Clarence's glared with the eyes of a sniper peering through a rifle scope. "How is that fair? Huh? How is that fair?" I demanded.

"Fair? In the last two hundred years nothing about the white man's treatment of the black man has been fair. Fair is a concept which does not apply. Nothing about this is fair."

Fury overtook me. I could feel it in my chest and hear the blood slam in my ears. I had nothing to do with any of this. I never owned slaves, I never made anybody sit in the back of the bus, I did nothing to deserve this treatment, this crap. Yet, here I was, being scolded by some kind of black king in a dashiki and left to wait for his henchmen to carry me off to the boiling pot. I was innocent!

Chapter 9

Melissa swept through my life like a breaking wave. We were soon seeing each other every day, but it was never enough. A few minutes here, a short little get-together there. We would meet for dinner, then at the library. She helped me with my French homework just like my mom had predicted. My grades started to improve. The more involved I got with her the less I gave a damn about anything else. Clarence became a minor annoyance as he and I both learned to avoid each other as much as possible. I understood that if Melissa and I wanted to enjoy each other's company, Clarence was not a good topic for conversation.

I began having imaginary conversations with her, talking to myself, running things by her, asking imaginary Melissa for advice. Should I wear this? Or this? Should I blow off this class and meet you for lunch or should I hit the books and call you later? She became my Jiminy Cricket, an invisible presence who never left my side, guiding me, telling me right from wrong. Every decision made me think, *What would Melissa want me to do? Should I put extra Cheese Whiz on the tater tots? Should I study or go to dollar beer night at the Salty Dog?* It was halfway through the year and I hadn't washed out yet. I wasn't on the dean's list, but I was still in college.

Soon Melissa was everywhere in my life. At least the invisible version was. My high school girlfriends became a distant memory; they felt like casual acquaintances compared to her. Was I in love? What did

I know? This was all new to me. Love was such a huge concept that I couldn't make myself think about it, much less talk about it. We never used the L word. That scared me more than Clarence did. But I was pretty sure of one thing: Was I in love? Yes. Was she in love with me? I had no idea.

I was still a virgin, despite my best efforts. One thing was certain: there was only one cure for that, and one doctor who could administer it. It became a thirst that only one thing, one act—with one person—could quench. It became a quest bigger than anything Don Quixote had ever chased.

Nineteen sixty nine was a rough year to be a college freshman. There was more going on outside of the classroom than in it. The war, social turmoil and racial tension; every time we turned around we were expected to take a stand for or against something. The draft claimed every guy who strayed too close to the academic edge. Lose your scholarship or your 2-S deferment and they'd pluck a guy like a ripe apple. Kids who had never been away from home before had to perform like trained seals to get through the semester without washing out. The world seemed insane to us and we held on to our Saturday evenings like a life raft.

Things were changing quickly. Even the clothes we wore evolved. The corduroy jacket with the patched elbows got stuffed into the back of the tiny closet, where it would remain unless I needed it for a costume party. Blue jeans, a sweat shirt and a denim jacket became my winter outfit.

One day, when the thermometer was bouncing off ten degrees, Melissa slid the box containing her beloved fur coat, which had belonged to her mother, under her bed. She could no longer drape herself with the skins of innocent animals. Its replacement, a thick navy pea coat with two rows of big buttons, was more suited to her new mood as an enthusiastic member of the proletariat. She traded her tailored slacks for some sailor bell bottoms, the kind with the drop front secured by thirteen buttons. I couldn't believe that the navy ever had a sailor as tiny as Melissa. When I saw her in her nautical outfit, I knew that if all sailors looked like her, I would quit school and enlist in a second. Then I laughed because I knew that nothing on the earth could make me enlist.

While we both searched for our own political identities, Melissa leaned farther to the left. "Liberal" is how she put it. Some of the stuff seemed flat-out crazy, but I followed along. I trotted at her heels like a willing dog. Every now and then she'd pat me on the head and throw me a treat. The treats were nice but not enough. Making out with Melissa was about the most fun you could have with your clothes on. And that was the problem.

Chapter 10

The most private place on campus that a freshman could get to was the floor of Uris Library. Almost no one went up there unless they had the same idea I did, the day I lured Melissa with the promise of the best view in Ithaca. We pulled two chairs up to the big window and just as the sun went down I made my move. I had even remembered to keep my hand in my pocket, against my leg, to warm it up so she wouldn't freak out when I slid it under her sweater. Once again, it didn't work.

"No, not here," she whispered. "We can't. Someone will see."

"It's dark out. It's dark in here. No one will—"

"Not now." This was driving me crazy. I needed some advice. But from who?

I thought of Country Bob.

Bob was a sophomore from Orchard Park, a farm community outside of Buffalo. He was the guy I gave the meerschaum pipe to. His room was at the opposite end of the hall where Clarence and I shared the prison cell. His dad owned a huge dairy farm. Country Bob came from money—big money—but he worked hard to keep up the country boy, hillbilly thing. He had a homey, rural saying for just about every occasion. When he happily accepted the gift of the pipe, he wandered off saying "Some days, the bear eats you. *But some days, you eats the bear.*" I knew right away that Bob and I would get along fine.

Bob was political, like most of the kids, but not crazy-whacko about it. He was against the war and the draft, of course, but I had the feeling that if they came for him, he would go. We had other stuff in common: we both smoked pot. Nearly everyone did. Except for Clarence. If he had ever rolled a fat one, I would have fainted dead away.

I had taken to hanging out in Country Bob's room, a big double that felt like a luxury suite compared to mine. He was the sole occupant, which seemed unfair as I was forced to share a single with Clarence. But I had chosen not to ask for another roommate and nothing would make my father happier than me begging for a change midyear.

I opened the conversation. "Bob, did you ever have a girl friend?"

Country Bob looked up from the big Animal Husbandry textbook occupying his attention. Above his head, stuck to his wall, were pictures of prize milk cows, gigantic creatures that could produce huge amounts of milk and were worth tons of money. The cows adorned the walls of his room like *Playboy* pinups. Bob tucked a piece of paper into the open book, then closed it, as if he expected this was a conversation that would take some time.

"Cain't say as I have," he drawled in an exaggerated rural accent. "Don't rightly need one, seein' as how we raised sheep." Bob was probably the most intelligent and articulate guy I had met on campus, yet he could turn on the country bumpkin thing as easily as he might switch on his reading light.

"That so? I figgered as much," I said, trying to sound like I had just fallen off the hay wagon myself.

"What's the problem? Are you having trouble with the ladies? I thought you were doing pretty well with Melissa. She's a Grade A filly, my boy. A blue ribbon winner."

"A filly is a horse, Bob."

"And I thought you were an English major." He dropped the accent. "To answer your question, I actually have two girlfriends. One here in Ithaca, and one at home. It's more convenient that way. I've had the same girlfriend back in Orchard Park since fifth grade."

"Since fifth grade? Are you kidding?"

"There were only forty kids in my graduating class; not a lot to pick from."

"So you've had some experience. In, uh, animal husbandry, so to speak?"

"So to speak. What specific aspects of that subject concern you?"

I let it rip. I hadn't spent a lot of time with Country Bob, not enough to call him a good friend. But he was my *best* friend right then. Something about him made me trust him. I started at the beginning and brought him up to date on all the details. He was especially interested in the details.

"I'm pretty frustrated," I summarized. "We've only made out a few times. It's worse than high school. We're never alone. She has almost no free time and we always go to the same places. There's always a bunch of people there. It's driving me crazy."

"You need to find yourself a hayloft."

"That's not the only problem. I can get just so far. I mean, it's great, but it could be a whole lot greater. It's like she thinks someone is watching. Like her father. It's almost as if she's got, you know," I tried to think of a farm analogy…"an electric fence around parts of her…"

"The good parts, I assume," said Bob.

"Yeah, the best parts."

"The ripe fruit…"

"Yeah, let me finish. I get, you know, ready to go, and then I can only go so fast…"

"Then a governor kicks in. We had a governor on our tractor. It would only go so fast. Big pain in the ass."

"What did you do about it?"

"Took it off, of course. That's what you do with governors; you take them off."

"I'm not making much progress and I'm not sure our relationship is going anywhere. I don't know what to do next. I don't know whether she's my girlfriend or what."

"Do you love her?" This came out of nowhere.

"I have no idea," I lied. What else could it be? When would I admit it to someone?

"Then you don't. Yet. When you do, you'll know. But you like her, right? And she likes you?"

"Yeah. At the very least. But it's not much of a relationship."

"Sure it is. You'll realize that if you ever let her get away. Don't worry about it. It ain't broke. You know what we do on the farm with stuff that ain't broke?" I knew he was about to tell me, so I just waited. "We don't fix it. You guys will figure it out. Takes time."

"How much time?"

"In my case, let's see. Fifth grade…I was ten. I'm nineteen now…hmm…."

"Yeah. I got it. A long frigging time."

"Maybe. But while you wait there is one thing that you could do. Find yourself a hayloft."

Chapter 11

Was that all there was to it? I just needed a private place, the desire, and a willing partner? Something else might be missing, in addition to "means, motive and opportunity." I needed ability. No, more: I needed talent.

Was I a lousy lover? I had no idea. I hadn't actually made love. Not yet, anyway. I was pretty good at making "like," but that's not the same thing. I knew, in general, how it was done—after all, I had seen *Deep Throat* at the crappy theater on 42nd Street, like every other guy I knew. But the up-close details were a mystery. You don't learn much about love from watching porn movies. Even I knew that.

No one ever talked to me about any of that stuff. I received plenty of feedback about myself in every other part of my life. I even got notes from Juanita, the Mexican woman who brought the clean sheets, offering suggestions how I could keep the room cleaner. But about lovemaking, I was totally in the dark. What was I doing wrong? It must be something. There was so much stress and grief in my life, I didn't need more. Not something as monumental and unbearable as that.

Christmas break was just a week away. The school shut down for intersession, three weeks for the holiday and a winter recess. Many of the kids lived too far away—maybe the West Coast, or even China, or South Africa, to go home during the break. The school kept the dorms and the main dining room open so the kids had some place to eat and sleep. Melissa's family lived in Washington State. She would be staying in Ithaca. My family lived on Long Island, a couple hundred miles away.

I was expected to make an appearance at home. Once again I sought out some of Country Bob's counsel. I knew he would have a thoughtful, practical solution. He was also usually good for a buzz.

Bob and I sat in his room and shared a bowl of homegrown grass he had scored from someone who worked in the Cornell greenhouses. The meerschaum pipe was a wonderful replacement for the lumpy, brittle joints I was able to roll. The pipe smoked cooler and tasted better. You got a different high from smoking a fine pipe. Bob's room felt less like an opium den and more like an English club—one decorated with posters of giant cows.

"Why do they call it intersession?" I asked as I exhaled a cloud of smoke.

"That's when you finally get to have intercourse," he replied. "You get to have intersession intercourse. Of course."

"How is intersession going to help someone get laid?"

"Think about it. Three weeks of no classes? No studying? No tests? Just a few kids? No crowds…no pressure…lots of privacy? What else are you going to do? If you can't get laid during intersession, you ought to unsaddle the horse and hang up the bridle."

This heady dose of country wisdom hit me like a horse-drawn plow. *Of course!* I thought. *He's right!* But where? Even if Clarence went back to Chicago for intercourse, I mean intersession, I still had a dangerous top bunk barely thirty-two inches wide. I couldn't visualize even getting Melissa up there, especially after all the wine we'd probably need.

"That won't help me," I said. "We sure do need some time alone. But my room sucks. We need some space to spread out. We need a hayloft. A big one." I looked around his spacious room. Hint. Hint.

Bob flopped on his bed. It was a regular size single bed, but compared to mine it looked like something out of the Playboy Mansion. "Bring her here. Use my room. I'm going back to Orchard Park and help my old man on the farm. I'll give you the key. Knock yourself out. Just make sure to change the sheets before I get back." *Yes! Attaboy, Bob.*

"Really?" I did my best to sound astonished. "Far out. Thanks. You're a real friend, Bob. But my parents expect me to go home for intersession."

"So what? Just tell them you have to stay here and study. It works every time. They're expecting it. They don't want you home! They just got used to not having you around! Just go back for a couple of days. That's how it's done, Tony."

Now I had the means. I had the motive. Actually, motive was the least of my problems. But what about the opportunity? How in hell was I going to get Melissa into Bob's room? No matter what complicated strategy I cooked up, would she want to go? If she did, *then what?*

Chapter 12

Y ou know the expression about the best laid plans of mice and men? For me it was the *best planned lays*. I was over-thinking this. In fact, it was all I thought about. Melissa and I didn't see much of each other in the two weeks before Christmas because we had to study for finals…especially me. I hadn't exactly been a model student for the first few months. Now I had a great reason to stay in school—even better than avoiding the draft. Melissa would be here—and no place else— next semester. So I had to be here too. That meant I had to pass my finals and turn in all the papers. It was crunch time. With that hanging in front of me, like that famous carrot, I whipped myself with the stick. Bob turned out to have a ready supply of diet pills which we ground up and snorted through rolled-up dollar bills, and I didn't sleep for three days. I felt like total crap, but I got all the work done.

Finally I finished the last test for the semester. Even better, I was pretty sure I hadn't blown any of them out my ass, and that my 2-S deferment was secure for the time being. I relaxed. Clarence came and went and I barely noticed him. He had added a red fez to his dashiki get-up. He looked like a character in a Mr. Moto movie. I ignored him. On the last day of classes, Clarence left with a small leather suitcase, fez perched on his head, mirrored sunglasses in place and a bus ticket to Chicago in his pocket. He didn't say good bye and neither did I. I didn't think of him again for three weeks.

I had a bus ticket of my own, to Long Island. I was obligated to a four day visit with my family, just long enough to catch a Greyhound, drink an eggnog toast with my parents who pretended to be happy to see me, and look excited Christmas morning, unwrapping presents I didn't need or want. It might have been tolerable if not for the constant hammering my long hair and newly-minted political views received. To my dad's delight, Nixon had been elected, squeaking by on a tiny margin, and my father—Lou—slapped the table and extolled his mandate to win the Vietnam War, no matter what it cost, deriding the pinko kids who hid behind their college deferments. His own kid—me, for instance, but I kept my mouth shut. He didn't seem interested in what I thought of Cornell or how I got along with Clarence. All he talked about was the war. The four days on Long Island were about four days too long. I could never have survived two weeks. I was back in Ithaca before New Year's Eve.

Chapter 13

Melissa and I met for dinner at the Straight dining room the same night I got back to Ithaca. She was really happy to see me…but not as happy as I was to see her! Even the cafeteria food was great. The usual crowds were gone and the food was a big improvement over the boring stuff they always served. Broiled chicken with cranberry sauce, actual baked potatoes instead of the usual whipped tasteless fluff that came out of a box. Even the coffee was better. I guessed the staff felt sorry for the poor kids who couldn't go home for the break.

"How long have we been seeing each other, Tony?" Melissa asked me, stirring her coffee long after the one packet of sugar had dissolved. I didn't answer. Even though we had been going out for almost two months I didn't feel the least bit secure in my status. I was really bad at predicting what she would say next. Was I her boyfriend? Good question. We hadn't done or even talked about the one thing that would definitively answer it. As far as "How long have we been seeing each other?" She was just as likely to say, "I think we should stop," as "We should see more of each other." Before I could answer, she blew my mind.

"Don't you think it's time we had a real date?"

Very carefully, and as calmly as I could, I replied, "Yes. I do. I've been thinking the same thing. We always have people around. We're never alone. We don't really get to talk…" I paused, rapidly considering and discarding ways to end this sentence that didn't sound so hokey and worn out. I settled on, "to talk about, uh, us," which was just what I wanted to avoid.

"We should go on a real date," she said.

"What…what did you have in mind?" I knew what a *real date* meant to me, but what was a real date for Melissa? A trip to Paris? A suite at the Waldorf Astoria? A cruise on the Queen Mary? I had so little money that when my mom gave me the bus fare back to Ithaca, I made the puppy dog face until she added an extra twenty. But I could definitely afford *my* idea of a real date.

"You know what a real date is, Tony."

I stood at the end of the diving board and she was pushing me off. She wanted me to say it. Was the pool empty or full of warm water? "A sleep-over?"

A glorious smile covered her face. She looked down at her chicken, and raised her eyes to mine. Her face glowed an incredible red. Just like the cranberry sauce. Melissa was blushing.

The only thing left to discuss was "When." "Now" was an answer that seemed to satisfy us both.

Chapter 14

We leaped to our feet, grabbed the dinner trays and jammed them through the hole by the dish room. Then we bolted out the door and down the hill to my dorm, our coats under our arms, holding hands tightly as if we were expecting the police to jump from the shadows and pull us apart. We must have looked like athletes in some kind of Olympic potato sack race. Melissa ran so hard the heel broke off her long black leather boot and she laughed when I tried to sweep her up and carry her the last few steps. We were out of breath when we stepped onto the fourth floor of Lyon Hall, my dorm. Instead of turning right to my room, I turned left towards Country Bob's.

"But your room..." she tried to say.

"Don't worry about it. Under control," I was breathing in short, fast gasps. Four quick flights of stairs, I guess. "It's okay. We're fine. I have the key...don't worry..."

"I got it, Tony. Relax."

Then I realized I had never looked into Bob's room since we had talked. I had no idea how he had left it. It could be a shit hole! His bed could be covered in dirty underwear and copies of *Playboy* and *Penthouse*! Empty Ripple wine bottles! Dirty Kleenex everywhere! Pictures of cows! I hadn't even looked in to see if it was clean. What if the bed was stripped? What if the mattress looked like...mattresses *looked!* I stood at the door and couldn't get the key in the lock. Right side up, upside down, it didn't matter. I rattled it frantically and tried to lift the door by the doorknob, but it wouldn't go. "Damn it! Damn it! Damn it!" I said.

"Tony. Please. Let me." Melissa took the key, slid it effortlessly into the lock, and the door glided open. "You're adorable, Tony. You are the cutest person I know. You're just adorable." I followed her in and flipped the light switch. The room filled with soft red light from his desk lamp, which was covered with a red T-shirt. I looked around. I couldn't believe it.

Bob's room was immaculate. The bed was made with fresh sheets. On the bedside nightstand (a nightstand! He had a frigging nightstand!) a thick red candle stood on a stolen dinner plate. A pack of matches leaned upright against it. The wonderful pipe rested next to the candle, the bowl stuffed with bright green bud. A bottle of Mateus wine, along with a corkscrew and two glasses stood on his dresser. All the guys knew that stuff was exclusively for dates and not for general purpose drinking. The most incredible thing were the walls: they had been cleared of every trace of livestock. Not a single bull or heifer would be looking down on us.

His record player sat on his desk, a Procol Harum album cued up, ready to go. "Look at this," said Melissa. "*A Whiter Shade of Pale*. The world's greatest make out song. How thoughtful."

On the pillow were three Trojan Natural Lambskin condoms in gold foil packets. A note in Bob's handwriting read, "It's all for you guys, Merry Christmas."

"This is lovely," she said as she sat on the bed. I sat down next to her. We were still holding hands.

"This is Country Bob's room. He said I could use it."

"Country Bob is quite a guy. Not everybody has a friend like him."

"Would you like, to, maybe smoke a little pot?"

"Pot just makes me sleepy. Do you want to?"

"Pot makes me horny," I said.

"Guys are always horny, Tony. Guys don't need pot for that." Boy, was that the truth.

"No, I guess not. Would you like some wine?"

"I don't need any wine. It's better without anything, don't you think? Then we can't blame it on anything. It's just something we did because we wanted to do it. Isn't that what you want? Two adults doing something they both want to do? No excuses?"

"Right. Yes. I agree, no excuses." I wanted to drain the bottle of wine and suck down the bowl of grass in one giant toke, anything to slow my heart down. She'll be able to hear my heart pounding. She'll feel it. She'll know. Then she said it...the big question.

"Have you done this before?"

"This? You mean…this? Yes, of course. Sure." I lied. I knew that question was going to come up, and I had planned to tell the truth. I had even practiced it before the mirror. I planned to say "You're my first!" But at the last second I chickened out and lied. I lied! "How about you?"

"Just with my boyfriend."

"You had a boyfriend?" This was news. It felt like being shot. "What was he like?"

She tilted her head and looked up at me with eyes that were even darker than usual.

"The last thing in the world I want to do right now…*right now*, Tony, is talk about my old boyfriend. Okay?"

"Of course."

"Tony, do you like me?"

"Of course I like you. You know that."

"How *much* do you like me? Tell me. Tell me how much you like me."

"I, uh…" The room was silent except for the slamming kettle drum beat which was about to demolish my rib cage.

"Are you going to kiss me?"

Finally, a question I could answer. "Yes. I am." I wrapped my arms around her and pressed my body against hers. If I had ever kept any secrets about how I felt, they were gone now. It should be perfectly obvious how I felt about her.

But she twisted her face away and broke the kiss. The she turned back and stared into my eyes without speaking. I wanted to kiss her again but this was not what she wanted. Then she said, "Tell me how much you like me. How much?"

"I'm crazy about you."

"Close. Try again."

I knew what she wanted to hear. Of course I knew. I had never said those words—those exact words—to anyone outside my family ever before. I wasn't sure I could do it. *What the hell was I so afraid of?* It felt like coughing up a giant hairball. But I knew that once it got out of my throat the first time, the next time it would be a breeze.

"I love you," I said. It didn't sound ridiculous at all, even in my own voice.

"That's the right answer," she said. Then she sat up and slowly pulled her shirt over her head, turning her back to me. Her skin was flawless. Her bra strap hooked in the middle. She sat quietly as I undid it.

"Start the record," she said.

Chapter 15

I awoke to the soft scratching of the record needle in the run-out groove. We had replayed the first side of the Procol Harum album at least five times. Bob, I realized, was a true friend. Also a genius. Melissa was right; not too many people had a friend like Country Bob.

I almost always wake up bleary eyed and disoriented, in no hurry to resume my unspectacular life. But that didn't happen. I was wide-eyed, alert and ready to go. I carefully pulled the blankets back and looked at my sleeping companion. My guest. My lover. Her long, glossy brown hair spilled over her perfect back. Her rear end was fabulously displayed for my enjoyment. I had never seen a girl's naked rear end before…not a real one. Not up close. I didn't even get to see it last night. Melissa had switched off the desk lamp and had blown out the candle long before we had advanced to that stage. I just took it all in. I had barely slept. As I moved to sit up in the bed I realized a dull ache seeped out of my groin muscles, as if I had done too many sit-ups. I looked down at the expanse of my own pale naked skin. It looked about the same as it always did—nothing special. But it felt different. Everything felt different. Something big had changed. I smiled at my own body, laughed out loud at its eagerness to return to the activities of the evening. I gently nudged my partner. She grunted softly and didn't move. I stepped it up a little, poking her gently…somebody wanted some attention.

"Oh, no you don't," she murmured. "You're out of thingies, remember? There were only three."

"Good morning, gorgeous," I said. "Time to rise and shine."

"Do some more shining and less rising, okay? I'm sore." She turned to face me, smiling. She sat up, her naked body ablaze in the sunlight streaming through the window. Bob's room, opposite my own at the other side of the building, had a tremendous advantage over mine. Each morning, the southern exposure and the big window gave you a great look at whomever you went to bed with the night before.

I realized I was staring at her. She blushed and I looked away. Then she said, "No. Look at me. I want to look at you too. Let's see what you look like in the daylight. It's okay to do that. We should do that. We made love, last night, remember?"

"Yes," I said, "I do remember that. Then it wasn't a dream after all!" *Interesting*, I thought. What she said. "We made love." Not, "We screwed" or "You finally got laid" or any other crude way of stating the obvious. No, we had made love. And, boy, was it ever obvious. I glanced at the room. Our clothes were all over the floor. Bits of the shredded foil condom packages were everywhere. Piles of crumpled Kleenex. Melissa's sailor pants...thirteen buttons? Hardly. Those things must have had a thousand buttons, at least. When they had finally yielded I whipped the pants off her feet and flung them over my head. Somehow they landed lying upside down and hanging from the window latch, like a sign announcing, "Hey you guys! Eat your heart out!"

She leaned against the wall behind the bed and looked me up and down. "Not bad. You'll do. Did you have fun last night?"

"Are you kidding? Yeah. Absolutely. The most fun I've ever had. You're like a one-girl amusement park. It was great. How about you? Did you have fun?"

She paused. "Uh huh."

"Just 'Uh huh?' That doesn't sound good. That's it? 'Uh huh?'"

She looked away, then said, "Are you sure you've done it before?" This was my chance to come clean, to tell her she was my first, to throw myself at her feet and beg for mercy, beg for an indulgence, most of all, beg for another chance.

"Well...sure! Of course." I lied. Again. What the hell was the matter with me?

She giggled. "You are such a liar. That's okay. All you need is practice. You'll come around. Don't worry about it."

"Practice? Like now? No time like the present, that's what I always say." To be honest, that's what my mom always said, but it didn't seem like a good time to mention my mother.

"No. Not like now. Down, boy. Tony, tell me something. What would you have done without Country Bob's thoughtfulness? The room? The music…the rubbers? Don't you have your own?"

"Melissa, you surprised the hell out of me. I wasn't…ready. I didn't expect…"

"You wouldn't make much of a Boy Scout. You know. Be prepared? Remember that? Weren't you even thinking about it?"

Another question I could answer! "Sure! That's all I thought about. Twenty-four hours a day. That's what I thought about. That's what I'm thinking about right now, if you want to know the truth." Then we were both quiet, as if we were in a play and one of us forgot our lines.

After a few seconds she said, "You're welcome."

"Oh…Yeah. Right. Of course," I said. "I mean, thank you. Can I see you tonight? We have the room till the end of inter… Intersession…"

"Not tonight, lover; I need a break. And you need to go shopping." She called me 'lover!' She stood up and let the sheet and blanket fall away. She reached her hands over her head and stretched. She wasn't shy at all. She didn't race around the room holding her hands in front of her breasts in a comical gesture of modesty. She looked comfortable, naked, not the least bit embarrassed or ashamed or regretful. Instead, she looked happy. And proud. Yeah, proud is absolutely the right word. She pranced around the room like a kid at an Easter egg hunt, finding each item of discarded clothing, then stopping in front of the window to pluck her sailor bell bottoms off the window latch.

"Now what in the world could have happened that my pants ended up over here?" She turned to me, laughing, holding the pants at arm's length.

"Damn, I love you," I said. I didn't even think about it. It just came out, effortlessly, easiest thing I had ever done. Just like I thought would happen.

"Hold that thought, Tony. I like hearing that. You can say that all you want." I said it again. Then I waited for her to say something.

She dropped the little bundle of clothes on the floor, and turned to me. "Are you sure you don't have any more thingies?"

Chapter 16

I hope I live to be the oldest guy in the old age home, but I doubt I'll ever be happier than I was those two weeks. I kept my promise to Country Bob. I changed the sheets before he came back. Juanita, the dorm maid, had returned to Mexico for the holidays, so I trudged the sheets down to the student laundromat. Four times. It's amazing how often you have to do that under the right circumstances. Two other guys I knew stayed on campus for the same reason and we'd run into each other. We acknowledged each other with a knowing smile and a thumbs up as if we had all joined some secret society. We had limped into winter break as boys and we were marching out as men.

Melissa and I gradually moved into Bob's room, even redecorating it with stuff she brought from her own dorm. We lived in glorious luxury, without classes to go to or tests to study for. We'd get up about ten in the morning, eat a leisurely breakfast, and then entertain ourselves with the winter weather. We'd steal trays from the cafeteria and sail down the snow covered hill like toboggan racers. We skated on the little lake by the girls' dining hall. Melissa did, anyway. I hobbled. Melissa skated like a champion, but that didn't surprise me. There was nothing she couldn't do. Evenings we spent at the coffee house, or in the Echo Chamber, singing and playing music together. We worked out an arrangement of *Visions of Johanna* that would have made Bob Dylan cry his eyes out. We called it our song. I actually learned all the words. Then we'd return to the room and the festivities would begin again.

Within a few days, my groin muscles didn't hurt anymore. A day or two after that, Melissa reported my performance as 'terrific.' I was going for 'absolutely fantastic,' and I received that assessment at the end of the second week. I smiled all that day. It was very gratifying to see my grades improving. If I had to find one word to describe those two weeks, it would have to be 'heaven.'

It all ended with a messy, dull thud. Intersession was over. The university reopened. The students came back... and so did Clarence. I had barely thought about him, but there he was, standing in front of our shared room with his suitcase. Country Bob returned and came looking for his key. Melissa gathered up her stuff and I helped carry it back to the other side of campus.

"Maybe I'll see you next Saturday, Tony. Great winter vacation, don't you think?" She kissed me on the cheek. "The best."

On the cheek? Like she was my Aunt Gloria? What was this "cheek" crap? How in the world would I live until next Saturday? I felt like I had severed an artery, my blood spurting into the snow. How would I survive?

Minutes later I was slogging through the slush and sleet. The sun had disappeared from the sky the very moment Melissa walked through the door to her dorm. At twelve noon it looked like seven o'clock at night and gray clouds and cold wind kicked up again. I shoved my hands in my pockets and dragged myself back to my room like an inmate in a prison yard, alone and cold.

Chapter 17

A thick depression moved in with the bad weather. Instead of Country Bob's big room and nice wide bed, filled to the brim with Melissa, my tiny top bunk bed and Clarence Carter waited for me at the bottom of the hill. The one word I could use to sum it all up would be, 'not heaven.' The other place. Bizarro Heaven.

I didn't need to write the date of my next meeting with Melissa anywhere. I wouldn't forget it. I counted down the minutes until I would see her again and time slowed to a crawl. I couldn't even call her. Twenty kids used one pay phone. Calling her was next to impossible. I stood vigil by our usual table in the dining room each day at lunch time. I didn't know her new schedule, or whether she even had a free period to eat lunch. Our Saturday date seemed like a distant promise.

I was wasting away from a severe Melissa shortage. Then, the Friday before I could see her again, there she was, pea coat, earrings, boots, the works. She was the sunrise after a month of rain. But the joyful reunion was brief.

"I hope you're not mad," she said, "Saturday evening is the only free time I have right now and I've got an invitation to meet with someone I'd really like to get to know a little better."

"Saturday night? But that's our night. Why would you make a date with someone else on Saturday?"

"It's the only time I'm free, Tony, remember?"

"But you're not free. What about us? We haven't seen each other for over a week." She stopped smiling. She stared into me like she was drilling for coal.

"Back up, Tony. What does that mean, I'm not free?"

"I just mean you have a date with me. I thought we promised each other."

"We did?" she asked. "How come I don't remember that? When did we do that? What are you so worried about? It's not even a date. Don't get so excited, Tony. Nothing has changed. I just want to talk to this guy and tomorrow night is the only chance I'll get."

"But what about..." I began but she stepped all over me.

"I spent two whole weeks with you, Tony, remember? Just you. You shouldn't be so selfish." I didn't reply. After a few seconds her voice softened. "Look, Tony... my good friend..." Now I'm a good friend. That's a hell of a demotion...down from lover. She put her hand on mine. I expected it to be warm. It wasn't. "Stop worrying about this. Try to see it through my eyes. That whole thing, you and me...it happened so quickly, we didn't have time to think." She smiled at me as if nothing was wrong. But I knew all her smiles, and not all of them were genuine. This one was a real stinker. "Maybe we just need some time."

I didn't need any time. *That whole thing?* It was broken. This was all wrong. The alarm bell going off in my head could empty the building.

"But why are you dating someone else?" I heard my voice begging for an answer. "I thought you and I were...together." The sounds in my head were like cracking of the roof timbers. "I thought you loved me." I sputtered this last part, frantically searching my memory for a specific, concrete example of when she said exactly that in so many words. I couldn't do it. A wave of nausea moved in. Lame! Lame! I was a homeless puppy scratching at her door.

"Does that mean I have to ask permission to spend time with someone else?" she asked. There was only one possible answer.

"No, of course not," I said quickly. "That's not what I mean at all. But I've been waiting all this time to see you. And you said..." But she wasn't finished. She swatted the puppy with a rolled-up newspaper.

"Tony, you had my undivided attention, *my mind, my body, my everything*, for two weeks. Two weeks! Now I'm asking you to share just a little of me for one measly night so that I can do something for myself...to talk to someone I want to get to know better. And you have a problem with that?"

"But we're sleeping together..." *Yip, Yip! Whine!* Then I realized what I had just said and what kind of swat would follow. I had pulled the pin on a hand grenade and I couldn't let go of it.

"We 'slept' together," she corrected me. "Is that what you want? You're the English major. Pick a tense, Tony. Is this past tense or future? I don't know what's happening here but I don't like it. I'm not used to people telling me who I can and can't spend time with and what I can and can't do. This shouldn't be that much of a surprise to you. You should know me well enough by now. This is a real turn-off for me, Tony." The Queen had spoken. The only thing missing was, "Off with his head."

"Okay. Okay. I'm sorry." I could hear the pleading in my own voice. It was embarrassing. "Your life is your own. I have no claim to you. Can you at least tell me who this guy is?"

"It's just going to make you more upset."

"Why? Who is it?"

"Clarence."

Chapter 18

Country Bob took a sip from his beer and watched as I tried to line up the pool shot. No use. It was still my turn, but this would be as far as I would get.

I had managed to sink three stripes—two on the break and one more on my second shot. I finished my beer and poured the last of the pitcher into my glass. Two dollar bills lay on the edge of the pool table, one of mine, and the other belonged to Country Bob. I tried to arrange a complicated bank shot but the geometry gave me a headache. This was not a good night for me to solve puzzles. The biggest puzzle of all occupied every second of my thoughts. I took the shot and missed, as I knew I would. Bob snatched his cue from its position, leaning against the wall just under the giant velvet painting of dogs playing poker. Then he proceeded to run the table of all the solids.

When you played eight ball with Bob, the rule was simple. Don't give him a chance to shoot. On his next to last shot, the cue ball rolled smoothly to a stop directly behind the eight ball. The side pocket looked as big as the Grand Canyon, just a few inches away.

"Don't bother," I said. "I concede."

Bob took a drag from his cigarette and stubbed it out in the glass ashtray on the sticky tabletop. "Nope," he said. "Can't do that. Have to play by the rules." In a second it was all over, the faintest click, the plop of the eight ball, the two dollar bills whisked away and stuffed in his pocket.

"Tell me," he said. "What kind of hell has come crashing down on you that would put you here in this God forsaken Collegetown bar to shoot pool and lose to a humble farm boy? Don't you usually spend Saturday night dancin' the horizontal mambo with your lady friend?"

I told him the whole story, at least up to the point where he held up his hand, muttered, "Hang on," and then returned with a new pitcher of Genny Cream Ale. "You're going to need this, big fella."

"I'll get the next one," I said.

"Then I'll get the one after that, then it will be your turn again."

"I'm gonna have to go back to my room at some point," I said.

"When you do, your friend Clarence will be there, so I'm betting you're not in a big hurry to do that. What do you think is going on here? Why is Melissa in such a hurry to spend time with the guy?"

"No idea. I don't get it. I can't see why anyone would want to be anywhere near him. The guy's an unfriendly asshole."

"Unfriendly?"

I refilled my glass. "You think Clarence Carter is friendly? Are we talking about the same guy?"

"I never had any problem with him," said Country Bob.

"You know him?"

"Tony, he's your roommate. You guys just live at the other end of the hall! I also see him at the fundraisers for Father Dan."

"He talks to you?"

"Yeah. He speaks English and everything."

"What do you talk about?"

"I don't know. I didn't know I was supposed to take notes. Stuff. Sports. Economics. He's an officer of the B.L.F. He's pretty involved in university politics."

"What the hell is a B.L.F.?"

"What planet do you live on Tony? Don't you read the *Cornell Sun?* The Black Liberation Front. He never told you that?"

"He never speaks to me. We live in the same room and he never says anything. If you know so much about him, tell me this: What does Melissa find so irresistible about him?"

Bob waited for me to answer my own question. I finished my beer in one gulp and poured another. The beer was doing its magical thing. I finally had an audience. I could give him the whole story. "I'll tell you what. He's *black*. And she's a crazy-ass flaming liberal and she's afraid to say no. She doesn't want anybody to think she's prejudiced."

"And is she? Prejudiced, I mean?"

"She's no more prejudiced than I am."

Bob nodded gravelly and said, "That bad, huh?" That was all I needed. I stopped myself from another round of shouting denials.

"I'm sick of hearing that crap. That's not funny anymore," I said.

"It wasn't meant to be." Bob reached for his pack of Camels and stuck another one in the corner of his mouth.

"So you think I'm racist?"

"Not racist. Maybe prejudiced." He lit a cigarette and took a long drag. I waited for him to offer the pack to me. He didn't. "Racist and prejudiced aren't the same thing. You don't think you're maybe just a little prejudiced? Hell, everyone is prejudiced about something, Tony. Some folks don't even like farmers."

"Oh, bullshit," I said. "I'm tired of hearing this crap."

"I came here to play pool. You want to shoot another game? Or what?"

"Screw it." I made no effort to hide the anger in my voice. Bob backed away from me before replying.

"So what are your plans for the rest of the evening, after you drain the pitcher? Are you planning to punch a few more holes in the bathroom wall?"

"Screw you, Bob."

"Lovely. I just remembered I have to wash my hair tonight. It's time I was on my way. Enjoy the beer. Try not to hurt yourself. Call me if you ever calm down."

Chapter 19

I jammed another quarter into the table and the balls tumbled into the box. I slammed each one into place in the triangle, and made enough noise to attract the attention of the bartender. He was huge. Not just huge, but huge and ugly, two hundred fifty pounds of ugly. In the light from the neon beer signs hanging from the stained ceiling, he looked like King Kong in an apron. He would have looked right at home clinging to the side of the Empire State Building, swatting biplanes like mosquitoes. I ignored him.

I lined up the cue ball and drew back the stick as far as it would go, then fired it forward like an artillery shell. The break shot exploded the balls in all directions and four of them lifted off the table and crashed into the cinder block wall just under the beagle with the full house. The eight ball rolled across the floor and tapped the bartender's shoe. It takes a lot to get the eight ball off the table in a break shot. King Kong picked up the ball and brought it to me.

"If I gotta recover this table you're gonna give me three hundred bucks. We understand each other, buddy?"

There were a lot more bars in Collegetown than just the Royal Palm. I went into a place that I had never seen students go into. We called it the old man's bar. A dozen guys sat on stools or in dark booths lined up against the wall. They were all old, in their forties at least. One woman sat at the bar, all alone on a Saturday night, chain smoking Kool cigarettes, the pack lying open on the bar, the ashtray before her filled with lipstick smeared butts. A half full wine glass on the bar. In the dim light, with the cigarette hanging from her mouth, holding the wine glass with two hands, she could have been my mother. Except for the tight black skirt and the high heels.

The place looked and felt like a zoo to me, and I was an animal in the wrong cage. I didn't belong here. I didn't sit down. Maybe, I thought, I should just leave. After all, I had a pint of bourbon in my coat pocket. But it was cold as hell outside. Then it hit me. This was the perfect place. This was just what I needed. No one who knew me would wander in. The chance of running into Melissa and Clarence was virtually zero.

How do you get a drink around here? I didn't see the bartender. A handwritten sign taped to the mirror behind the bar offered the Saturday night special. Eighty five cents bought a shot of Four Roses and a mug of Utica Club beer. The price was right. A dark bar where no one knew me and sold cheap booze was just what I needed.

A door behind the bar was suddenly pushed open and the bartender clomped up the final steps from the basement. He was even bigger than the gorilla at the Palm. He wore a white apron over a white shirt and a black bow tie. He was the first bartender I had seen wearing a bow tie who wasn't in a movie. Over his shoulders he carried a fresh half keg of beer. I knew what that felt like. I had carried one of those before. Well, me and another guy, anyway.

I was already bombed. I had stopped keeping track of all the beers. Maybe it was time to try something else. I swayed a little. Did the bartender notice? If he thought I should leave I would agree right away and go quietly. No sense in causing trouble. This wasn't a TV show. No sense getting hurt. What did I have to prove? Nothing.

I pushed a handful of coins into the cigarette machine and pulled the handle on a pack of Kools. *I must be hammered; I never buy a pack of cigarettes.* Why Kools? My dad would kill me if he caught me smoking. But everyone in here had a cigarette dangling out of their mouths. That's just what you do in a shit hole like this, right?

Where should I sit? No one looked too friendly. There was just one woman in the whole bar, and she wasn't exactly my type. But what the hell? I could sit next to her, strike up a conversation. See what happened next. *That's what you do, right? Right? And just how would Melissa feel about that? Who gives a shit? Because Melissa's not here, is she?*

I sat down on the stool next to the woman and ordered a Saturday night special. I peeled the wrapper from the pack of Kools and tapped one out.

The woman glanced at me and smiled. She lit a match and offered the flame as I put the cigarette between my lips. I took a drag and the smoke burned my throat as if I had sucked on a bottle of Ben-Gay. Kool, my ass.

"Slummin' it tonight?" she asked. In reply I exhaled the smoke through my nose, like they do in the movies. It burned like I had shoved a sparkler up there. She studied me, then looked away. "You don't smoke, do you? Here's some advice. Don't start tonight." The bartender placed my shot of whiskey and draft beer in front of me and swept away my dollar bill. "What happened, honey?" the woman asked, "Did Igor throw you out of the Palm?"

I took a tiny sip from the shot glass before I answered. "How did you know?"

"Oh, I know lots of stuff," she said. "I know you're not a whiskey drinker. Try this. That'll go down easier if you just drop the shot glass into the beer mug. It's still nasty but you'll be able to drink it."

"Just drop it in?"

She nodded. "Just drop it in." I held the shot glass about a foot over the beer. She took my hand and gently lowered it to an inch over the mug. She nodded and I let go. It splashed through the foam and settled to the bottom.

She picked up her wine glass, and held it out in a toast. I picked up my mug and downed it in one long gulp. She smiled as she watched me, then looked away, shaking her head.

"What else can you teach me?" I asked, and banged the glass on the bar.

"Oh, I think school's over for tonight, honey. You're not driving, are you?" She finished her wine, stubbed out her cigarette and picked up her purse.

"You're leaving?" I asked. "Alone?"

"You get used to it. Don't get too comfortable on that bar stool, my friend. Don't make a habit of it."

"You didn't even tell me your name..." I said.

"Lorraine." Then she slid off the chair and headed for the door, as if I was frigging radioactive.

The hell with you too. I fished out another dollar from my wallet and waved it at the bartender. He returned with a fresh shot and another mug of beer. A bar towel draped across his shoulder. "Last call," he said.

"I just got here. Last call's at one AM. It's only twelve-thirty."

"Last call for you." He was polite about it, I'll give him that. "Can I call you a cab?"

"No thanks," I said. "I can walk. I'm a shh…shtudent." I dropped the shot glass into the beer from a foot away and drenched the bar with Utica Club.

"A student, huh?" asked the bartender. "No kidding." He waited till I had drained the last of the whiskey and beer, then flapped his hand the way a little kid says, "Bye bye."

Chapter 20

I walked home in the cold. I knew the route by heart, had taken it nearly every day since I arrived in Ithaca. Collegetown was barely a half mile from my dorm. Every kind of store you needed, you could find on College Ave. A grocery store, a bookstore. Bank, record shop, drug store, bagel shop. Two liquor stores. Ugh. Maybe a bagel would be good...Yeah, a bagel.

There had to be a shorter way to get back to my dorm. No reason to go the long way, across the bridge. Which way would Melissa go? But I didn't want to see Melissa. She'd be with Clarence. What if they were kissing? No, they wouldn't be doing that. What *were* they doing? Go back another way. Find a shortcut. There must be a shortcut.

I had to force my eyes to stay open; I even slapped myself on the face with my open palm. My cheeks were numb in the winter breeze but I barely felt it. Everything looked familiar but somehow nothing looked like what I expected. I had seen it all before, but nothing really made sense. If I went that way, what would I see? I couldn't remember. Where was the bridge to campus? Had I ever been in this neighborhood before? Why couldn't I find College Avenue? I tried holding one hand over my left eye, then my right, to see if I could focus better, but then I nearly fell over. I couldn't feel my feet. I hadn't dressed for a frigging trek to the North Pole. There were stairs I had to walk up. Stairs on a sidewalk? Where the hell was I?

I needed to rest.

Maybe I should sit down. The street was pitching and swaying like the suspension bridge on a windy night.

A bench! Here's a nice bench. I reached out to hold it still so I could sit on it before it moved away again. I dropped on it, grabbing the sides so it would know who was boss. Finally. I just needed to close my eyes for a few seconds.

Thump. Thump. What the hell was that? I shooed it away with my hand. It was hard. It came right back.

Thump. "Wake up, son."

"I'm not asleep." I opened my eyes. A policeman poked me again with a nightstick.

"You can't sleep on a bus stop bench. You need to wake up and go home, son. You'll freeze to death tonight, and I'll have to fill out a lot of paperwork. You don't want me to have to do that, do you?"

"No."

"Have you been drinking tonight, son?"

"Maybe a little. It's Saturday night. Of course I been drinking. I'm nineteen, for chrissakes."

"Can you stand up?"

"Sure I can…"

"Well, I hope you can. Because if you can't, I have to give you a ride downtown. And you don't want that. You don't want to spend the night in the drunk tank, do you?"

"No, sir."

"Of course you don't. And you don't want to go through life with a public intoxication charge either, right?"

"Right."

"All right then. Up you go. Where do you live?"

"Lyon Hall."

"You're in luck, son. You're a hundred feet from Lyon Hall." He pointed his nightstick at a tall stone building lit pale yellow by a street lamp. I thought hard. Had I ever seen it before? "That's it, right there. You're going to be all right. Go on home now, son. If I see you like this again it won't go so easy on you. Okay? Do you understand?"

"Yes."

I needed to throw up. I waited until the cop had walked into the shadows before I doubled over and vomited violently, clutching the back of the bench and heaving till my stomach muscles cramped. It was the loudest, most terrible sound I had ever heard. The cop didn't turn around.

Chapter 21

Cold air burned in my lungs with each deep breath as I made my way back to the dorm. I was blind drunk and I knew it. I had puked just a few feet away from a cop. I had barely escaped being hauled in for vagrancy, public intoxication, who knows? How did this happen? *What would Melissa think?* Would she ever talk to me again? What should I do now?

Then I remembered. It didn't matter. Melissa wasn't here. She was absent, away without leave, out of the office, gone fishing. What did I care what she thought about me? Why should I? Who gives a crap? The truth was all around me: once again I was alone. Then I remembered Clarence. My head throbbed and a burst of heat formed in my throat. I puked again. Right outside the dorm.

I began the long stomp up the four flights of stairs to my room. Clarence would be waiting for me. It was after two in the morning, so nothing was open. The movies and the bars had closed. Even frat parties had shut down. Everything was finished for the night. Clarence would be in his bed, staring at the door. I'd see the whites of his eyes and his teeth. He'd be laughing at me. I'd have to face him. The son of a bitch. I stopped to hold myself up while I sucked in a huge lung full of air, my heart pounding. The stairwell swirled around me. Despite the cold, my face was dripping with sweat.

I let go and continued to climb the stairs. I started over: Okay, so this is how it's going to work: *If he gives me shit I'm calling him out. I don't give a damn how big he is. I don't care if he's got a knife. I don't care if I live or die.*

He can beat me to death right here, right now, I don't care. If I'm going down I'm taking him with me. I'll kill him first. I'll break my typewriter over his head. I need to get this over with. If he gets out of bed I'll kick him in the chest like Bruce Lee. Then I'll hit him with his desk chair.

I stopped at the first landing and grabbed the banister, panting like a wild animal. The pain in my side—the one I always get when I run too hard or climb too many stairs—had kicked in.

By the time I reached the fourth floor I was pulling myself up with the railing. My heart was racing, I could feel it in my ears. A powerful, sour taste in my mouth made me desperate for a drink of water. Every part of me ached. Somehow, some way, I would kick Clarence Carter into the next county, if it was the last thing I ever did.

I jammed the key into the lock and threw the door open. It crashed into the side of his desk with a noise so sudden and loud I was sure a hundred guys would pile out of their rooms to watch the battle explode.

But the room was dark. Clarence was not in his bed. His bed had not been slept in. There was no sign that anyone had been in the room since I had left it to play pool with Country Bob. Confusion blotted out all my brave thoughts. If Clarence was missing—at two in the morning—where was Melissa? *She must be with him.* I nearly vomited again, just at the thought of it.

My knees gave way and I tumbled onto the bottom bunk. I needed to sleep. I needed a shower, a glass of water. I needed to get my shoes off, to climb up on the chair, stand on the desk, and get in my own bed. I needed to sleep...I needed to sleep.

Chapter 22

The pounding gradually grew louder. The pillow over my face did nothing to muffle it. It wouldn't stop. I opened my eyes. I was still alive—that was the only thing I was sure of. I flexed my fingers and toes, then ran my right hand over my legs and left arm. Two arms, two legs. No wounds. What had happened to me? Two more bangs sounded on the door.

The tiny room was washed in the milky gray morning light that seeped through the dingy window. After a few moments I knew I was in my dorm room. But the perspective was all wrong. What was I looking at? What was that thing above my head? It's not the ceiling. *Am I on the bottom bunk? On Clarence's bed?* What *happened* to me?

"Shut up!" I yelled to whoever was doing the incessant banging and rattling. I didn't need visitors. "Go away! Get out of here!" I sat up on the tiny bed, just missing hitting my head on the bed frame above it. The pressure filled my skull and my head felt like it was about to pop open like an over-inflated tire. I threw myself back down onto the mattress. The banging continued.

"Go away! Beat it!" I yelled. My voice was hoarse and gravely, and nowhere near as loud as I wanted it to be. But it was as loud as I could make it. A horrible taste filled my mouth. Had I been smoking cigarettes? My skull throbbed and my eyes burned. Some big nameless, faceless anxiety hung over me and I struggled to make sense of it. Melissa. Melissa was gone.

"Tony! Wake up! Are you all right? Are you still alive?" It sounded

69

like Country Bob. Bob...why did that name scare me? What had I done to Bob? Did we have some kind of fight? "Tony, for God's sake, let me in! I brought you a cup of coffee."

Why would he bring me coffee? I sat up again, but more slowly. I pulled myself to my feet and waited for the room to settle down before walking to the door, carefully, measuring each step, as if I were a blind man. My eyes were as wide open as I could make them. I unlocked the door. Bob was dressed in blue jeans and a blue flannel shirt. His hooded parka hung open, and dripped with melting snow. He held a large coffee in his free hand, a big red C printed on the white cardboard cup.

"Why did you bring me coffee?" I asked him.

He didn't answer. He stared at me. "Jesus! What the hell happened to you? You look like you just got out of the rodeo rink. And you lost. Did you get in a fight after all?"

I reached for the cup. "Why did you bring me coffee?"

"Because I figured you'd need it. You do, too. You look like hell." He looked around the room. A trail of blankets and sheets led from the bottom bunk to the door. I was still clutching a pillow. He looked at the rumpled bed. "What happened in here? Did you sleep with Clarence? Did you two kiss and make up?"

I took a sip from the cup. The coffee was hot and black. I drink it with lots of milk and sugar but didn't complain. The thought of milk and sugar made me nauseous. "Very funny," I said. "He didn't even come back to the room last night."

"Oh crap. That's not good," said Bob.

"I gotta sit down," I said, and slumped into my desk chair and stared off into space, sipping from the steaming cardboard cup.

"What happened to Melissa?" asked Bob.

"I have no idea." The words hissed out of me. "Maybe they're still together. I don't know where she is. Did the hall phone ring last night? Or this morning?"

"Would you have heard it if it did? You were pretty out of it. I'd say you were plenty hammered last night."

"Give me a break. Didn't you ever go out drinking?"

"Plenty of times, but never like that. Hell, even the sheep and the goats have the sense to stop—"

"Oh shut up, Bob. I don't need a lecture. I'm never going to drink again."

"Uh huh. I'm sure. Did you see the note on your door?"

"There's a note on my door?"

"Crap, Tony, finish the coffee and wake up. Yes, there's a note on your door."

"Who's it from?"

"How the hell do I know? I don't read other people's mail! Come here." He grabbed my hand and pulled me into the hallway. I spilled some of the hot coffee on my foot. I still had my socks on. Somehow, I had gotten my shoes off. He pointed to a folded piece of paper hanging from a safety pin stuck into the wood. "See, Tony? A note. What did I tell you?"

I put my face up to the note so I could see it without my glasses, without a good part of my brain in working order. It was written on a slip of paper the size and shape of a check; it looked like a deposit slip torn from a checkbook. Across the front was written "2:45 AM" in a familiar color of lipstick. Kind of red, kind of pink. I knew that color well. "It's from Melissa," I said, tearing it off the door as fast as my arms could move. I pulled the scrap of paper open and read it. Instantly my hangover vanished. My blurry vision cleared, a rush of air filled my lungs, and blood surged through my veins and into my brain, closing every switch.

"Is she all right?" asked Bob.

"No!" I held it up for Bob to read. Written in the pink lipstick, in letters top to bottom, it read, "HELP."

"Wait! Tony!" Bob called after me as I careened down the stairs three at a time. "Slow down! It's freezing out! Call her first!"

"Her dorm phone is always busy. It's faster to go over there!"

"It's *Sunday morning!* Call her! That's why God invented telephones! And put your damn shoes on. My hound dog has more sense than you do." Bob stuffed his hand into his blue jeans and held out a coin. "Here. Dime. Phone. Now."

I jammed the coin into the payphone and spun the dial. I hardly ever got through but I had the number memorized from the moment she gave it to me. I couldn't remember my mother's birthday, but Melissa's phone number was burned into my skull. "It's ringing!" I told Bob. "It's still ringing…still ringing…"

"I got it, Tony. Get a grip. Calm down. Everything's going to be okay."

The phone clicked and a girl's husky voice, heavy with sleep, said, "Risley Hall, third floor. Umm, good morning."

"I need to speak to Melissa Kolaski, please. It's important."

"What room is she in?"

"Three twenty three."

"Oh God. That's like a mile away. Hold on." The phone made a sharp cracking noise as the receiver at the other end smacked into the cinder block wall. I knew the girl had simply dropped the phone and shuffled off.

"Hurry up…please…" I called into the phone. I could hear my own voice echo in the hallway on the other side of campus.

"Come on! Come on, come on, come on, come on, come…" I hissed through clenched teeth.

Bob shook his head. "Calm down, Mr. Vitelli."

"Bob, what's your last name?"

"Crawford. Why?"

"Shut the hell up, Mr. Crawford."

"You're going to give yourself a heart attack, Tony."

"Too late. I think I'm already having one." I slammed the receiver back into the cradle. "I'm leaving. I'm putting on my shoes and leaving. Are you coming with me?"

"I think I'll pass," said Bob. "I'll stay here and keep an eye out for Melissa. What do you want me to do if I see Clarence?"

"Kill him."

Chapter 23

When I got to Risley Hall I charged past the reception desk. The girl called after me, "Excuse me! You have to sign in! Hey!" The girls' dorm had an elevator. The guys had to stomp up four flights of stairs in the boys' dorm, and the girls got to use an elevator. But I couldn't wait for it. I took the stairs two and three at a time. After running the half mile across the campus, uphill, I practically flew up the stairs. I reached her room and pounded on her door, breathing hard. No answer. I did it again. The banging reverberated down the corridor. A girl wrapped in a bathrobe came towards me.

"Are you the guy who called for Melissa? Stop with the pounding already. Give us a break. It's Sunday morning. She's not there. She went out last night and hasn't come back yet. Who are you?"

"I'm her boyfriend," I said. The statement seemed very much in doubt. "I'm her boyfriend" sounded like the dumbest thing I could have said.

"Uh…yeah. Okay. Sure you are," she said. "Well, I'll tell her you were here."

The walk back to Lyon Hall gave me plenty of time to think. As a hero, I had flunked miserably. Passed out drunk the very moment she needed me. Who needs a guy like that? I was a total waste of a human being. No wonder she slept with Clarence. That must be what happened. What a worthless piece of shit I am. I tried to pick up a woman my mother's age. I threw up in front of a cop. What in God's name was I going to say to Clarence if he ever came back?

I began the long climb up four flights of stairs to my room. As soon as I opened the thick door to the hallway I could hear it. The whirring of the electric motor. The tiny *clack clack clack* of the keys against the roller. Clarence's typewriter. He was in the room.

Chapter 24

I stood in the open doorway at the top of the stairs. I had to make a choice: hang a right and ten steps away, behind the half-closed door, would be Clarence, sitting at his desk, typing some endless paper he never seemed to finish. A whole confrontation awaited me, probably even physical violence. The night before, I was all for it. I was ready. I was an idiot. I wouldn't have lasted thirty seconds with Clarence; he would have beaten the shit out of me. Now, I felt even worse: exhausted, depressed and hung over. Now was not the time for a fight. I'd never survive. I turned to my left and walked to the end of the hall.

Bob's door was a welcome sight, even though I knew very well that behind it I would not find beautiful Melissa; I would find Country Bob. I knocked. He opened.

"Did you find her? How is she?" he asked.

"No one's seen her. What happened? You were supposed to kill Clarence."

"Yeah, I know, and I was going to, honestly. But I remembered that murder is, like, you know, illegal, and I could get in big trouble for it. I chickened out, sorry. But *you* can do it. He's in your room."

"I know where he is," I said. "That's why I'm in here."

"How is that going to help? Don't be such a wimp. At least go and talk to him. I'm telling you, he's not such a bad guy. Maybe there's a simple explanation for all this."

"Simpler than, like, for instance, 'I took her to a motel, then dumped her body in the woods?'"

"Don't waste time jabbering with me. Your girlfriend's missing. Go ask Clarence."

"What am I supposed to say to the prick, Bob?"

"That's easy. Let me help you with that. Just say this: 'What happened to Melissa?' You better rehearse that before you get there."

"Gee thanks, Bob, you're a big frigging help." I turned in the direction of my room.

"Say it, Tony. 'What happened to Melissa?'"

"What happened to Melissa?" I droned obediently.

"Good. Once more with feeling."

"What happened to Melissa?" I recited again, with no more feeling than if I were counting to a million and I had just reached the halfway point. "What happened to Melissa? That's three." I dragged myself to the end of the hall. My legs each weighed at least a ton.

I pushed the door open. As usual, Clarence neither looked up nor greeted me. He just went on typing, his glasses pulled down to the end of his nose. I stood before him. I realized I was slouching. I could feel the slouch from my toes to my hair. My face slouched, my ears slouched. I made myself straighten up as if someone had pounded a four foot piece of re-bar up my ass, right through my spinal column. I filled my lungs with as much air as I could hold and threw back my shoulders. Clarence lifted his gaze, and for maybe the first time since I had known him, looked me directly in the eyes.

"What happened to Melissa?" I managed to get this out solemnly and calmly, in a tone which was neither aggressive or accusatory. I was going for authoritative. Clarence looked me up and down as I stood ramrod straight, my shoulders thrown back, chest out, arms at my side, my hands rolled into fists as tight and hard as cannonballs. I felt like a toy soldier.

"What the hell is wrong with you?" he asked.

"What happened to Melissa?" I asked again. This was the fifth time. I was getting the hang of it. He had to answer me. No one could ignore me. I gave it all I had.

He looked back at his typewriter. "How should I know?"

I gritted my teeth and advanced one step closer. I could feel the blood in my ears and the banging of my pulse. Muscles all over my body tingled from the adrenaline surge, like Popeye after a can of spinach. I took another step closer. "Where is Melissa?"

Clarence seemed unaffected by my surging hormones and spectacular display of bravado.

"Fuck you," he said calmly. "I don't report to you."

I looked around for a weapon. A stapler lay on the edge of his desk, and I reached for it. Clarence reacted with the reflexes of a cheetah. He jumped to his feet, grabbed my shirt just under my throat and threw me against the wall. He lifted me up until the tips of my toes left the floor, then even higher until we stared eye to eye. His massive hand encircled my throat and his other hand pushed my chest against the wall. The disparity between our physical sizes became very apparent. What was I thinking?

"Are you threatening me? You're going to do, what? Hit me with a stapler? A *stapler*? Have you thought this through? Do you know what a bad idea that is?" The air in my chest whooshed out of my mouth directly into his face. He turned away.

"Jesus! What did you do last night? Mop the barroom floor with your tongue?" He spat the words out. "What in the name of God did she see in you?" Then he dropped me like a bag of wet sand. I crumpled to the floor, pulled myself into a ball, and waited for a kick which didn't come. He didn't hit me, just looked down on the human puddle on the floor. "You're pathetic. Whatever problem you have with Melissa is *your* problem, not mine. Anything else you want to know, ask her. You are annoying me. And you must stop. You will get yourself hurt. Do you understand me?"

Now it was my turn to say it. "Fuck you."

He looked down at me. "You're an English major, so I'll say this slowly. Maybe you will understand it. Leave... me... alone." He stepped over me and headed for the door.

I scrambled to my feet and called after him. "What did you do to her? Why did she need help?"

He stopped and turned. "What do you mean? Why did she need help?"

"She left me a note. On the door. It said 'HELP.' What did you do to her?"

"Let me see it." He actually sounded concerned. He should have been an acting major. I almost fell for it. He held out his hand. I fished out the folded piece of paper from my pocket.

"She wrote it in lipstick."

He unfolded the note and frowned. "How do you know that this note is for you?"

"What do you mean? Of course it's for me!"

"It's not addressed to anyone. I live in this room too."

Chapter 25

It took me a few days to figure out what my problem was. I had spent most of the time wandering the campus and Risley Hall, looking for Melissa and asking everyone I could find if they knew anything about her. I hadn't been to any of my classes and returned to my room as little as possible. But Melissa was gone. I had a bad feeling about it. By dinner time I was tired and frustrated and pissed off, but I thought I knew the source of all my grief.

That evening, Bob and I ate dinner together at the cafeteria. He ate, or tried to. I talked. I had figured it all out. He was the only one around, so he got to listen. He wasn't happy about it.

"And that's the whole problem," I said. Bob held his fork in midair. A few baked beans plummeted to the plate.

"What's the whole problem?"

"What Clarence said. That's the whole problem with everything, Bob. Pay attention."

He was not impressed. The remains of his Sunday dinner of three hot dogs, baked beans and potato chips lay on the plate. I hadn't eaten. I wasn't hungry. I wasn't sure if I'd ever be hungry again.

"That's it?" he asked. "The whole reason why you can't find Melissa, why you have a permanent hangover—which I think is a medical first, even for college kids—and why you've been skipping almost every class since the semester started… all this you can blame on the fact that you have to live with Clarence Carter? You don't think that's a little bit of a copout?"

"Yes! Yes! Exactly. I know that sounds crazy. It never occurred to me until Clarence said it. 'I live here too.' That's the whole damn problem. I can't stay focused on my classes. I'm depressed and I think…I think I might drink a little too much."

"You? I don't believe it. I'm shocked."

"Yeah. Shut up. Look, he goes out with Melissa and she vanishes from the face of the earth."

"But she didn't vanish, TONY, She just didn't tell you where she was going. That's not the same thing. And it's only been a few days. Give her a break."

"No one knows where she is," I said. Bob was about to interrupt me again so I charged ahead. "And Clarence doesn't seem to give a shit. He thinks the note was for him! I'm, like, sick to my stomach. I can't eat. I don't want to go to class. I don't want to go back to the room. Everything that's wrong with my life is because he lives there too."

"Okay, so you guys don't get along. I got it. It happens. Kids take off without telling anybody all the time. They usually come back, Tony. Maybe she just got tired of you. It's not like…wait a minute. Was the note for him?"

"Bob! Of course not! Whose side are you on?"

"Did you call her family?"

"No, I didn't call her family! I don't know where they live, and even if I did, what am I supposed to say? 'Hello, Mrs. Kolaski. How are you today? Did you know that a black guy probably assaulted your daughter and now she's vanished?' Don't you see? Everything that's wrong with my life…it all started when I got put into a room with a psycho who wants to kill me. My father told me to get my room changed before I even got here. What the hell am I gonna do? Tell me that!"

"Okay," said Bob. "I'll give it a shot. How about this for a plan: get your room changed. Brilliant idea, huh? I won't even charge you for that one. Call your dad. He can make it happen in a second. So call him and tell him he was right all along."

"I'd rather cut my arm off."

"Well, if you're right about Clarence, he might do that for you."

Chapter 26

When I got my father on the phone I expected a tirade that started with, "I told you so," and ended with, "Of course! I'll call the housing department first thing in the morning." I also thought I'd hear something like, "Your safety is the most important thing in the world to me." It didn't happen that way.

"You made your bed, now lie in it."

"Dad! You're not going to help me?"

"You're a big boy, Tony. You ignored the advice of your prejudiced, hard-headed, *racist* father and now you've changed your mind. So go and tell your sad story to the college officials and get your goddamned room changed on your own. Spew the same blather to them that you just told me. See if they get all worked up over it. Maybe they'll get more excited than I am. This will be a lesson for you. You're in college now. That's what you get in college. Lessons. Some are tougher than others."

The lesson got even tougher in the housing office. The woman reminded me of Lorraine, but less sympathetic.

"You are more than halfway through your freshman year, Mr. Vitelli," she said. "I can't simply change your room without a good reason. There are very few vacancies available. You should have made this request months ago. Can you give me a good reason why you want a different room? Your roommate is Afro American, I see. Does that have anything to do with this?"

"Yeah. I don't think he likes white people."

"Really? Did he tell you that?"

"He didn't have to. It's pretty obvious. What he said was that I might get, uh, 'seriously hurt.'"

"Seriously hurt? That sounds like a threat. Did he threaten you?" Her expression changed. Suddenly she took me real seriously. She picked up a clipboard and pen and stared at me, ready to write down everything I said. "Please answer the question. Did he threaten you? Yes or no?"

I didn't answer. I had a lot to think before I opened my big mouth. How much of this story did I want to tell?

"Has he *threatened* you?" she demanded.

"Well, not exactly. We had kind of a disagreement which got kind of out of hand."

"It wouldn't be the first time that ever happened between roommates. We can't switch people around every time students have a disagreement."

I caught a glimpse of my reflection in the glass windows that served as the walls of her office. I stood with my arms folded across my chest, my head thrown back and chin up. This was just the pose my Psych 101 instructor called the Mussolini stance. Obnoxious, aggressive, stubborn. I was every bit of that. This would get me nowhere. I relaxed and sat down in the chair opposite her desk, and attempted a smile. When I saw my reflection again, I knew that it was the lamest smile the housing lady had ever seen.

"I just think," I said calmly, "that we'd both be better off if we had roommates who...were more like us. More like we are, I guess."

"In your case, that would be 'more white,' for example?"

"I think that he'd rather have a roommate who is more black, now that you mention it. Yeah."

"And we would rather that he didn't. We made the roommate assignments this year very carefully. No Afro American student was roomed with another. The university is trying to facilitate the process of integration, not exacerbate it." I nodded as if I, too, used words like 'exacerbate' all the time. "Even if that were true," she continued, "that would not be sufficient grounds to change your room."

"What would be sufficient grounds? What's it gonna take?"

"Safety issues. Drug use. Disruptive behavior, excess noise, extraordinary hygiene problems. Violence...real violence, not just an occasional argument. All these things are reasons to change rooms and they all prompt a thorough investigation. Do you have these issues with him?"

I was just about to jump on the safety thing when I remembered that I was the guy who had grabbed the stapler. So that wouldn't work. Clarence didn't drink or smoke, never touched drugs. He didn't make any noise, didn't even have a stereo. Hell, he didn't even snore. He was the cleanest guy I knew, he spent half his free time in the damn shower. In fact, all he did was work at his desk and go to classes and meetings. His part of the room was immaculate. I was doomed. I searched my brain for something that could work.

"How about irreconcilable differences?" I asked. I pulled that right out of my ass. My older sister had gotten a divorce from her husband of four months because of irreconcilable differences. Over their china pattern, for God's sake.

"This is the first we have heard of any differences at all, not to mention 'irreconcilable' ones. It's been seven months, Mr. Vitelli. I hardly think you can make a case for that." Then she stood up and extended her hand. She looked like she was about to walk me to the gallows.

Chapter 27

When I got back to Lyon Hall, I could hear the sound as soon as I began the climb up the stairs. The *whack* was sharp and sudden, like logs split by an ax, but not as loud. The closer I got to the fourth floor the more I was sure it was coming from my room.

Clarence hadn't even bothered to close the door. The smell of apples filled the hallway. The bare, tiled floor of the tiny room glistened with bits of apple, seeds, skin and puddles of juice. A grocery bag from the Collegetown IGA lay open on his desk. Everything on my dresser lay scattered on the floor as if Clarence had cleared it with one sweep of his beefy arm. He was splitting apples, on my dresser, with a big machete, the kind the marines in Vietnam were issued to clear the jungle paths. The top of the old wooden dresser looked like a chopping block in a restaurant, with deep knife scars and wood chips, all soaked in apple juice. He glanced at me when I entered the room but didn't acknowledge me. Instead, he took another apple from the bag and placed it on the dresser. He wiped the machete blade off on one of my T-shirts, raised the blade high over his head and brought it down with the speed and accuracy of an executioner dispatching Anne Boleyn Antoinette, or whatever her name was. The apple exploded into two halves which flew across the room. I stood in silence, watching the performance.

"What are you doing?" I asked quietly.

"What's it look like?"

"It looks like you're making an apple pie. On my dresser. With a machete. Have you lost your mind?" He brought the big knife down again and another apple disappeared in a blur of skin and juice. A piece hit me in the shoulder. "What are you doing?" I yelled. "What the hell are you doing? Are you going to talk to me?"

He wiped the machete off on my shirt again and held it up to examine the blade. I backed up into the doorway, not sure if I should make conversation or run out of the room screaming. He put down the big knife. "When I am ready to tell you what I am doing," he said. "I won't need to talk. Believe me, you will know. You will be the first to know."

Chapter 28

I made terrific time getting back to the housing office. There was a line outside the door. I ran past the kids and flew into the room. The housing lady tried to get out of her chair to stop me but I made it all the way across her office before she could stand up.

"You want 'safety issues?' You want 'threats?' 'Irreconcilable differences?' You want the *National Guard?* I can give you all of that, lady. Get me out of that damned room!"

Ten minutes later I was out of there, clutching the paperwork for a new room assignment. A half hour earlier, there had been 'very few vacancies.' Suddenly; out of nowhere, I had my choice. Amazing, I thought. All I had to do was get hysterical and scream stuff about knives and murder threats and soldiers with guns on campus and national headlines, and magically, a couple of vacancies appeared. The housing department lady couldn't have been more anxious to get me out of her office if I had been Godzilla with bubonic plague. She hustled me out her door with these parting words: "Just remember, Mr. Vitelli, the Safety Police will interview Mr. Carter to corroborate your story."

Go right ahead. While you're out there corroborating, you can exacerbate too. Hell, you can masturbate for all I care. I didn't say that out loud. I'm not stupid.

I went to the cafeteria to read the stuff she gave me. I needed a cup of coffee. Actually, I needed something stronger, but coffee would have to do. I sat at the long table where I used to find Melissa. I looked around. Melissa wasn't there. I opened the envelope.

Both available rooms were doubles where one of the occupants had washed out early in the first semester. The remaining guys had been enjoying the luxury of a half-empty double room as the sole tenant, but they were living on borrowed time. "Robert Crawford" was the name of the occupant of the first available room. I'll be damned. Country Bob! Small world, I thought, my problems would be over. Or maybe not. Bob's room was big and comfortable and had great morning sun. But it would be the sight of Country Bob in his underwear that would greet me upon arising, not Melissa in her birthday suit. That sucked. Worse…much worse, Bob's room was just down the hall from my old one. Clarence could strangle me while I took a leak in the john or stick a knife in me when we passed in the hallway, pretty much whenever he wanted. Bob's room was out.

The sole remaining room available belonged to a kid named Gordon Soloway: room 101, McFadden Hall. That was one of the original stone buildings built in the last century. That dorm was famous for having the biggest rooms…and for being a party dorm. It was mostly upperclassmen in there, not too many freshmen. A first floor room meant no stairs! Maybe I wouldn't be so exhausted from climbing those horrible four flights, maybe I wouldn't have to collapse in my bed every time I returned to the room. Maybe, in fact, I might even *want* to return to the room for once. But what if this Soloway guy was even worse than Clarence Carter?

As if that could ever happen. Gordon Soloway, here I come.

I finished the coffee and looked around once more for Melissa. I didn't see her. Ithaca was a big town, with maybe twenty or thirty thousand students. If I didn't hear from her or see her pretty soon I'd tell the campus cops about it. I doubt it would help. What else could I do? Hang up posters with her picture that said, "Lost Girlfriend?"

Chapter 29

McFadden Hall, home to Gordon Soloway, my new roommate—who didn't even know I existed yet—was right next to Lyon Hall. Big glass windows in heavy iron frames faced the street. Which room would be 101? The windows were right at street level. They opened like doors, each big enough to enter and leave through. Most of the windows had makeshift curtains made from tie-dyed sheets over them. One window had a curtain made from an American flag, pulled to one side, and was cranked open a few inches in the frosty air. I approached it carefully and peered in. A waft of warm, moist air, reeking of pepperoni pizza and cigarette smoke hit me in the face. A chubby kid with a mass of curly black hair sat at a typewriter with his back to the window. His blue denim work shirt had a big red fist and the word STRIKE printed across the back in stenciled letters. I couldn't hear the typewriter because the stereo was blasting out a song I had never heard before, at top volume, while the kid sang—more like screeched—along with the band.

"Inna gadda da VEEEEEEda, bayyyybee! Doncha know that I Luvvvvvvv you!" An electric guitar shrieked and howled in a duel with a thunderous, evil electric organ in what sounded like a death match between two raging dinosaurs. Then the kid stopped typing and began pounding on his desk top, then one of his books, then began simultaneously banging his coffee cup, spastically accompanying a gathering storm of a drum solo. I could feel myself being sucked through the window and into this new world.

The drum solo was endless, so I had time to study my new home. A pyramid of beer cans on the long windowsill blocked my view, but I could still see where the source of the pizza smell was coming from. Two aging slices wrapped in foil sat on the radiator, which ran the length of the wall just under the two windows. Two six packs of Rolling Rock beer sat on the wide windowsill. The radiator served as the oven and the windowsill did duty as the refrigerator! Brilliant! This Gordon kid had his shit together! A black guitar case lay on one of the two beds, a mountain of dirty laundry obscured the unused second bed and added to the room's aroma. Posters of various sizes, all printed in neon psychedelic inks, hung from the walls at various heights—Bob Dylan, Grateful Dead, Big Brother and the Holding Company, Vanilla Fudge, Alan Ginsburg, The Fugs. Who were The Fugs?

Around the perimeter of the room, below the ceiling, individual sheets of computer paper had big capital letters made up of thousands of small typed characters, spelling out SDS…SDS…SDS. A black light poster of a bright green marijuana leaf, three feet across, hung over the occupant's desk. Photos of LBJ and Tricky Dick Nixon bristled with a dozen darts. Books, magazines, comics and record albums covered every surface.

I'm home!

Chapter 30

I almost missed the room's most intriguing feature. On a small rug in the center of the otherwise bare concrete floor lay a sleeping girl, with her back to the window. She had long, bright red hair, which flowed over a frayed army blanket that covered all but her naked shoulders. She must be nude! Damn shame she had her back to me. The curly-haired kid ignored her as he found new things on his desk to tap, smack or beat on, in time, more or less, to the drummer on the stereo, pausing only to take a long drag from his cigarette. He held it with his fingertips, sucking noisily as if it were a giant, perfectly rolled joint. Could this be the famous Gordon Soloway? I tapped at the window gently. No response.

After what seemed to be an hour, the drum solo finally gave way to the organ player who tore it up it like Captain Nemo, and the kid's desk became a massive imaginary organ. He squeezed his eyes shut, stood up and wailed away with both hands on an invisible keyboard. When would this song ever end?

I looked down at the girl on the floor. What kind of person makes his girlfriend sleep on the floor while dinosaurs maul each other just inches away? I took another deep breath of the warm air coming from the window. Maybe this guy *was* worse than Clarence. I had second thoughts. What had I gotten myself into?

I banged louder and the kid stopped playing his desk. He turned around to face me, his expression wide-eyed with surprise as if I had startled him. He had a full black beard and thick glasses with black frames.

"Are you Gordon Soloway?" I shouted over the roar of the stereo. "Who's asking?"

I took one more look at the anti-war posters, the dart firmly embedded in the end of Nixon's nose. "Who are you expecting?" I shouted back. "The FBI?"

"Well, we're not exactly *not* expecting the FBI." He peered at me over his glasses. "You're not them. Yeah, I'm Gordon. Who are you?"

"Turn down the stereo!" I yelled. He made a face to indicate that this was an unusual request, and turned the knob on the record player. There was no discernible difference. "I'm your new roommate!" I yelled again. "I'm Tony Vitelli."

"Damn it." he said. "I knew this wouldn't last forever." He turned the stereo down another notch. "You may as well come in. Use the, uh, formal entrance." With a grand sweep of his arm, he indicated the actual door. Apparently, it was something of a compliment to be offered the use of it. "Room 101."

I found my way through the main entrance to the dorm, then down half a flight of stairs and down the hall to where Gordon now held open his door. He extended his hand. "Welcome to paradise, comrade," he said.

"The Housing Department sent me. Here's the paperwork." I offered the envelope full of forms and other crap that I had been given.

Gordon pushed his glasses down over the end of his nose and squinted. He held the envelope high in the air and pretended to twist the right side of the frame as if it was a monocle. Then he turned to me, snapped to attention and clicked his heels. Except for the beard and T-shirt, he looked just like Colonel Klink. In a ridiculously bad German accent he said, *"Ah! You haf paperzz. Dat is goot. Very goot. Now, vee must zee ef zey are een orderrrr."* He rolled his r.

I looked down again at the sleeping woman. She had burrowed completely under the army blanket, seeking privacy or warmth. She looked more like a body bag with red hair than a human being. Then she began to snore.

"Maybe we should talk in the hallway," I said. "I don't want to disturb your girlfriend."

"Don't worry about it. She's not my girlfriend." The snoring abruptly increased in volume. The last time I heard a noise like that I was at the zoo. Between the never-ending song on the record player and the ferocious snorting from the figure on the floor it was hard to make conversation. I thought of how Melissa slept. *Not only did she not snore, but her gentle, rhythmic breathing was the sweetest, most calming sound in the natural universe. You just had to hear it and you were instantly transported…* I was lost in thought and had to fight my way back to the subject at hand. What was this poor girl's story? I pointed again to the record player and twirled my finger counter clockwise. Gordon turned it down to level where we could hear each other. The organ and the guitar were engaged in mortal combat. I found myself taking sides; rooting for the organ.

"Hang on, it's almost over!" he shouted. "Anyway, not only is this girl not my girlfriend, she is not, in fact, even a girl." He bent down and peeled the blanket off the face of who or whatever occupied the rug. "Behold! See? A genuine man—or boy, your choice—of the non-female variety. Complete with a full set of the required anatomical paraphernalia. Decidedly male. Check it out."

Chapter 31

It was true. A full beard, bright red, a perfect match for the pile of hair that fell from his head, was revealed. His skin color was fish belly white, as if he had spent his life living under a highway overpass. A wave of relief hit me when I realized that this was not a woman. Thank God.

"Meet the Freak," said Gordon. At the sound of his name, if that was his name, the Freak pulled the blanket up tighter to his face. He had stopped snoring. He appeared to be waking up, but I couldn't be certain.

"Wake up, Freak," Gordon told him. "We got company. Besides, it's almost dark; it's time you got up anyway." The pale and slender figure pulled himself to a sitting position and let the blanket fall away. He was, indeed, without clothes. And he was, indeed, a male. Also, a natural red head. I was certain of that. He opened his eyes, which were a pale, almost transparent blue, and stared at me. His eyes were fixed and glassy, exactly the way you're supposed to look when you're in the school play and you're the murder victim. I was surprised when he spoke. First, at how soft and gentle his voice sounded, and secondly, that he could speak at all.

"Pleased to meet you." He almost purred. "I'm Steve."

"I thought you were the Freak. Which is it?"

"My parents always called me Steve," he said, staring at me without blinking. "But here they call me the Freak. I don't know why."

"You said your name is Tony?" Gordon asked me. I nodded, unable to break eye contact with Steve the Freak. "Well, Tony, here's the thing. You can't move in here just like that, even if you have papers. You have to pass the interview. Right, Freak?"

"Oh absolutely," came the response.

"So you have to answer a few questions so we can see if you'll fit in here, you understand. First of all, do you play guitar?"

"Yes," I said, but immediately backtracked. Perhaps I had over-promised. "Kind of. Sort of. A little."

"Do you sing?" asked Gordon.

"Better than you."

"That doesn't make you special," chuckled the man on the floor. "What are your favorite bands?"

I looked around at the posters covering the walls. This was a lot easier than my college interview. "The Dead. Dylan. Joplin...the Fugs." Were the Fugs a band? For all I knew they could have been a gang of assassins.

"Are you now, or have you ever been a member of the Communist Party?" A trick question! I shrugged my shoulders.

"Probably."

"Do you have a girlfriend?"

Damn. The questions had gotten a lot harder. Did I? Still? Steve the Freak rolled his hands as if to say, "Hurry up."

"Tick...tock...tick...tock," said Gordon. Then without warning he put his lips to his forearm and made a loud farting sound.

"Time's up!" said Steve the Freak.

"Yes!" I said. "Absolutely!"

"Good. Now, the most important question of all. Does she have a *sister?*"

"Yes! Absolutely!" I lied.

"What do you think, Freak?" asked Gordon.

"Oh, he's in. He's absolutely in."

I was in! I passed the interview! I was among friends. Instantly, I felt at home. This was now where I lived. But now it was my turn to ask a question—an important one, considering I needed to sleep in this room where I now lived.

"So, uh, Freak, what's your story? Do you live here too? I thought this was a double."

"Let's just say I'm 'in transit.'"

"In transit?" I asked. "What's that mean? Are you, like, a student? Or what?"

"Well, I'm *like* a student," he replied.

"He's more of an 'or what,'" interrupted Gordon.

"I'm sort of a potential political prisoner," said the Freak.

"He's a draft dodger," said Gordon, with a wave of his hand. "The pigs are looking for him. He's hiding from the FBI. I thought you were them."

Chapter 32

No one has ever moved from point A to point B—with point A being my old room and point B being my new room—with greater speed and efficiency than I did. United in purpose, and spurred on by our battle cry, "Safety in numbers!" my band of volunteers marched up the four flights to my old room. I went first. Behind me clomped Gordon and The Freak. The fourth guy was CJ, the kid in my psych class, who lived down the hall from my new room.

"Yo, Tony, my man," he said when Gordon dragged him into the room as a conscripted volunteer. "How's your foxy girlfriend? Are you still doin' the deed?" He was reluctant to join the work party but practically begged to help when he heard actual violence might be involved. Steve the Freak, on the other hand, expressed disapproval of any physical activity that might involve any actual physical activity, but Gordon explained that his participation would be required if he expected a comfortable concrete floor to curl up on in the future. I expected a confrontation with six foot two inch Clarence Carter, and possibly, but hopefully not, his machete, still dripping with the blood of innocent apples. I warned my moving crew to expect the worst, and got out my key.

The door to the room was closed and locked. The floor in the hall was spotless, mopped clean of any evidence of the wholesale fruit slaughter that had occurred a few hours earlier. We approached the door like four feral cats sneaking up on a vicious dog sleeping on a fresh fish. I put my ear to the door to listen for the typewriter. Nothing. I slipped the key into the lock, turned the knob and cracked the door open. I peeked in. Clarence was not in the room. I threw the door open and stared in astonishment.

Not a trace of apple carnage could be seen. My dresser had been wiped clean and a cloth covered the top, masking any chips or scratches. Everything had been scrubbed down with something that smelled like Windex. The crime scene had been thoroughly cleaned. It would be my word against his. In the middle of the floor, everything that belonged to me was neatly packed and arranged as if the bell boy was expected any second. My suitcase, my old typewriter, my twelve-string guitar. A milk crate packed with books. My duffel bag. My posters had been removed from the walls and rolled up and rubber banded together. Apparently, I was leaving.

"Did you pack before you even got your room changed?" asked Gordon.

"No. Clarence did this. He cleaned the room, too. He cleaned up after the apple mess. He must have known I'd get my room changed."

"Wow," said the Freak, "He did a damn good job. I've never seen such a clean room. Was he always this neat?"

I was still a little stunned at all my stuff being packed. "Yeah," I said, "he was always this neat. Always."

"No wonder you had to move," said the Freak. I opened all the drawers to my dresser and desk; everything was empty. I took a deep breath and not even a teeny bit of the smell of apples remained. It was creepy, thinking of Clarence scooping my clothes out of the dresser and sticking his hands in my dirty underwear.

"Where do you think the guy is?" asked CJ, disappointed at the lack of fireworks.

"He's probably up in the housing office, corroborating, right this minute."

"Disgusting," remarked the Freak. I grabbed my big suitcase and the guitar, and my moving crew grabbed the rest. All but the typewriter, a 1938 pre-war Underwood that weighed about thirty-five pounds and covered anyone who picked it up with grease and black ink like some sort of iron octopus from another planet. As soon I saw all my stuff in a pile, I knew that carrying the typewriter would be my job.

Chapter 33

Waking up in my new room in McFadden Hall presented a few challenges which required a change to my routine, but after a week or so I was very comfortable with the bed, the room, and my companions. I had been used to being the only occupant in the morning; Clarence was out the door by 6:30 and in the gym by the time I opened my eyes. Now I was usually the first one up, which felt all wrong.

In my old room, I would carefully climb down from a top bunk, stepping first on my dresser, then my desk, then chair, then finally to the floor. Now, I could spring out of bed, (if I was the kind of person who did much springing, which I wasn't). I just had to remember not to step on Steve the Freak, who lay curled up on the concrete a few feet away. I had no idea what time he went to bed, or even when he got up. All I knew was that he wasn't there when I turned out my light at two AM, and he wasn't there when I came back from dinner at seven PM. But every morning he'd be huddled under his army blanket, directly between me and the shortest distance to the bathroom, snoring like a frigging steam locomotive.

Except I couldn't hear him. I had taken certain measures. Each day I awoke to a strange and complete silence, as if my bed was a sarcophagus and my dorm room a crypt. I sat up in the bed and pulled my bulky headphones off, then dug my fingers into my ears and yanked out the waxed cotton earplugs. The return of the sense of hearing was a rush.

In my old room, the path to the door was always clear and I could sprint to a urinal unimpeded. In 101 McFadden Hall it was a different story. First I had to evaluate what objects, in addition to the Freak, lay in my way. It was an ever-changing obstacle course, strewn with guitar cases, speakers, a ten speed bicycle, pizza boxes and a giant conga drum, which belonged to CJ. I had recently become quite good at the intricate dance moves required to get from the bed to the door without stepping on something I didn't want to step on. Soon I was able to complete my morning routine in the comfort of the cavernous first floor bathroom. I returned to my room and sat on my bed, brushing away the pile of *Zap* comics, which served as my evening reading when I got tired of the assigned text books.

This happened earlier and earlier each evening. I had a paper due on *Confessions of St. Augustine*, and had not yet been able to penetrate even the first chapter. I looked at the thick, mind-numbing book lying on the floor between copies of *Captain Piss Gums* and *Mr. Natural Comics*, and knew that I would have to hunt down the Cliff Notes, or, failing that, a Classic Comic version. Did they even have a Classic Comic for *Confusions of Saint Augustine?* I hoped to hell.

Chapter 34

Without Clarence in my face, life was easy. I didn't really worry about classes. I would go to two or three each week, and took turns going to a different one each time. My attention was focused on one thing: finding Melissa. But even that began to fade as I settled into a routine of all-you-can-drink beer nights, poker games and the expertly rolled joints that the Freak could produce so effortlessly. Gordon was a cigarette smoker with an unusual quality—generosity—and soon I was a few pounds heavier and grubbing his Winstons maybe three or four times a day. There were plenty of chicks that looked like Melissa from the back, a girl five foot four inches tall with long, shiny, perfectly brushed dark brown hair. But none with hoop earrings. None even came close when I saw their faces. None of them were Melissa. Two months went by and I could find no trace of her. I met a few other girls but I didn't do much more than just meet them. None of them could compare to her. That's all I did: compare.

I was in deep trouble. I knew why I got good grades when Melissa was around. I wanted to. When Melissa was with me, I was a different person. I felt smarter. I was funnier, even my crappy guitar playing sounded better. I wanted to work harder. I even looked better. I laughed when I remembered my sports jacket with the patches on the elbow and the pipe in the pocket. I still had a pipe, but now it was a twenty-five cent corn cob with a piece of aluminum foil in the bowl, and it stank of half-burned pot. I had gotten good grades because I wanted to get them. Also because Melissa wrote all my French essays for me. That helped too.

But now, I just didn't feel like doing that much work. There wasn't anyone to impress, if you didn't count my parents, which I didn't. It sure didn't matter to Gordon or the Freak. Everything about school seemed irrelevant. "Irrelevant" was a great word that I had been using a lot. All kinds of stuff seemed irrelevant. It sounded so much better than "stupid and boring," which was pretty much how everything felt.

Who really gave a crap about what Saint Augustine felt guilty about? Not me. I couldn't care less. I was *supposed* to care, but I just didn't. Also, I was supposed to feel guilty about not caring. I didn't care about not feeling guilty, about not caring. And so it went.

One thing led to another, and everything led downhill. The one thing that could drag me back was if Melissa magically reappeared. She had been a straight A student and she quit school with no explanation. Her address was listed in the Pig Book only as Olympia, Washington. No phone number. I figured that Olympia was probably a pretty small town and everyone would know about the Kolaski family, so I wrote her three letters. But I never got an answer.

At first, all I did was think about her. I missed most of my classes and spent each day hanging out in the places where we used to go. But she never appeared, not in the cafeteria, the coffee house, the library or any place else. Her roommate said she had no idea what happened to her. Or why. She had just vanished.

Pretty soon my average tanked. My grades sucked. Not just in the lit course, but also French, which they made me take even though I had taken French every year since junior high school. Without Melissa's help, I was too embarrassed to even attend class. The teacher heard my accent and from then on called me "Pauvre Antoine." Kids in the class laughed whenever I had to read something out loud.

An art history course that I had counted on for an A, or at least a B plus, turned out to be boring and pointless. In the face of all the crap going on—the social unrest, racial problems and the escalating Vietnam war, it just seemed completely irrelevant. I had been lured in by the ridiculous course name: "Cubism and Eroticism." Everyone called it "Cubes and Boobs." I went to the first few classes but the professor was so boring I could barely stay awake. He reminded me of one of my dad's drinking buddies from work, overweight, balding, tired of his job. I was about to fail Cubes and Boobs, which seemed incredible. At the rate I was going, if something didn't happen pretty soon, I'd get my draft notice at the end of spring semester.

How had this happened? I had a C minus for most of first semester, then, after meeting Melissa, my average had rocketed up to a B. Now, without her, it had fallen to a D plus. I would only get that if I passed Cubes and Boobs. I couldn't tell a Cubist from a sado-masochist. As far as erotic art was concerned, you needed a hell of an imagination to believe that those were pictures of naked women, no matter how hard you tried. Hell, I could draw better than that when I was eight years old and running a 102 fever.

All the great stuff that Melissa had brought to my life was slipping away. I started getting fatter. The weight crept up on me as surely as the stack of pizza boxes got higher, as if one thing had to do with the other. Then the trips to the laundromat grew fewer and fewer. I discovered that whipping my dirty socks against the radiator and then spraying them with Right Guard made them soft, flexible and ready to wear again. Necessity, as the saying goes, is the mother of invention.

The time I had spent with Melissa in Country Bob's room felt as if it had happened sometime in the last century. I hadn't been back to the fourth floor of Lyon Hall, and I hadn't seen Clarence again either. I avoided every place I could have run into him. Instead, I took to frequenting the places that Melissa and I had been to together, especially the Echo Chamber, where I had met her. I also spent a lot of time downtown, drinking and grubbing cigarettes at the Haunt and the Salty Dog. I spent more time playing guitar than I did studying. Gordon and I would carry our guitars to the Echo Chamber on the weekends and play one Dylan song after another. *Mr. Tambourine Man, Desolation Row, Like a Rolling Stone, Subterranean Homesick Blues.* Gordon knew them all.

There was one song we never played.

We never did *Visions of Johanna.* That song was on the blacklist. I couldn't even listen to it, much less play it. Whenever I heard that song, I'd be thrown face first into the sad wall. I'd remember the way I felt the first time I heard Melissa sing, in her soaring, crystal-clear voice, weaving in and out, with my own. I'd never experienced anything like that, not before. Not since. Then I'd be done for. If *Visions of Johanna* came on the radio or somebody played it in the dorm, I would leave the room. There was a reason my father called me crybaby.

Maybe I needed a shrink. I was living my life in the land of make-believe...sitting on the floor of the Echo Chamber, guitar in my lap, waiting for Melissa to open the big door. So we could start again. That's all I wanted: the chance to start again.

Chapter 35

Spring in Ithaca had arrived, finally. The weather changed as if God had reached for the wall switch and changed it from "Terrible, miserable, cold and yucky winter" to "Wonderful, beautiful, warm and sunny spring." Gordon, a sophomore, had already spent an entire year in town and warned me that spring, like autumn, lasted about a week. Then the switch was snapped again and it became "Hot, humid, with afternoon thunder showers summer," which was almost as bad as "Cold and yucky winter." In Ithaca, winter lasted eleven months. Summer lasted two months, spring and autumn a week each. Gordon said Ithaca was the only place in the world where this happened. It made me laugh when he said it the first time, but after the winter was finally over, I believed him.

Today was one of the rare spring days, and my schedule was jammed with studying, writing the damn paper, trying to convince myself I cared even a teeny bit for whatever the hell Saint Augustine was so worked up about, and showing my face at four classes I hadn't attended since the first week of the semester.

We had no choice but to take our guitars up to the Arts Quad and sit in the grass, playing everything that we knew, hoping to attract the attention of a couple of girls. At least one, anyway. Eventually, I returned to the room alone, leaving Gordon to finish a bizarre duet rendition of *I Got You Babe*, singing both parts. As Cher, he sucked, but he nailed Sonny's part. His voice was even more nasal, if that was possible. The Freak was in the room, clipping his toenails, sitting on

Gordon's bed. I tried not to watch, although it was grotesquely fascinating. The intensity of his concentration was breathtaking.

"It's not right to call you 'the Freak,'" I said. "Is it okay if I call you Steve?"

"Call me whatever you want. But you can call me Freak. I don't mind. I'd rather that nobody knew my real name."

"But it seems so disrespectful."

"It's just a name."

"Not a real name. Steve is your real name. Why do you have a problem with Steve?"

"That's my father's name. When I hear it I get all weirded out 'cause I think my father's here."

"Yeah. I got that. But still. I want to call you Steve. That's a pretty good name. A lot of neat people have that name. You should get used to it."

"Okay. If you want. What's your dad's name?"

"Lou."

"Okay. Then I'll call you Lou."

"You're a pain in the ass." Most of my conversations with the Freak, I mean, Steve, evolved into some kind of word game. He was really good at word games. "I'm going to try it out," I said. "I think it will do you good to get a little respect. So ...*Steve*, do you want to get high?" He didn't reply. Instead he studied the toes on his right foot intently.

"Hey you," I said.

He looked up. "What?"

"I asked you a question. Do you want to get high?" He smiled.

"Of course. I'm sorry. I thought you were talking to my father."

We stuffed a wet towel in the crack at the bottom of the door and hunkered down in the corner of the room, which wasn't visible from the window. As soon as we fired up the pipe, I got to talking about my favorite subject: Melissa.

"It's a mystery," I told him. "No one knows what happened to her. Even her roommate and her friends."

"Did you ever consider alien abduction?" he asked. "It's a classic case. All the signs are there. They're probably probing her right now as we talk." He sat on the edge of Gordon's bed and sucked on the corn cob pipe, then passed it to me. No matter how much smoke he inhaled he never seemed to cough.

"Don't you feel better with me calling you Steve instead of Freak? Isn't it more dignified? Don't you feel more like a human being?" Before he could answer, the big window that led to the street was pushed open and Gordon, still howling, "I got you, Babe!" stepped onto the radiator, almost stomping on a triple meatball and cheese sub. He held his guitar case in one hand, and jumped to the floor.

"Hey!" he said. "Bad Freak! You're not allowed on the bed! Off the bed! Off! Bad Freak!"

Steve shrugged and exhaled a stream of smoke that would have alerted fire spotters to a major conflagration. He turned to me. "While we're on the subject, you said Melissa had a sister. What's she look like?"

"She doesn't have a sister. That was a lie. Besides, what do you care? I thought you were a homo."

He giggled. It was hard to tell because he worked hard to keep a straight face but his mustache and beard vibrated. It was a dead giveaway. "What makes you think I'm a homo?"

"You never have a date."

"By that criteria," said Gordon, "We're all homos."

"Well, damn," said Steve, "Now you tell me." None of us had gone on a date since I had arrived. In fact, of the three of us, I was the only one who had dated a girl since arriving on campus. This was almost the end of Gordon's second year. I was rooming with two virgins. If things didn't change pretty quickly, I was sure I would become one again.

"I think we all need to get laid," I said. I added quickly, for Steve's benefit, "by women. Let's go downtown tonight. It's 'all you can drink night' at the Salty Dog. We need a total of three bucks."

"What if we get lucky?" asked Gordon.

"Then we'll need six bucks."

"I thought you were going to study tonight, Tony," said Gordon. I didn't reply. I gazed over his shoulder as if I hadn't heard him.

"Tony?" he asked. "Yoo hoo. Can you hear me? Tony?"

"Call him Lou," said Steve. He leaned forward and looked me in the eye. "Hey Lou, do you play poker?"

Did I hear that right? I answered him slowly. "Maybe. I might…play poker." This could be interesting. "What do you have in mind?"

"A game of course!" Wait a minute. This barely conscious human hookah wants to play cards? "How about it, Gordon?" Steve reached into his army blanket and produced a worn deck of cards.

"Not me," said Gordon. "But you go ahead, Tony."

"You need money to play poker, Steve," I said. "Since when do you have any bread?"

"Since the minute you lend me some."

"You gotta be kidding. No one's gonna lend you money." But Gordon chimed in.

"If you're playing poker, he's good for it. Trust me on that." Gordon's face was buried behind his Labor Relations textbook but his voice sounded like he was about to laugh.

Steve nodded. "Okay," he said, "We'll cut for the deal. High card takes it." He held up the deck. Somehow, all the cards magically leaped from his left hand to his right. He fanned the cards and showed them to me, all in order. He snapped the fan closed, split the deck and shuffled the cards in mid-air, his eyes never leaving mine. The cards fluttered back to his left hand. He slapped the deck face-down on my desk.

"Cut."

"You know what?" I said. "Gordon's right. I really need to work in the library tonight." I stood up slowly, watching Steve like I expected him to draw on me.

"Looks like Tony has had a sudden attack of scholarship," said Gordon. I could hear them cackling as I headed up Libe Slope with a notebook—any notebook—under my arm.

Chapter 36

I had finally stopped keeping time by how many hours or days or weeks it had been since I last heard from Melissa. It had been months since that Saturday night that Clarence had taken her out, Bob and I had played pool, and Lorraine, a woman older than my mother, had shot me down, I had barfed for a cop and all that other stuff had happened. I hadn't seen Clarence either. I didn't go looking for him. I did everything I could to forget him. All that weed and Utica Club and Boone's Farm apple wine was doing a great job smoothing out the wrinkles in my brain, which now must have been as smooth and shiny as a bowling ball. I could barely remember which classes I was taking.

I expected to find a warning notice in my mailbox any day. I had no idea what my exact average was but it couldn't have been much above a D. For some reason, even though I knew that flunking out meant a draft notice and a free ticket to a Southeast Asian country along with a new set of clothes, I just couldn't get too excited about it.

The last communication I had with my family—actually just my father; my mom almost never picked up the phone unless my dad told her to—had ended in another argument. That happened sometime in April. I made a lot of promises I had no intention of keeping, and then I forgot what the promises were. I got pretty stoked up by the argument, though. I remember it took quite a few bowls and a bottle or two of Boone's Farm to calm me down. I don't even remember what we were arguing about. Probably whether we should be in Vietnam. Gordon didn't argue with his dad. That guy was an actual Socialist, maybe even a

Communist. Gordon came by his radical politics honestly. The thing was, he never shut up. He knew every statistic, every fact about the war, and all the scandals and cover-ups.

Gordon was fast becoming a raving lunatic as far as I was concerned. I wasn't much of a debating opponent, I simply agreed with him about everything, whether I had thought much about it or not. Most stuff, I hadn't thought about. But you didn't have to be very bright to know that war was wrong and kids had no business fighting it. If Gordon was for something, so was I. If he opposed it, then I did too.

Gordon was really into politics. I didn't really get it. It was like he completely believed that the government couldn't do anything right. Whatever the politicians said, we had to do something else. I didn't argue with him. It was like arguing with my father, only Gordon and my dad were exact opposites. Whatever the truth was, I was pretty sure it lay someplace in the middle. It would be a cold day in hell before I let Gordon meet my dad. That would be like Godzilla and Mothra having breakfast with each other.

Or Freak. My dad could never meet Steve the Freak, either. Just the thought of that made me nervous. Steve slept most of the day, stayed up most of the night, and spent a lot of time either unconscious or incoherent. We never heard from the FBI or anyone else about bringing him in for draft evasion. If the FBI wasn't paying attention, neither were we. We didn't pay attention to a lot of stuff.

Sometimes, I had an uneasy feeling that I was wasting my life—that time was flying by. Fall had changed to winter, winter had changed to spring. But nothing else was changing. I was still alone, living in a messy room, eating meatball subs from Johnny's Big Red, picking through my dirty clothes and boring myself to sleep each night. Was this forever? Was this my life? What the hell had happened?

Then I would tell myself everything would all be okay again as soon as I was back together with Melissa. It was only a matter of time. It didn't register on any of us that the end of the semester was behind the next curve, at the end of the block, turn right, go straight, fall off the cliff.

Chapter 37

"You are, *of course*, going to Paci-Fest, right, Tony?" Gordon and I were filling the shopping basket with supplies for the big event. What could I say? Gordon had been nagging about this ever since the posters went up on campus, back when the weather was still cold and dreary. Now it was hot and sunny, and the weekend looked to be the perfect time for the giant combination peace demonstration, anti-war rally and folk music festival. Not to mention it was shaping up to be the biggest street party of the year, maybe the decade.

Anybody who was anyone would be there. The rumor was the National Guard and maybe the governor was going to make an appearance. It was like hearing that the Stones or the Beatles might show up for your dance. Paci-Fest was not to be missed.

Gordon carried the wine and I carried everything else: a dozen eggs, a jar of Vaseline, Hellman's Mayonnaise. A stop at Woolworth's got us three bandanas like cowboys wear out on the range. We tried to buy three of those yellow hard hats like construction workers wear but they were sold out. "Beware of enterprises that require new clothes"...I couldn't remember who said that. I wasn't sure that I wanted to be involved, but I didn't want to miss it.

Country Bob and Gordon wouldn't miss it for the world. I wanted to do my part, but I didn't want to get hurt. I think soldiers must feel like that. I know Steve did. He planned on spending the day under the bed.

When we got back to the room I was surprised to see Steve awake and sitting at my desk, drawing a new cartoon. Steve had an annoying habit of chuckling—kind of laughing but pretending that he wasn't laughing so you wouldn't say, "What are you laughing about?" but you knew he was laughing about something, which was probably you. I put the shopping bag full of supplies down on my bed.

"Lou called," He was looking at me when he said it.

"Lou who?" I asked. I sounded like a cuckoo clock.

"Lou, your father? Remember you told me his name was Lou?"

"Oh crap." This would be bad news. "What time did he call?"

"About ten this morning. Where were you guys? Did you actually go to class this close to the end of the year? What's the point?"

"Yeah, right. Not hardly," I said. "What were you doing up at ten AM?"

"I had to answer the phone, remember? Anyway he had some stuff to tell you. He had me take notes. I got it right here."

"He had you take *notes?*" Steve was now in full chuckle mode and looked about to lose it any moment and break down and just pass out from laughter. If Steve thought this was that funny, I would think it was equally terrible.

"Let's see," he began. "First off, he hasn't heard from you, and you forgot his damn birthday…AS USUAL. So don't be surprised when he forgets *your* birthday! But that's not why he called. Oh, and is it SO DIFFICULT to write a goddamn letter? Seeing as how you're an ENGLISH MAJOR, he'd have thought you'd KNOW HOW TO WRITE BY NOW, don't you think? But that's not why he called either." Steve had to stop and catch his breath. The effort to not laugh was having an effect on his breathing.

"Gee, Steve, did he happen to tell you why he *did* call, by any chance?"

"Yeah, I'm getting to that. Right here. He says the university sent him a letter, addressed to HIM, by the way, a WARNING LETTER—it was even printed in red ink—about how you were on academic probation and you had one C, three Ds and an F so far, and that means you're going to lose your Regents Scholarship. That's the LEAST bad thing that will happen. But probably what will really happen is they'll throw you out, and you'll lose your 2-S deferment. And THEN you'll see what the REAL WORLD IS LIKE, 'Buddy.' He called me Buddy, it was like he forgot who he was talking to. And he said, let's see, how did he put it? Oh yeah, he said that in case you wanna know why they sent the letter to HIM and not YOU, it's probably because he PAYS the

BILLS for your GODDAMN EDUCATION, in case you've FORGOTTEN that little point. But he's not gonna do it anymore, you are on your OWN, and then he asked me if I would give you that message and I said, sure."

I had to remember to close my mouth so I could talk. Up until then it was hanging open and motionless, just like my eyes. Finally I managed, "Anything else?"

"Yeah…you're gonna love this part. He also said that he thinks it's time you and him had a face-to-face TALK, in PERSON, not over the phone, and since you're probably REAL BUSY studying for finals— he said that as if maybe he thought you *weren't* real busy studying. Like how did he know that? Anyway, he's gonna come up to Ithaca and pay you a visit. He said he wants to see your new room." Steve began to sob and wheeze. He couldn't go on. He collapsed in laughter. Tears ran down his face. "I'm sorry. I'll try again."

"Did he say when he was coming?"

"No. Maybe he wants it to be a surprise. He said for you to call him back as soon as you got in. Oh, and this part's great: He said you better not try that 'old bullshit,' let's see, I gotta get this right. He sort of changed his voice for this part, but I won't be able to do it as good, 'But Dad! I did call, you guys weren't home!' because that's not gonna work this time. He said not only will he be home the rest of the day but now they have one of those new answering machines, he said he 'borrowed it from the office.' Check that out, he 'borrowed it!' and it takes, um…yes, he said it takes FUCKING MESSAGES so call him, 'goddamn it.' He curses a lot, doesn't he? I wanted to wash the telephone out with soap."

"Holy crap," said Gordon. "Your father is coming *here?*" Gordon looked around the room, a quick sweep to take in the beer can pyramid, the SDS signs, the *Zap* comics, the bong, all the outrageous examples of stuff that I absolutely, no doubt about it, 100% guaranteed my parents that I would not get involved in. I could barely fill my lungs with air. I could feel the sweat collecting on my forehead.

Steve sat up on the floor where he had collapsed and said in a tiny voice, "This mess is so big and so wide and so tall…"

"…that we can't clean it up. There is no way at all," finished Gordon. "Yeah, we get it. Are you going to call him, Tony?"

"Call him? Are you out of your frigging mind?" I realized I was shouting. "No! I'm not going to call him! I have to find another place to live! Right now!"

"But we have to get ready for Paci-Fest..." said Gordon.

"Screw Paci-Fest! My life is on the line, guys!"

"Holy hell, you don't think he's coming tomorrow, do you?"

Steve was back on the floor, wheezing and gulping for air. "This is too beautiful. There IS a God," he said.

"I have to find another place to live for a couple days!" I screamed this as I raced around grabbing for magazines and beer cans and album covers. "He can't ever see this room! You understand? He can't see this room! If he sees this place, the world will end! That is the TRUTH! It will END! Period!" I headed for the door.

"Where are you going?" yelled Gordon.

"To see Country Bob!"

Chapter 38

I had a genuine, life-changing crisis on my hands. If my old man suddenly arrived and saw my current life, in glorious living color, my life would change. Or end! He'd shut off the dough. That would be all it would take. With the war going on, there was no life after college.

I had no time to think of a Plan B; this was Plan A all the way. If this didn't work, I was doomed. I'd trade rooms with Country Bob, take down the cow posters, put up the Hendrix and Janice posters, carry my damn half-ton, grease-dripping typewriter back up the four flights, throw the twelve-string on the bed like I had just finished playing it, spread my as yet unopened copies of Wordsworth and Yeats around the room. Then I'd be golden. My dad would be blown away by how neat and organized I had become. I never kept my room at home as neat as Bob's. I could make this happen in a half hour...if the guys were on board. It was pure genius. All that needed to happen was for Bob to agree.

I hadn't been back in Lyon Hall since I switched rooms. Running up the four flights of stairs told me I had made the right choice—not that I had a choice, of course. I hadn't noticed it before but Lyon Hall had its own unique aroma, a signature scent, a mix of sweat, English Leather, pizza, and a cigarette snuffed out in a tennis shoe. But I could also detect a faint whiff of perfume. Was that Melissa's? I wasn't sure. Could she be here, in the building? But why? Could she be with Clarence? Impossible.

The more stairs I climbed the more real the memory of Melissa, and the time we spent in Bob's room, became. By the time I hit the fourth floor, I was back to the winter break, with Melissa in my bed. Well, Bob's bed, anyway.

I threw open the heavy fire door and looked at my old room. The door was shut. No typewriter clackety-clack. So far so good. I sprinted to the other end of the corridor and banged on Bob's door.

"Just a minute!" he called. It was way more than a minute. I stood outside his door tapping my foot and nodding my head, breathing hard through my nose, snorting like an animal. Hurry up, Bob. I banged on the door again.

"Hold your horses!" he yelled.

"Bob! It's me, Tony! Open up! I need to talk to you!"

The door opened. Bob wore his bathrobe and had the contented look of someone who had just enjoyed the best part of waking up. But it was close to dinner time! The room was warm and the air was moist. The big window, wide open, let a heady breeze blew through the door. There was something new in his room, something I can only describe as…one of his girlfriends. Oh my God! What a doll. A few inches shorter than Bob, but still taller than me, her light brown hair fell almost to her waist. Her blue jean shorts were cut off so high that a good three or four inches of her pockets stuck out from the bottom. She had just tied the tails of one of Bob's red plaid short-sleeve shirts high above her flat belly. No bra, I noticed. I guess that was the first thing about her that I noticed. She was drop-dead cute. The bed was not only unmade, it could have passed for a playing field after a big game. The room smelled like sex, a lot of it, and recent.

Bob made the briefest of introductions. "Wendy, meet Tony. Tony, Wendy."

"Hi, Tony," she said, smiling. Perfect white teeth. She grabbed her large shoulder bag. A purse? Luggage? and finished the short conversation. "Bye, Tony. Sorry, but I must be on my way." Exactly the way Bob said it. Holy crap. Good for you, Bob.

Wendy walked down the hall toward the stairs. Wait, that's not exactly right. She pranced down the hall, the big shoulder bag swinging from side to side. I think she was whistling.

"Well," Bob said, "If it isn't the prodigal son. If you wait long enough, all the pigs come back to the trough. To what do I owe the pleasure?"

"I need to borrow your room."

"No."

"Bob, it's really important."

"No."

"It's a matter of life or death."

"Then it's a matter of *your* life or death. No. You don't understand one syllable words anymore? Also, are you blind? Did you somehow miss the gorgeous girl that just left, the one with the perfect ass and great legs, the long hair, you missed all that?"

"Believe me, I saw her! But Bob..."

"No. I need the room. Change the subject."

"I'll trade you. You can use my new room. It's just for a few days."

"That's a riot. You're a funny guy. Tony, I've seen your room. Everyone has seen your room. You leave the windows wide open to the street and every morning you play the *Fish Cheer* to the whole campus, remember? I've looked in there. I'd rather entertain a girl in the cow barn back home than in your dorm room. Get serious. Get a motel. I'll even lend you the money if I have to."

"That won't work. It needs to be a dorm room. My dad is coming. I can't be living in a motel."

"Your father is coming here? You do have a problem! I thought you needed the room for more shenanigans with your filly."

More farm crap. I didn't have time for this. "What filly?"

"Oh, I'm sorry. I'm speaking upstate English. Maybe I should talk Lawn Gyland English. Your GOIL friend."

"My what? What the hell are you talking about? Nobody talks like that on Long Island. Nobody talks like that period."

"Mah-LISS-Ah. Your girlfriend. Remember her?"

"Yeah, I remember her. She's the one who skipped town on me and disappeared. What about her?"

"She's back, dummy. She's back. You haven't seen her?"

Chapter 39

Melissa is back! These three words pushed 'My father is coming' to someplace way in the back of my mind, stuffed it into a some dark mental cubbyhole, along with 'I'm flunking out,' and 'The paper is due tomorrow' and a bunch of other statements that just a few minutes ago had seemed important. Now the only thing that I could think about was, "Melissa is back!"

My lower jaw dropped into the position where Bob could have given me a root canal if he wanted. "Where?"

"I've seen her at the Straight. And the library. Saw her a couple days ago."

"Why didn't you tell me?"

"If you ever came by sometime when you didn't need something, I would have."

"She never called me…"

"Does she know you changed your room?"

"No…did she come here, to my old room? To see Clarence?"

"How would I know? I'm actually what they call a 'student' here. This is a 'college.' Some of the students go to what they call 'classes.' I'm not here twenty-four seven. Also, your friend Clarence hasn't lived here for quite a while, now."

"Where did he go?"

"That's a deep, dark secret. If I told you, then I'd have to kill you."

"I've got to find Melissa."

"No Tony, if your dad is coming, you have to find another place to live. Then you can find Melissa. You have to get your priorities straight, my man, or you won't live long enough to find her."

My head was spinning. What did all this mean? How much time did I have to figure it out? Why didn't Melissa contact me? I leaned against the wall, dazed, trying to put all the things I had to do in some sort of order.

Bob already had it all figured out. In the time it took me to decide I was dead meat, he had found a solution. This was why he was on the dean's list and I was on probation.

"Okay, here's what you're going to do," he told me. "Are you ready? You don't look ready. Pay attention."

I straightened up and tried to look a lot more confident than I felt. Why had she not come looking for me?

"Sit down." I sat on his rumpled bed. I had to move out of the way of the wet spots. "You need to use another dorm room for a few days, right? And there is no way on God's green earth that you're getting my room. So we find you another room. An empty room. And where are you going to find an empty room? At the end of the hall. Clarence's room. It's been empty for weeks. It's almost the end of the year. The maid doesn't even look in there anymore. No one's going to use it. You can tell your old man it's yours. Once you get that problem out of the way, you can go find Melissa."

This man, I thought, is a genius. I will give him all my worldly possessions when I die. Which could be soon. "Do you have a key?" I asked.

"Why would I have a key? I didn't live in the damn room. Don't you have one? You moved out in such a hurry, you remembered to get your big one dollar key deposit back?"

Chapter 40

I did have a key! Someplace.

When Bob and I got back to my room, Gordon and Steve the Freak were waiting for me. Steve gleefully greeted me with "Yoo, hoo. Did you do Lou?"

I didn't respond. Instead I turned to Gordon and asked, "What did you do to him?"

"Nothing. He's been like that since you left."

"If you didn't do Lou," said Freak (it was hard to think of him as 'Steve' under the circumstances), "it's doo doo for you."

"He called while you were looking for Bob. He sounded pretty hot. You better call him," said Gordon.

"Call your father, Tony," said Bob. He looked around the room, which looked like a small tornado had just blown through a head shop. "Is this where you think I ought to shack up with my girlfriend? What a riot. I hope you can find the key."

"You guys got a *key*?" asked the Freak, suddenly snapping out of the rhyming word game prison he had built for himself. "Woo hoo!" he shouted. "We're in business! Do you have a scale? Let's roll some joints!"

"Not that kind of key. The kind that opens the door to my old room."

"Never happen," said Bob. "If it's in here, it's gone for good."

"This kind of key, you mean?" Gordon reached into his desk and produced the very object of our search. "You left it on my desk the first day you got here."

"Now we can go look for Melissa."

"No," said Bob, "now you can call your father."

Lou picked up on the first ring. He didn't sound surprised when the operator asked him if I could reverse the charges. He wasn't as crazy mad as I thought he'd be. I was able to calm him down with an endless stream of soothing lies. The warning notice, I assured him, was a mistake, and was sent before I aced a few tests. I was sure to get a terrific grade on my art history project. I mean, come on, who fails an art course, right? My French was improving. Me and Saint Augustine were buddies. I laid it on thick. My dad responded with a few "uh huhs." No big deal. It was all a misunderstanding.

In truth, my whole college education had been a misunderstanding. I had one goal throughout the conversation: hang up the phone and get my ass to Melissa's side of the campus to see if she was back in her dorm.

"By the way," I said, steering the conversation away from my grades. "Happy birthday! I called you to tell you that but you guys must have been out celebrating."

"Really? What day was that?"

Uh oh. A trap. "On your birthday, of course."

"And what day is my birthday?" He waited just a few seconds before the tirade began. "You don't know, do you? Nineteen years old and you don't remember your own father's birthday. Not a card, not a call. You can't even tell me the day. I'll tell you something else, buddy. You and I are going have a face-to-face, because I'm not buying this wagon-load of bullshit. I'm dropping by for a visit."

I had experience with this. Dr. Jekyll and Mr. Hyde had nothing on my father. "Okay, Dad, I think that's a good idea. Just when are you coming?"

"Tomorrow."

Chapter 41

I hung up the hall payphone, grabbed the key from Gordon and headed out the window again with Bob running to keep up.

"Is he really coming up here?" asked Gordon.

"Tomorrow," I growled. "He'll be here tomorrow."

"Wonderful," said Steve. He'll be here for Paci-Fest. Wouldn't want him to miss that, would we?"

"Thank God he's not coming today. We've got time." Then I was out the window and running for the other side of campus. Bob, who towered over me, followed at a lazy trot. Running all the way to Risley Hall was plenty familiar: I had done it dozens of times. Every time I went there, it seemed like I was in a gigantic hurry. But none as urgent as this. Melissa was back? Could it be true? We sprinted over the suspension bridge which bounced up and down with every foot stomp and headed into the Risley Hall parking lot. I charged past the sign-in desk and headed for the stairs.

"HALT! Hold it right there!" yelled the girl in charge of the sign-in book. "I remember you. I'm supposed to call the Safety Division if I see you again. I need to see your ID and you need to sign in or I'm calling them. Get back here."

Bob stopped dead at the words "Safety Division." The Cornell cops were legendary. The rumor was they were ex-Nazi SS officers.

It took me a second or so to tally up all the trouble I was already in, or about to fall into face- first. I decided that since I actually had an ID and could sign my name, I would comply.

fortune. I'll go get it. You guys finish. You know what the room is supposed to look like. A little messy."

"Just a little messy?" asked Steve. "You don't need me for that."

I turned to head back down the four flights to get the guitar. I had just made it to the first floor when I heard Bob's voice echoing in the stair well.

"Tony! You better come back here. I just thought of something."

I huffed and puffed my way back to the room. "This better be important, guys. It's almost nine o'clock. And we don't know what time he left, so—"

"Tony," said Bob. "This is a bad idea. This isn't going to work."

"What are you talking about? How can it be a bad idea?"

"Your dad told you to get your room changed, right?"

"Yes..."

"And you did. What did you tell him?"

"I told him I got my room changed, like he wanted. So what?"

"So when he drove you up here in September, what room did he take your stuff to?"

DAMN IT! Bob's right. Problem! I hissed like a flat tire. "This one. Maybe I could tell him Clarence moved out."

"Good luck with that!" Steve was grinning and chuckling, both. He had a weird sense of humor.

"So what do I do now?"

"So now it's YOUR turn to come up with a plan, don't you think?" asked Bob. "What do we do, General? Do we attack, retreat, what?"

"Commit hari kari?" offered Steve.

"We do the only thing we can. We move me BACK into McFadden Hall. And...and we move STEVE into Clarence's room so his shit isn't all over my new room and it looks like only two people live there."

"I get my OWN ROOM? Woo HOO! Yahoo for LOU!"

"Shut up. We're gonna need every minute. Let's go! Let's go!" I had a terrible headache. It was hard enough keep the past and the present straight without having four frigging flights of stairs in the way. Where I actually lived became a foggy memory.

The three of us ran around the room stuffing the papers and coffee cups and clothes into the cardboard box and trash can. The boys were out the door before I had a chance to suggest that someone else might want to carry the typewriter. Well, at least I didn't have to go back for the guitar.

By the time I made it down the two million stairs and across the lawn, my three volunteers had decided that now would be a great time for a smoke break. All my stuff was piled in front of the big window. The sun had set, and most of the rooms in McFadden Hall were lit with desk lamps as the university's finest hit the books to study for finals. Something I should have been doing.

Bob and Steve and Gordon were relaxing on my duffel bag and sitting on the boxes of books and miscellaneous crap outside my window, as I hefted my nasty, heavy, pile-of-shit 1938 monster typewriter. I dropped it at Bob's feet. He tapped out a cigarette and offered it to me.

"I don't smoke," I said.

"Yes, you do. And this one is going to be the last one you're going to get until your father leaves. Better take it."

Chapter 43

I never finished a cigarette. If I did, I would have to admit to being a smoker. I also never bought my own. Okay, maybe just once, but that was in a bar. Everyone smokes in a bar. For those two reasons I could tell anyone who asked me if I smoked, "No." My father, who put away two packs of Marlboros a day, would pretty much kill me if he caught me smoking. But right then, I needed one. I took a few puffs and tossed the butt away. "Back to work. We gotta move me in, Steve out, and clean up the remnants of the commie pinko stuff that's all over the room."

"Including the smoke bombs and tear gas repellent and the flags with the red fist on them?" asked Steve.

"Especially those." I placed the typewriter on the ground outside the window and looked in. The light switch was all the way on the other side of the room. The floor was covered with crap of every size and shape. It looked like a bomb had gone off in a thrift shop, but it looked normal.

"It's dark as a cow's asshole in there," said Bob. "Be careful." I steadied myself on the window ledge, then dropped to the floor. Immediately I realized I had made a big mistake. My feet landed on a hard object which gave way with a simultaneous loud crack and a horrible, evil musical chord, which I couldn't identify but was certainly in a minor key. It sounded like Wiley E. Coyote had dropped a piano through the roof and just missed the Road Runner.

I had broken the neck off my twelve-string guitar.

Chapter 44

The room filled with light as Bob hit the switch. He had walked around to the main entrance to the building, and entered the room through the official door and switched on the light. "What just happened?" he asked.

I looked down at my feet to confirm what I already knew. The long, wide neck of the twelve-string, made from three pieces of polished birch wood, laminated together with a rosewood fret board, studded with twelve brass Grover tuners and inlaid with white ivory scroll work all the way up to the sixteenth fret; this gorgeous piece of the guitar maker's art lay a good three feet from the rest of the instrument. It felt like I was looking at the body of a beautiful woman, whose head had rolled into another room.

The enormity of what had just happened was slow to register on the three of us. Steve spoke first. "Well, that should make it easier to tune."

Bob asked, "Does your dad ever ask you to play?"

I took a deep breath. The first words were just raspy squeaks, but eventually I was able to say, "No. Never. He always finds a reason to go work in the garage when I play."

"Lucky boy," said Bob. "You don't need the guitar. Just the case. He'll see the case and that's all he needs to see. You're saved, Tony."

"Yeah," I said. "Sure I am." I picked up the pieces of my precious instrument and arranged them carefully in its coffin. Like a soldier collecting the remains of his buddy. No time to grieve. Shells flying overhead. I closed the cover and clacked the clasps shut. Nothing has ever sounded so final.

"Let's keep going," I said. "Get that crap off the walls."

Steve backed up against one of the posters and threw his hands out. "No! Not my favorite! Not this one!" It was a three foot by two foot black and white photo of a bare chested, long haired, unshaven man extending his middle finger to the camera, a joint hanging from the side of his mouth, a tattered American flag tied across his forehead. The words, "LBJ! Pull out like your father should have!" completed the sentiment.

"Yeah," I said. "That one too."

Chapter 45

I was very, very close to losing it. I could feel all the screws letting go, the nails popping out. Shingles began to fly off the roof, parts fell out on the highway, pieces of my brain started to overheat, smoke, sizzle, and shut down. The realization of what mountain of crap had fallen on me became crystal clear.

Now I had nothing to lose. I had lost it all: my girlfriend, my comfy hideout from the draft, my meal ticket, and now, even my guitar lay in ruins. I was down to stems and seeds. My loyal crew seemed to realize that the bottom had been hit, and penetrated. Bob, Gordon and Steve began to quietly pick up the room, solemnly, as if cleaning up after a messy suicide. It was clear they wanted to be anyplace but here. The smell of death was in the air.

A knock sounded at the door. All I could think of was The Inquisition. Was it my father? I didn't care. If it was my father, then so be it. Let it rip. Let's get on with it. If he was a screaming maniac, let him scream. If he took me out of school, if I got drafted, if I had to learn to eat with chop sticks, then get it over with. But I didn't care. *Do your worst. I'm ready.*

The banging on the door sounded again, and I threw it open, ready to face whatever was on the other side. Ready to face my crazy father.

But it wasn't my father. It was CJ. He handed me a piece of paper.

"Your old man called about half an hour ago. He said he can't call you again; you'll have to call him. He said to tell you 'please.' Like, as in, *please* call him. Here's the number."

It with an unfamiliar area code. He wasn't on Long Island. That area code was 516. And he wasn't in upstate New York; that one was 607. This area code was 845. Where was that?

"He said 'please?'" I asked CJ.

"Call him, Tony," yelled Bob.

What the hell? Every other time anybody ever tried to call me either the damn phone was busy or nobody gave me the message. Today I had receptionists coming out my rear end.

"Also," said CJ, "he told me you can't call collect. Do you mind if I hang around? This sounds like it's gonna be good."

It took all of Gordon's beer money, mostly in quarters for Pint Night, to scrounge up the cash needed to coax the pay phone to call the mysterious area code 845 and number. It rang four times and then a woman's voice answered.

"Stovertown Police Department."

Chapter 46

I had never actually called a police department before, not in Stovertown, wherever the hell that was—not on Long Island, not in Ithaca, and I didn't know what to say. I asked for Mr. Vitelli.

"We have no officers by that name."

"He doesn't work there…he might be…a guest…I mean, a… He's my father. I'm returning his call."

"I'll transfer you to the holding area." Then I waited. And waited. Several minutes passed. The old black pay phone donged again and I stuffed another dime into it. Finally an unfriendly voice answered, "Officer something or other."

"I'm sorry," I said, on my very best behavior, "I didn't catch your name."

"Who's this?"

"This is, uh, Anthony Vitelli. I am Louis Vitelli's son…He called me. I got a message…he said to, uh, please call him."

"Oh, in that case why don't you ask Mr. Louis Vitelli who I am. As far as he's concerned, my name is Officer Fascist Pig."

"He called you that?"

"Close enough."

"Why would he call you that?"

"Because he was intoxicated. That may have played a role in it."

I put my hand over the phone. "Guys!" I whispered out loud. "My dad's in jail!" Steve collapsed onto the floor clutching his throat. I put my hand over the phone and tried to shush his shrill cackling.

"Are you there, Mr. Vitelli?" said the cop.

"Yes, sir," I said. "I just find it so hard to believe that my father was drinking and driving. He's never done that."

"Oh yeah, he has. He's been picked up before. On Long Island. He's an old hand at it. Also, he didn't exactly want to cooperate and he failed the field sobriety test. Couldn't walk a straight line. Couldn't say the alphabet backwards."

"I can't either..." I said.

"Well, you better learn it before you drive through Stovertown with a load on. Hang on, I'll put him on the phone."

I put my hand over the phone and said in a loud whisper, "He called the cops fascist pigs!"

"I wonder where he got that from." said Steve. His mustache shook like a clothes dryer full of wet sneakers.

"He's in the Stovertown jail. No, I don't know where that is. But it's in New York someplace. I think. They got him for speeding."

My father's voice came through the phone, sounding very different from when I last spoke to him. He spoke calmly, as if he called from jail every evening at this time. "Tony, you have to come get me. You have to bail me out."

"What happened, Dad? What did you do?"

"I'll tell you when I see you. Get in the car and come and get me." *And what car might that be?* I thought.

"Were you drinking? The officer said you were drinking."

"One beer! I had one beer. With dinner."

"How fast were you going?"

"Tony, we don't have time for this. Bring three hundred in cash."

"Three hundred bucks? Write them a check!"

"They don't take checks. They won't take my Diner's Club. You need cash to bail someone out. Also, they took the car."

"What does that mean, 'they took the car?' Dad, let me talk to Officer...let me talk to the cop." The tone of my voice did not require that I add, "Just do it. How do you like being treated like this, 'buddy boy?'" which I wanted to say but didn't. Steve, Gordon, CJ and Bob were doing some sort of dance around the dorm room, trying not to laugh while waving their hands in the air and hopping up and down. I put my hand over the phone while I waited for Officer Fascist Pig to come back on the line. He took his time.

"This is the greatest thing that's happened all year," gushed Gordon.

"But why is he in the pokey? They don't lock you up for speeding. You pay your fine, you're on your way."

"They lock you up if you argue with the cops. And you've been drinking."

"Lou is doomed," said Steve.

"I got a ticket in Stovertown," said CJ. "They're very big on law enforcement there. They run the whole town on the speeding fines. God knows what they do to you for a DWI."

"He says he wasn't drunk," I said quickly. "He said he just had one beer."

"Ah, yes," said Gordon, "The old 'one beer' defense. I've tried that myself. It never works."

"Especially in Stovertown," said CJ. "That place is like just one street. The cops hide under the overpass on Highway 17. Why did he argue with the cop? Is he nuts?"

Officer Pig came back on the line. "Make it quick, son."

"My dad said you took the car."

"Impounded it. Yes, we did."

"Why would you do that?"

"You can't drive a car while under the influence. I'm not going to drive it back to the station. The tow truck takes it to the impound lot."

"How does he get it back?"

"When he's sober, and the impound lot is open, he pays $70 for the tow and $20 a day storage and gets the car back." This just got better and better. It was Friday night. I knew the answer to the next question, but I still couldn't wait till I heard Officer Pig actually say it.

"And when will the impound lot be open?" I took a deep breath and crossed my fingers. I held the phone out so all the boys could hear the triumphant answer.

"Monday."

You would have thought the end of World War II had just been announced. If there was a girl in the room, any girl at all, I would have swept her into my arms, bent her over and kissed her on the lips like that famous picture.

"With the $300 bail, the tow charge and two days storage, that makes $410 cash," the cop went on. "Plus $15 a day board and $50 processing, that's $490. Then he has to come back for the hearing, unless he wants to plead guilty and save himself the trouble and expense of visiting our lovely town again. We'll call it 'driving while impaired,' which is a misdemeanor, with a $100 fine. Speeding is $10 for every one mile over the speed limit, so that's another…$200. So that's $790, son."

Seven hundred ninety bucks! I repeated the amount to the boys and they assumed the expressions of people who have just been struck by lightning.

"What about 'insulting an officer?'" I asked.

"Assaulting an officer?"

"No, insulting an officer. He called you a fascist pig," I said.

"Oh, heck, everyone does that. If I locked up everyone who called me a fascist pig I'd fill all the jails in New York. Tell you what, I'll throw that one in for nothin'. How's that?"

"Can you do me a favor, Officer?"

"I suppose I can. What can I do for you?"

"Ask my father where I'm supposed to get $790, if you would please." There was a pause.

"He says, 'Call your mother.'"

"There is no way this can happen before sometime Monday at the earliest," I told Officer Pig.

"Then we'll see you Monday. Your father will enjoy a leisurely weekend in peaceful and law abiding Stovertown." Then the phone made two jarring dongs signaling the time was up. "I'll tell him you said goodbye." The line went dead.

Chapter 47

I hadn't eaten all day. Sometimes I go a whole day like that, because I'm upset about something. Maybe something awful has happened or I'm worried about something big. My eating habits over the past week were not what my mom would call healthy. I hadn't been hungry all day and had nothing but coffee since I woke up. But knowing my dad was locked up in a small town holding cell, with nothing but a tin cup to rake across the bars and a spackle bucket to take a dump in, now my appetite was returning fast.

Gordon, Bob, Steve and CJ had clasped hands and were reenacting a song from Wizard of Oz.

"Ding Dong! The witch is dead! Which old witch? The wicked witch!" they sang, each in his own key. I waved at them to quiet down.

"It's late and I'm hungry," I announced. Gordon, Bob and CJ reacted as if this was an odd thing to say, given the recent events.

"So am I," said Steve. This was not significant. He was always hungry.

"What about getting your old man out of jail?" asked Gordon. "Don't you have stuff to do?"

"Like what? What am I supposed to do?"

"You have to get the money!" said Bob. He seemed pretty agitated about my lack of urgency. "You have to call your mom! You have to get a car from somewhere! Tony! *You have to get your father!* What's wrong with you?"

"I do? Why do I have to do that?"

"You're just going to leave him there?"

"If I was the guy in jail for DWI and resisting arrest, and I didn't have the bail money, and I called HIM, what do you think he'd do?"

"He'd let you rot in jail," said CJ. "I never met your dad, but that's what I'd vote for."

"You have a death wish, my friend," said Country Bob. "You don't know enough to come in out of the rain. Your old man has power, Tony. He can crush you like a bug. Get your dad out of jail. Don't be an idiot."

Bob made a good point but I had this figured out. I had a plan. "Bob," I said, "you're a farm management guy, right? What do they teach you there? Aren't you supposed to solve the biggest problems first? Isn't that how all the problems get fixed? In order? Hell, that's what they taught us in eleventh grade business class. I figure I have three big problems right now. And bailing out Lou doesn't even make the list."

Bob stared at me as if I had been babbling incoherently. When he didn't reply and just looked at me blankly, I elaborated. I almost sounded like I had thought this out ahead of time.

"My number one problem is I gotta find Melissa." Problem number two is that tomorrow is Paci-Fest."

"If Melissa is problem number one, why aren't you out there looking for her?" said Gordon.

"Think about it. Melissa is the biggest liberal on campus. She hates the war more than anybody. She was one of the people who silk-screened those big red fists on the shirts everyone's gonna wear tomorrow. She loves animals. She traded her mom's million dollar fur coat for a surplus military jacket as soon as she got here. She knows the words to every Phil Ochs song, hell, *every protest song* ever written. Melissa can sing *Eve of Destruction* backwards, probably."

"That's not exactly a marketable skill," said Bob.

"She sounds irresistible," sighed Steve. I went on with my speech.

"So, if you wanted to find her, and you didn't want to look under every frigging rock in this whole town, and in every corner, library, language lab, dorm room and lecture hall in one of the biggest college campuses in the whole frigging world, *where would you be... tomorrow?*"

With one voice, except Steve, they said, "Paci-Fest." Steve said something that sounded like "taking a nap."

Gordon turned to Steve and asked, "You're not going?"

"Of course not! I'm a wanted man, remember? You know who else is gonna be at Paci-Fest? Thousands of them, like *maggots*, all over the place…FBI agents. And guess whose picture is hanging on their office walls?" With that he flashed a big smile, tilted his head, pointed to his face and said, "I'm ready for my close up!"

"Well," I said, "that's where I'm going to be. If Melissa is anywhere in this town she'll be on the front lines tomorrow. I'll knock off two problems at once."

"When are you gonna call your mother and tell her she has to come up with eight hundred clams that she has to wire to you like super pronto?" asked Gordon.

"Don't exaggerate," I said. "Seven hundred ninety bucks."

"You owe me for the phone call. Also you're buying us dinner. What's problem number three?"

"I don't have a car."

"No! Forget it," said Gordon. He was a sophomore and could have a car on campus. His 1960 Ford Falcon was legendary in Collegetown for the number of parking tickets stuffed in every free space of the beat up sedan, which only lacked a big Demolition Derby number spray-painted on the door. "Borrow Bob's truck."

"Hey," said Bob, "I lent him my room. We all have to do our part to help those less fortunate."

"Didn't someone mention food?" asked Steve.

Chapter 48

Bob fired up a cigarette and took a deep drag, then let the smoke out slowly. "So, General, if the enemy isn't going to invade tonight, can we stand down?"

"At ease, men," I said, "The crisis is over…for the time being. The enemy is contained. There will be no attack tonight. Who wants to get some food?"

"If you're buying, I'm eating," said Bob. I reached for my wallet. It wasn't there. This happened all the time. What did I do with the damn thing? I slapped my pockets.

"You left your wallet in the other room, when we were moving stuff. You're not getting away that easy."

"Okay," I said. "I'll pony up for one cheese pizza. Nothing on it."

"With mushrooms, sausage, pepperoni and anchovies," yelled Gordon.

"No anchovies!" yelled Steve. I stepped over the guitar case, onto my chair and then the window ledge. I looked down at the catastrophe that until recently had been my precious guitar. Would it ever sing again? Bob followed me to the dark street.

We began the climb to the fourth floor one more time. "Are you sure you want to go for pizza?" he asked. "When your dad finds out you're leaving him locked up for the weekend it might be your last meal. Maybe you should get steaks?" We rounded the first flight of stairs and began the next one. It was a good thing I didn't live here anymore. How did I ever deal with all these stairs? I dug out the key and opened the door.

"Please don't tell me that we have to move you back into the other room," he said. "I'm sick of the musical chairs crap with all your stuff."

"You and me both. I'll figure out what to do tomorrow, after I've found Melissa and I've talked to my mother. Maybe a night in jail will cool him off. Don't worry, he won't show up here. I know my dad. When he gets the car back, he'll turn around and boogie on home to Long Island." I flipped on the light. I didn't see the wallet.

"On the bed?" asked Bob.

"Not there. What the hell? Wait, I remember I took it out of my pocket when we were carrying all that stuff. Did you see where I put it?"

"There! On the floor." Bob pointed to a barely visible corner of brown leather poking out from under the dresser. I knelt down and swept my hand under the dresser and whisked away the wallet. And something else. A scuffed and dirty envelope slid out, streaked with dust. I held it up. It was sealed. I turned it over. In a familiar handwriting it said, "READ ME!"

"Another note from Melissa?" asked Bob. "Boy, how long has that thing been under there?"

I turned it over, then over again. "I don't know. Could be weeks...months. No idea."

"Aren't you going to open it?"

I stared at Melissa's handwriting. "I guess I am," I said, as if I were talking to myself and not to Bob. For some reason I wasn't in a big hurry to do that. Something didn't feel right. It had been a long time since I had heard anything at all from her. Holding the note felt a little like holding a message from beyond the grave. Was I ready for it? "I wonder how long it's been there," I said. I tore the little envelope open and pulled out the folded slip of paper. Inside were another two words, in big capital letters. I read it out loud to Bob.

"'I'M LATE.' It says 'I'M LATE.' late.' What the hell does that mean?"

Chapter 49

Bob backed away from the note the way Superman recoiled from a piece of Kryptonite. "Uh oh."

"I don't get it," I said. "Why would she walk all the way over here to tell me she was late? Late for what? Why would I care if I wasn't here anyway?"

"Tony, look carefully. Is there a date on that thing?"

"No."

"Does it have your name on it? Are you even sure it's for you?"

I looked at both sides of the envelope. "No. Why is it such a big deal that she's late? She was always late. One day I waited for her..."

"Tony. Take your wallet. Turn off the light. Lock the door. Let's walk over to the Royal Palm. I'll explain the mysteries of the universe to you over a beer. You're going to need one. I'll talk real slowly, because, Tony? You're the dumbest motherfucker on the planet."

"What about the pizza?" I asked.

"We'll worry about the pizza later. I have a feeling you might not be hungry."

We walked in silence to the Royal Palm. It was a warm evening. Bob put his hand on my shoulder and pointed me this way and that, as if guiding a blind man. We walked in silence; I was lost in thought. The last time I had been to the Palm, it was cold and the streets were covered in slush. The bartender, what was his name? Lorraine called him Igor...he threw me out because I was a lousy pool player. I hoped the big oaf wasn't working tonight. Why hadn't Melissa called me?

When did she get back? What did the note—I stopped walking and turned to face Bob.

"She's pregnant," I said.

"Bingo. Give the man a cigar."

"How do I know it's mine?" I asked quickly, as this enormous fact sunk in. The only thing I could think of was, "It's not my fault!" but what I said was, "How do I know the note was even meant for me? Clarence lived there too. It could have been for him! The note has to be for him!"

"You never told her you moved?"

"I moved after she disappeared. No. I couldn't. When did Clarence move?"

"Pretty soon after you did."

"The note was probably for him. It has to be."

"Do you really think Clarence had sex with her? Are you sure? Did you ask him? What did he say?"

"I was afraid to ask him. Besides, what good would it do? He'd have denied it."

"Do you think they did it?"

"Of course they did. Who wouldn't want to do it with her?"

"But you don't know for sure."

"No. Not for absolute, a hundred percent, sure.

"But you guys did, uh, have sex, right?"

I smiled. "You *know* we did. More than once."

"More than once?"

"Yeah, like way more than once. Way, way more."

"How many times?"

"You know, a bunch. I don't know exactly. Why?" I asked.

"She's your first, right?"

"Yeah…" And only…and how did Bob know? Was it that obvious?

"So stop with the bullshit. Every guy knows how many times they did it with their first. So how many times?"

Was this true? I should have been counting? How come I didn't know that? I had to think. Two weeks… fourteen days. Three, sometimes four times a day. A couple days just one or two times. One night five times…

"How many times, Tony?"

"I guess maybe forty, forty two times."

"Tony, Tony…" said Bob. "You think maybe *Clarence* is the father? Are you kidding me? Forty two times?"

Chapter 51

That night would have been a great time to get a good night's sleep. But it was not to be. I felt like I had fallen into my mom's Veg-O-Matic. If I didn't keep hopping and jumping out of the way I'd be chopped into coleslaw. My dreams—if they were dreams at all—were stuck together like one endless movie about changing diapers, paying bills, warming bottles and getting up, day after day, to drive a rusted out car to Triphammer Mall to work a lousy job for a buck and a half an hour while Melissa did one load of laundry after another, frowning the whole time. Whenever I looked at the baby it was a different color. Then my father would appear, and I'd have to go and get him out of jail. Over and over. I no sooner had one problem solved when the dream would reset and the baby would start crying again. What had I done to myself?

The gravelly, liquid eruptions of the twin snoring beasts, Steve and Gordon, served as my alarm clock. But I had never really been asleep. The relief that always came when I realized that everything was 'just a dream' didn't happen that morning. It wasn't a dream. It was real.

Flat on my back with my eyes wide open, I knew that today was going to be one brutal, bastard of a day. Today was the day that the giant anti-war demonstration and peace rally was going to shut down the campus. Today I had to find the dough to bail out my old man. And the very first thing I had to do was call my mom and tell her a whole mountain of miserable crap that she didn't want to hear.

I sat up in the bed. Along with the noises Steve and Gordon were making there was another noise in the room, some low frequency shake that I could feel rather than hear. Something that even the ferocious snoring couldn't drown out. Then someone banged on the door.

"Open up the door, you bunch of subversive, seditious perverts. It is I, the Voice of Reason." It sounded a lot like the voice of Country Bob Crawford. I pulled myself out of bed. The room seemed to vibrate with a low rumble. Was that my imagination? I opened the door.

"Did you call your mother?" he demanded.

"What the hell is that noise, Bob?"

"The rumble, you mean? Tanks."

"Tanks?"

"You're welcome. I'll get to that. First things first. Did you call your mother?"

"Not yet, but I will. I swear. What do you mean, tanks?"

"Call your mother first. Right now. Before the festivities start. Here's some change." He picked up my open hand and dropped three quarters and two dimes into my palm.

"Call your mother," yelled Gordon as he, too, crawled out of bed and searched for his glasses. Steve chimed in with something that might have been, "Call your mother," or pretty much any other three word sentence you could think of. Maybe even, "Leave me alone." It was asking too much of Steve to expect coherent speech first thing in the morning. I joined Bob in the hallway and plugged the change into the payphone. Gordon moved in on me to listen. Bob held his finger to his lips to shush him.

My mom picked up right away and I could hear the concern in her voice right from the word *hello*. She was having a crappy day too. Join the club.

"Where's your father? Is he there? Let me talk to him."

"He's not here, Mom. He's in jail."

"Where?" It was a simple question. No outrage, no surprise. It seemed as if she had taken this kind of phone call before. She sounded more irritated than surprised.

"Some Podunk place called Stovertown." I said. "It's on Highway 17 somewhere, down south. They nailed him for speeding. The cop said he was drinking."

"Is he alright? He's not hurt, is he?" No fear, no disbelief.

"I think he's fine. He was pretty upset yesterday. They threw him in the clink to cool him off."

"Drinking. Huh. Again. What are we supposed to do?"

"He wants me to bring the bail money and the money to get the car…"

"They impounded the car, I suppose."

"Yeah, that's what the cop said."

"How much is the bail?"

I was about to say "Seven-hundred-ninety dollars," when Gordon lifted up the pizza box and waved it back and forth. Steve thrust up his left hand and wiggled three fingers on his right. That made eight. But I needed gas money…and something to make it worthwhile. I said it very slowly and carefully, because I knew she would yell, *"WHAT?"* if I didn't. "Uh, the whole thing, including the fine and the tow and all, is like, uh, nine…hundred…dollars." I could always come down.

"WHAT?" she yelled. "Nine hundred dollars?" Gordon and Bob mouthed it along with her, as if the three of them had been practicing.

"Yeah, Mom, that's what the cop said. Dad told me to call you for it. You can wire it to the Collegetown bank where you send my food money. I'll pick it up and bring it to Stovertown on Monday. Dad said they only take cash."

"Oh, it's as simple as that, huh? That's all I have to do is just find nine hundred dollars someplace? Maybe I'll check behind the couch cushions. How are you going to get to this place? Do you even know where it is?"

"I'll find it. Don't worry about that, Mom, I'll get it to him." Then she stopped speaking and I got ready to say, "Thanks, okay, bye bye," which is how I ended all my phone calls to my parents. She started speaking again.

"Tony, the radio is full of news about a big anti-war demonstration at Cornell today. Do you know anything about that?" Just then a big truck downshifted to climb the hill to campus. The noise was loud enough for my mom to hear it. I looked out the window to see a huge brown vehicle that looked like a cross between a big pickup and a covered wagon, loaded with soldiers wearing helmets and carrying rifles. "What was that noise, Tony?"

"Nothing, Mom. Some construction equipment. They're working on the road."

"Is there a demonstration going on today? There is, isn't there? Stay out of it, Tony. Please tell me you're not involved with that, honey."

"Don't worry, Mom. Violence isn't my thing."

"Promise me."

I was sure that Bob and Gordon could hear her. I swallowed hard and said, "I promise."

"And something else, Tony. Your father says you're failing, that you're going to flunk out. Is that true?"

"Mom, relax. I'm not going to flunk out. Don't worry." At this Steve the Freak held his hand over his head as if he was holding a noose and shut his eyes and stuck out his tongue.

"Tell me the truth, Tony. I have enough to worry about without you getting thrown out of school."

I spoke quickly. "I'm not going to flunk out, Mom. I have to hang up, I'm out of change. Wire the money, Mom. I'll take care of this. Eight...I mean nine hundred bucks."

"Call the bank first thing Monday, Tony. It'll be there. I'll find it. But first I have to make a few phone calls."

"Don't worry, Mom, I'll take care of this. I love you, Mom."

Her voice had been strong for the whole conversation but it broke when she said, "I love you, Tony," just before she hung up. Why did that sound so strange? Then I realized that it was the first time anyone had said the words "I love you, Tony" the whole damn year.

"You lied to your *mother?*" asked Bob, horrified. "I can understand lying to your father. Hell, everybody does that, but lying to your mom? You go to hell for stuff like that."

"I didn't lie to her."

"You sure as shit did," said Steve.

"Yeah, you did," said Gordon. "You lied to your mother. You're doomed to burn for eternity."

"How did I lie? What did I say?"

"You told her you weren't flunking out."

"No, I didn't. I told her I would not 'flunk' out. That's not the same thing. And that's not a lie."

"How's that different?" demanded Bob. He seemed to be taking this personally. As if I didn't have enough trouble, now I had a brand new Jiminy frigging Cricket up my butt. "You have all Ds and probably an F or two. How's that not flunking out?"

I turned to Bob, filled my lungs with air and expounded, with authority, on the subject of lying to one's mother. "The word 'flunking' is an infinitive and implies an on-going process. 'Flunk' is a verb and implies a definite action, an…um… irreversible action. An action that's in *progress*, like flunking, can be stopped or reversed. Something that has *flunked* is an action that is completed…finished. I may be 'flunking' but I will not 'flunk.'

"How about that?" asked Gordon, "You're an English major after all. I'll be damned."

Bob added, "You're so full of shit, Tony. That's why your eyes are brown."

"Don't believe him!" yelled Steve from under the army blanket. "He pulled that all out of his ass. Genuine English major gibberish. Flunking is a freaking *gerund*, for Pete's sake." It was just possible that Steve might be right, which by itself was incredible enough.

"Regardless," I said. "I do not lie to my mother and I will not flunk out."

"You still lied to your mother, Tony. You told her you weren't going to the demonstration," said Steve quietly. He had me. All that great oratory was for nothing. I had been caught fair and square. I didn't even think Steve had been awake.

"Okay. True. But it was just a little lie. I mean, compared. Anyway, I have a plan. Gordon, I will require the use of your car on Monday, if you could please. I have a humanitarian mission to the wilds of Stovertown."

"I knew this was coming. You can't use the car. The last time you used it you brought it back empty with three parking tickets under the wipers."

"I happen to know you don't have any classes on Monday next week."

"You can't use the car. Here's my best offer. I'll drive you and you pay for the gas. Also lunch. But I got one big question. What are we gonna do with Lou once we spring him? Are we bringing him back here for the grand tour?" I shook my head. "Is he going to follow us?" I shook it again. "Because I'm not up for any more cleaning or moving or any other crap." He walked around the room waving his arms around. Gordon was on a rant and it was best not to interrupt until he took a break to catch his breath. "I'll drive you to Stovertown but that's it. I am beat. *Beat*, I tell you. I didn't go to college to schlep boxes. I'm here to get an education." Gordon finally stopped and reached under the bed and withdrew the bong.

"How are you doing with that education thing?" Steve asked from under his blanket.

"Don't worry," I said. "Lou will not be coming here to see the room, or me, or for any other reason. Lou will get in his car and drive right back to Long Island."

"How can you be so sure?"

"Because Lou will have spent the previous three nights and two days eating bologna sandwiches and cold oatmeal, sleeping on a board and pissing in a bucket in a room with bars for a door. Lou is going to hightail it back to his comfy house on Long Island. We'll have our little face-to-face chat, which should last maybe a whole minute, and he'll hit the road like Richard Petty. He'll be home, tearing into a steak and a six pack before we get back to Ithaca. I frigging guarantee it."

Another rumble from the street made the three of us run to the window. Steve leaped out of bed in a startling burst of speed I had never seen before, and yelled, "I know what that is! That's the sound of bad news."

"See?" said Bob. "Tanks."

Chapter 52

It wasn't an actual tank, not that it made any difference. My dad had dragged me to every military museum in the state before I was eight years old. I knew a half-track personnel carrier when I saw one. As the giant truck, pushed by tractor treads, rounded the corner and headed up the hill, we got a close look at the faces of the soldiers in the back. Every one of them looked directly at us. If not for the haircuts, we could have been them. They could have been us.

"Gentlemen," said Gordon, "it looks like the opposing team has arrived on campus. Let the games begin."

"The other team has some serious hardware, guys," I said. "What do they need that for? We're just a bunch of hippies. Poor, unarmed, long haired peaceniks." This was way beyond anything I had signed on for.

"What does your father call us, again?" asked Steve.

"Commie pinko faggots."

"And proud of it," he said.

"You know who joins the National Guard, don't you?" asked Gordon. "Guys who don't want to go to Vietnam. They're not real soldiers. Those guns they're carrying? They're wooden training rifles. They're toys."

"The hell they are," I said. "Those are M-1 rifles. My dad has one hanging over the fireplace. He carried it in the war. That's about as real as a gun can get."

"Then they're not loaded. Why would they give kids live ammo on a college campus? It doesn't make sense. Don't worry about it."

"Bullshit," I said quietly.

"What's the matter, Tony? Isn't this how you wanted to spend a nice Saturday?" taunted Gordon. "Are you gonna chicken out? Why did you want to go to this thing anyway? Tell me that. You don't give a crap about politics."

I had been trying to avoid answering that question, even to myself. There wasn't an easy explanation. Had I succumbed to Gordon's non-stop bitching about raising our voices against an unjust war? Or did I just not want to miss a party? But I didn't get to answer. Steve did it for me.

"He thinks he can find Melissa there. Remember? That's why he's going." He nailed it. I had to admit it. It was all the answer Gordon needed. I didn't have to dredge up lofty liberal justifications that I only half believed in. "Follow your heart" was all the explanation anyone—especially me—needed. I was about to put myself in harm's way to find my soul mate, my one true love. This was all that anyone could do. It was a pure motive; I needed no other reason.

"Is that it?" asked Gordon. "You really think Melissa will be there?"

"I know her as well as I know myself. She'll be there."

"Plus," added Bob, "Tony doesn't want to miss the party."

"Move out, men," said Gordon. "The concert starts at oh-one-thirty PM, or whatever. The music starts in an hour. Drop your cocks and grab your socks. Time to boogie. Freak! Are you coming?"

"I'll pass. Too many FBI agents with my picture in their wallets. If you need me I'll be hiding under the bed."

"Don't forget the signs," said Bob. "I must have spent at least ten minutes making the damn things. Take your pick." He handed me a stack of large cardboard signs that he had painted with big, black letters. Paint dribbles ran from the words to the edges of the cardboard and down the handles, made from a broken yardstick. I spread them out on Gordon's bed to keep the paint off my own. Gordon grabbed the one that said STOP THE DRAFT, I took HELL NO WE WON'T GO. Bob picked OLD ENOUGH TO FIGHT OLD ENOUGH TO VOTE, and we left the HO HO HO CHI MINH on the bed. I had no idea what the hell that even meant.

It was a beautiful, sun drenched late spring day in upstate New York, one of the few times of year it made any sense at all to be there. One by one, we hoisted our knapsacks and shoulder bags to the sidewalk and climbed out the open window. Hundreds of other kids were doing the same, streaming out of dorms and frat houses. Cars pulled onto the lawn in blatant violation of the parking regulations and disgorged hippies and jocks alike, along with kids dressed 'normally' as my mom would say. There were plenty of them as well. We joined the crowd that had assembled across the street, and together we began the trek across campus to Barton Hall, a huge field house which would house the opening concert.

If it was just a concert that would have been great. I could do with a little music right then. But there would be endless speeches and rhetoric and rabble-rousing that would bore me to death and try my patience and my commitment. My commitment? What commitment would that be?

American flags were everywhere. Even on a few flagpoles. The Stars and Stripes served as bandanas, flags were sewn across the back of Levi jackets, on the seats of pants, and served as tops or bottoms to bikinis. Good God, what would my dad, Captain Lou Vitelli, U.S. Army, Retired, think of all this? The fact that he was sitting on the corner of a cot in some Stovertown hellhole jail seemed almost merciful. It's funny the way things sometimes just work out for the best. He'd go stark raving off-the-wall crazy if he saw this group.

The crowd swelled with every kind of person imaginable. Kids from nations and races which weren't even involved with the war, kids who weren't U.S. citizens and wouldn't be drafted stood next to healthy nineteen year old guys—guys like me—who would be the first to go. Beautiful girls in cut-off shorts and halter tops, who looked ready for a day at the beach, walked with young girls in dungarees and fatigue jackets who looked as if had they just run away from home. Many had sleeping bags or bedrolls, paper grocery sacks packed with junk food, wine skins and six packs. The morning breeze stank of pot. This was shaping up to be a hell of a party. As long as no one got killed.

We weren't the only ones out in force. Young guys, kids like us, only wearing uniforms, formed lines on each side of the street. They could have been trick-or-treaters dressed as soldiers if they were a few years younger. One guy in a helmet strapped tightly under his chin watched us trudge along with our stuff. I held up my sign to him, HELL NO WE WON'T GO. He loosened his middle finger from the stock of his M-1 and held it up. I think, if I had been close enough, he would have spit on me.

Screw you too. "What's that all about?" I asked Bob and Gordon. "I'm not the enemy. I didn't start the war. I didn't make him be a soldier."

"But somebody did," said Bob. "And he's not happy about it. I think he doesn't like your sign."

"Hey Tony," said Gordon. "Your dad was in the army, wasn't he? What was he doing on December eighth, 1941?"

"Standing in a line with everyone else he knew, trying to enlist in the army. Which is where I would have been. How about you?"

"Yeah, we all would have been there. So what do you think: why would we have enlisted back then and now we're protesting the draft? Did you ever ask yourself that?"

The truth was, I hadn't really asked myself much of anything, other than, *Do you want to get shot in Vietnam?* To which my answer had always been a big fat *No.* "That war was different, Bob. That was World War Two! The Japs attacked Pearl Harbor! Remember?"

"Would you have gone if you got drafted?"

I didn't have to think long. "Of course. Wouldn't you?"

"We all would. The draft isn't the problem."

"No, it's not…the *war* is the problem," I said completing the thought. "Some wars you have to fight. Some you don't. This isn't our war."

"Am I getting this right?" asked Gordon. "You think there is such a thing as a good war?"

"That's what that soldier boy is pissed off about," I said. "He doesn't want to fight this frigging war any more than we do. But he doesn't have a choice. They're making him go. I'd be pissed off too," I said. I stopped walking and set my bag down. Then I folded the sign in half, and half again so it couldn't be read, and I dropped it on the ground. "We're bitching about the wrong thing. No wonder these guys don't like us. We've got it all wrong. It's not the draft that's the problem, it's the damn war. We look like a bunch of selfish, spoiled brats."

"Whoa, Tony," said Gordon. "That's heavy stuff. Coming from you, anyway. Did Melissa tell you that? You didn't think that up all yourself, did you?"

"Bite me," I said. I wanted to say, "Go fuck yourself," but Gordon was my friend and I needed all of those that I could get.

Gordon tossed me what appeared to be a large pair of gloves, clipped together like a little kid's mittens. I caught them. They were heavy, worn leather, work gloves of some sort.

"What are these for?"

"Welder's gloves. My old man is a welder in the shipyards. He gave them to me, told me we might need them." Gordon's father was a union organizer, a genuine card carrying Socialist, a guy who might have something to teach this vast crowd of revolutionaries-in-training.

"Why do we need welding gloves?" I asked. "Do any of us know how to weld?"

"I do, as it happens," said Country Bob.

"You don't count. You know to how to do everything," I said.

"You'll need the gloves if the pigs start throwing tear gas grenades," said Gordon. "They'll burn the hell out of your hands when you pick them up. You have to wear gloves."

"*I've* got to wear gloves? For what? What am I supposed to do with a tear gas grenade?"

"You pick it up and throw it back, of course!" he said, as if any idiot would know just what to do with a live grenade.

"Yeah? Not a chance. I'm not picking up any frigging bombs and throwing them anywhere. Here, Bob, you take them." I threw the gloves to Bob.

I stopped on the concrete stairs that led to the foot of the cafeteria and looked at the procession of trucks painted in blotches of green, gray and brown. They looked like an army of duck hunters coming up the hill. "Jesus, Gordon, what are we doing? What's the point?"

Gordon stopped and turned and shielded his eyes from the sun. "There's a lot of the bastards."

"They're not all Guardsmen," said Bob. "You got your Cornell Safety Division, the Ithaca police, also state cops. And, I see a couple of TV news crews. See those white vans? I'll bet those guys are from the TV networks. We'll be all over the TV tonight and in the front pages tomorrow."

"And that, Tony," said Gordon, "is the point. News coverage. We're here to engage. To be seen and heard so the whole damn country can see just how many of us there are, and how angry we are and how we're opposed to the war, and how we're willing to take some lumps to do that. If a few heads get knocked together, that will be bad, but that just means more coverage. You know what they say in journalism, 'If it bleeds, it leads.'"

"I don't plan to do any bleeding, guys."

"Nobody *plans* that Tony. It just happens."

"It's not going to happen to me."

"See Bob? He *is* a chicken. It's not too late to go back to the room and hide under the bed with Steve," said Gordon.

I stood on the hill, in the warm sunshine, a beautiful day, blue sky, perfect weather. What kind of terrifying nightmare hurricane was about to be unleashed on a bunch of unarmed, naïve, innocent students? Could anything we did make the slightest bit of difference to the politicians and generals in Washington that controlled everything that happened to us? The old men in jackets and ties that put rifles in kids' hands and sent them to fight a war that we didn't understand for people who didn't want us there and didn't like us? What was my role in all this insanity?

What would Melissa want me to do? I'd have to figure that out for myself. It had been a long time since I had asked myself that question. I used to ask that a dozen times a day, before I moved into McFadden Hall, back before my grades cratered, before I barfed for the cop, before I lied to my mom, before my dad got busted, before I knocked up my girlfriend. Before...before *all this*. Good God, what had happened to me?

A fire truck and two ambulances passed us, headed up the hill toward the field house.

"Tony," said Gordon. "We gotta keep moving. Come on." I didn't budge, just stared at the kids and the trucks and soldiers and the ambulances. What would Melissa want me to do? Would I do it?

"Tony," said Gordon again. "What's it gonna be? Are you coming? Yes or no?"

Chapter 53

We trudged along with the crowd of kids, all headed for the concert at Barton Hall. Ithaca cops and National Guardsmen lined the sides of the road, watching our every move. We rounded the top of the hill and the huge building came into sight. Police cars and National Guard vehicles were parked along the roads. Instead of commenting on the size of the opposition, Bob instead remarked, "Do you honestly think that Melissa will be there?"

"If she is anywhere, she'll be here today," I said. "Melissa's probably running the place by now. She is the most radical person I ever met."

"I hope I'm there for the blessed reunion," said Bob. "Ah, the thought of two lovebirds flying into the sunset. Why, it brings a tear to my eye."

Gordon snorted. "That's not all that's gonna bring a tear to your eye. Those blue canisters the soldier boys are sporting is tear gas. You guys are gonna be glad we brought the 'jiz' jar."

"Soon we'll be covered in jiz. I can't wait," said Bob.

Gordon passed the jar to me. The label said "Hellman's" but the glop inside was not something you'd want on your sandwich. For one thing, it was the wrong color. "Don't wait until the first shots are fired before you put this stuff on." He said. "You might not have time before the gas hits you."

I studied the syrupy orange goop in the mayonnaise jar. "This is disgusting. How do you even know it works?"

"We don't. But it's better than nothing," said Gordon. "It's supposed to coat your skin and dry on there to keep tear gas and pepper spray from getting into your pores. You also need to soak your bandana in vinegar so you can breathe. Tear gas is nasty stuff. I got gassed at a demonstration in Syracuse last year. Here." He stopped walking. "I'll show you how to do it." He pulled a red and blue piece of fabric out of his back pack, along with a plastic bottle that had at one time held shampoo. He squirted the bottle on the scarf—it smelled like pickle relish—then tied the scarf over his face just under his eyes. "How do I look?"

"You look like Jesse Frigging James," I said.

"Wait till you see me covered in that orange crap. Then I'll look like Jesse Frigging James after he fell into a cheese omelet."

"And this sophisticated gear," I said, "that we made ourselves, from crap that we bought at the IGA, is supposed to keep us safe from the mighty U.S. Army. Right? You have to be kidding."

We stopped walking. We were at the top of the hill, on the main road through the center of campus. Thousands of kids converged on the enormous field house and were piling into the building through the giant double doors. National Guardsmen—kids my age—stood on both sides of the procession, watching us herding into the building like cattle. Some of them held rifles, some had gas masks, others carried riot shields. They all looked as nervous as I felt. Even guys carrying the biggest, scariest rifles looked like they would rather be at home watching a ball game. They had no business holding deadly weapons. Anything could happen, anything could go wrong. We outnumbered them, maybe by fifty to one, but did that even matter? Would a mayonnaise jar full of egg yolks and dish detergent mean a damn thing if some scared kid got excited and fired his shiny new gun?

The crowd came to a stop as it narrowed to file through the open doors. "Why did the university even let us use Barton Hall for a demonstration?" I asked as I passed into the building, packed in on all sides by kids wearing army jackets, holding signs and passing joints back and forth.

"They think this is a big peace rally and folk concert. A Peter, Paul and Mary concert."

"Peter, Paul and Mary? Are they actually here?"

"Did you pay money to get in here?" asked Bob.

"Not a dime."

"Then you can bet your ass that Peter, Paul and Mary aren't here," said Bob.

I stood on my tip toes to see over the crowd. The stage looked about a thousand miles away, with a million people between us. It was a just a few risers wheeled out onto the floor in front of a wall with a single door in it. No curtains or lights. Nothing like you'd expect to see at a real concert. A tall skinny guy with a beard was setting up a single microphone stand. I recognized him. He was Melissa's Government instructor, a guy name Gary Borack. He was president of The Students for a Democratic Society. My father—the guy in the jail, I recalled— would have just *loved* Gary Borack. Everybody called him the General. He never went anywhere without a megaphone and a torn military jacket with peace symbols sewn on the back. A small mountain of speakers were piled on either side of the platform, and an acoustic guitar leaned against a wooden stool. The stuffy air smelled of cigarettes and weed, and the floor was already sticky with wine and beer.

"Maybe it's not Peter, Paul and Mary," I said, "but someone is going to sing." The guitar looked familiar, even from far away. It was the orange macramé strap. I had seen it before. I had to get closer to the stage. I turned sideways and began walking like a crab, weaving back and forth through the crowd, trying not to step on the people setting up blankets and squatting on the floor.

"Hey, Tony, where are you going? We need to stick together!"

"I have to get to the stage!" I yelled to Gordon.

"Say hi to Melissa for me," said Bob, as I wove myself into the tangle of people.

The closer I got to the front, the more kids there were and the harder it was to pass through them without stepping someplace I didn't want to. About thirty feet from the stage kids were packed together like cocktail sausages and I had gone as far as I could. I was surrounded by kids who towered over me, maybe they were football or basketball players. My five foot six height had never felt so small. I couldn't see a damn thing. I tried pushing my way through the jammed-in kids.

"Cut it out, asshole," said the guy in front of me. I looked up at this human barricade. He wore faded dungarees and a tie-dyed shirt, with long, dirty brown hair. Wire rims. A bandana was tied around his neck. He looked just like me, except he was five inches taller. I stuck up two fingers in a 'V,' like I was ordering a couple of hot dogs in Yankee Stadium: the peace sign.

"Sorry, man, I need to find my girlfriend." I said. I added "Dig it, man," though I'm not sure it added much.

"Tough shit," he said. "That doesn't give you the right to knock people down. Do it again and I'll knock *you* down, you got that?"

"Far out, man," I said. So much for a peace demonstration. There was nothing peaceful about it. But I had to get to the stage, so I kept squirming my way through. Someone grabbed me by my shirt collar, and I stopped dead, afraid to turn around. I didn't want to see who—or what—disagreed with my right to part the sea of people like Moses. It was better to not confront anyone. If this was how brave I am—surrounded by hippies singing folk songs—what's it going to be like when I'm in real danger?

I couldn't see anything but the back of people's heads. Blue denim shirts with red strike fists stenciled on them were everywhere. The noise of thousands of kids chanting, singing and repeating slogans over and over roared in my ears, and I wished I had my anti-snoring ear plugs. A thunderous crackle and buzz exploded from the piles of black speaker boxes. Someone had jabbed a microphone into an amplifier. I still couldn't see the stage. I had to get closer.

Then I heard something I had heard many times before. The sound of an A string on an acoustic guitar burst out of the speakers. It was just a tiny bit flat, but the note slid into tune instantly, followed by the D, then the G, B and high E strings, each one in order, and each string struck just once. Then the low E string sounded, and the player paused. I knew exactly who was tuning the guitar. Seconds later the song began with a bright G chord, followed by the voice. I was ready for the voice. I knew whose voice it would be. The voice of an angel, clear and high, and it knocked the air out of my lungs.

"How many roads must a man walk down?" the voice asked, ringing through the huge building, echoing off the walls. "Before they call him a man?" Melissa! Singing to me! For the first time in months. I broke into wild applause, my heart beating as hard as my hands were slamming together. It was Melissa! I was seconds away from laying eyes on her, filling my vision with the girl I was crazy about.

But I was the only one clapping. Not many people even noticed the show had started. The crowd was too large, too noisy, the room too big. Was I the only one who knew how fabulous the performer was, the only one who wanted to hear every note, every word? I plowed into the crowd, away from whoever had grabbed me. I was an irresistible force, and no one could stop me, driven by an energy that I didn't know I even had. I couldn't be stopped and no one dared to try. Everyone around me could sense my determination and got out of my way. Seconds later I was at the foot of the stage staring up at Melissa, just a few feet away from her.

She wore a pair of faded denim shorts, cut off six or seven inches above the knee, and a bright yellow halter top, tied with a thin string around her neck and across her back. I stared at her perfect skin and hair and remembered—I had *touched* those things! I had touched her! *I had made love to her!*

I desperately tried to get her attention, waving, jumping up and down, and failing miserably. For some reason, she couldn't see me, even though I was just a few feet away. But she was the complete professional. Of course she couldn't acknowledge me, in front of the thousands of people. It's not like she was playing by herself in the Echo Chamber and I had wandered in off the street. I'd have to wait till her set was finished. Then I'd chase after her. She'd be thrilled to see me! I could barely keep myself from climbing on the stage and sweeping her off her feet in front of God and everyone.

One protest song followed another, all written by Bob Dylan, but the singing was delivered straight from heaven. *Blowing in the Wind*, then *Masters of War*, then *A Hard Rain is Gonna Fall* and *The Times They Are a Changing*. With each song the crowd got a little quieter, the group around the edge of the stage, with me in the middle, became tighter, more focused. Finally she ended with a sing-along, *Mr. Tambourine Man*, and shivers passed through my neck and face, like they had the night I met her. Little by little the crowd sang, first just me and the people at the stage front, then more and more until the chorus rang with a thousand voices. None stronger and more determined than mine. Melissa didn't look or sound even a little bit like Bob Dylan, but he must have had her in mind when he wrote *Mr. Tambourine Man*, he must have known no one would sing it like her. I was still shaking when she hit the final chord. She let her little Gibson guitar ring out till there was nothing left. She smiled at the crowd. I think she looked directly at me—how could she not see me? I was right in front of her and burning like a railroad flare. Then she turned and dashed off the stage. Alone. Leaving me leaning on the stage, breathless.

Some guy was jabbering away at the microphone, thanking Melissa 'Kolokoski'—he couldn't even pronounce her name correctly—for 'getting things started,' but I didn't care what happened after that. I knew what I had to do, and nothing in my life could go forward until I had talked to her. I tore off around the front of the stage, past the two guys wearing shirts that said 'Security" who were sharing a joint. I sprinted through the door behind the platform. Melissa was scurrying down the long hallway to an office, carrying her guitar, practically running. I called her name, then added "It's me, Tony!" She couldn't hear me. I ran to the end of the hall and followed her into the office.

I reached out to grab her hand. She stopped and turned. She stared at my face for nearly a second—a long, long time—before she said, simply, "Tony."

"Melissa," my voice said, all by itself. It was the voice of a moron. I hadn't rehearsed what I was going to say when I found her. I hadn't thought that far in advance. My big chance, and all I can say was, "Melissa?" No wonder she took off. We stared at each other in silence until she finally spoke.

"What are you doing here? You're not supposed to be here." The edge in her voice was familiar; I had been cut by that blade before.

I interrupted her. The questions spewed out. "Where did you go? What happened to you? Are you okay? Where have you been?" I spoke fast and piled them on, battering her with them. She cocked her head and examined me as if I was speaking one of the few languages she didn't understand. "You were sensational! You were great," I went on. "Why didn't you call me? I could have helped you!"

"You could have helped? Helped me with what?"

"With your, you know, your problem."

"What are you talking about? What problem?"

"Melissa, why did you run away?"

"You're not supposed to be here, Tony, and I can't talk to you about this right now. I have another set to do after the speeches are over, then I have to talk to the newspapers. I don't have time…I can't do this right now."

I stopped her. I looked her right in the eyes, like she had told me I should do, months before. "My eyes are up here," she had told me, but I couldn't stop myself from looking at the curve of the yellow halter top and the perfectly flat belly. If she was pregnant, it wasn't going to be twins.

"You disappeared," I said. She pursed her lips and almost rolled her eyes but stopped. There would be no small talk. I had to get to the point. I had seconds before she was out the door. "Why did you leave like that? Where did you go?"

"It's not important now."

"Yes, it is. It's very important. I've done nothing but worry about you. I have to know. Why did you leave me like that?" Her expression softened as if she took pity in me, as if I had gotten through to her.

"I needed time to myself. Maybe I wasn't thinking clearly. But now I need to go…"

"But why? What happened?"

"I had a personal problem. I don't want to talk about it. Really, Tony, you have to get out of here. Please."

"What was it?"

"Tony, don't you understand what a 'personal problem' is? It's something the other person doesn't want to talk about."

"I know about your problem," I said. A jolt went through me. This might have been the wrongest thing I could have said. I might be traveling down a very dangerous road. I had absolutely nothing to back me up. *Everything that I thought I knew could be wrong.* But I said it anyway: "I know about your problem and I want to help." I was breathing quickly now, I could feel my heart pounding.

Melissa stared into my eyes as if she was searching for something written on the back of my skull. "There is nothing you can do to help. I don't have a problem."

"Yes, you do. I know how to fix it."

"Really. And how are you going to fix a problem I don't have?"

I put my hand on top of hers. "I'm going to marry you."

Chapter 54

"Your name's not Tony anymore." said Bob. He was on a rant. This could take a while. "From now on your name is going to be 'Shit for Brains.' Seriously. That's what you said? 'I'm going to marry you?' You couldn't have scarfed up a 'Will you marry me?' or maybe even, 'We'll get married'? You just told her you were going to marry her and she had no say in the matter? Is that it? Aren't you the guy who just this morning said, 'I know Melissa, I know what she's like?' Oh wait, maybe that wasn't you. Maybe that was Gordon. Maybe Gordon is the guy who said he knows all about Melissa."

My breath hissed out of my lungs in a long sigh. I was getting the keel-hauling I deserved. "Nope," I said. "That was me. Mr. Shit for Brains."

I slumped against the tree where Bob and I had taken refuge from the gathering insanity of the field house. I was surprised that Bob had lasted this long. Confined spaces and big crowds were not his thing, and he'd usually bug out and seek a peaceful tree or nearby friendly animal to sit with. Gordon was somewhere in the building across the street, which was now filled with people. The air was thick with angry voices. I stared at the dirt between my knees and thought about how skilled I had become at slumping. If I slumped any more I'd dribble into the dirt and be sucked up by the tree roots. Bob wasn't done with me.

"If the love of your life is in that building over there," said Bob, "what the hell are you doing over here, propping up this oak tree?"

"She ducked out when her set was over. Now it's just maybe a hundred hours of speeches by that pompous asshole Borack and a bunch of other radicals. I can't take the speeches, they make me want to puke. It gives me a frigging headache."

"So where did she disappear to?"

"I have no idea. I spilled my guts and she hit the road."

Gordon ran up to us, breathing hard and smelling like cigarette smoke. He had run across the parking lot, waving his arm at us. "Tony, I gotta talk to you…"

"Hang on," said Bob. "Our friend here is having a crisis." He turned to me. "So are you going to tell us just how she reacted to the idea of spending the rest of her life with a guy she hadn't seen for months and who came out of nowhere with her life all planned out for her? What did she say, Tony? I mean, Shit for Brains? I'll bet she said—what do you think, Gordon, you think she said, 'No?'"

"Hey, Tony," interrupted Gordon, "You need…"

I had been pushed far enough. "Cut out the "Shit for Brains" or I'm going to beat your head in with your own jiz jar." This was the first time I had spoken up in my own defense, the first time that the constant ass-ragging had pushed me too far. The tone of my voice made it clear that I wasn't kidding. I knew I belonged more on a psychiatrist's couch more than I did slumping on a tree trunk. I could feel my face forming into a rigid scowl, a frown that sucked the light out of the afternoon. I knew that, even though I couldn't see myself. If someone had handed me a mirror, I wouldn't have taken it. I knew what I looked like.

"Tony," began Gordon.

Bob eyed me up and down, as if he, too, had noticed what a mess I was. "You look like hell, you know. You're going to disappoint your mom and dad tonight when they see you on TV."

"Not my dad. He's a guest of the village of Stovertown tonight. I doubt they even have electricity down there in the holler."

A loud bang, like a firecracker—a big one, maybe a cherry bomb— made the three of us jump. Someone had tossed it into the street a dozen yards away. A puff of smoke hung in the air.

"Shit," said Gordon, "That's all we need. I gotta talk to the General." And he ran in the direction of the tall guy with the goatee and the bullhorn. Two news photographers shot pictures of the General's every move. He posed for the cameras, throwing his chin up, his hand on his hip, like Patton and MacArthur. What an asshole.

"Did you notice all the fake hippies? The joint is crawling with them," Bob said.

"The guys with the flowered shirts and bell bottom pants? And the Beatle haircuts?"

"They looked like they were there to audition for *The Mersey Beat*," said Bob.

"Don't tell me you watched that show."

"Of course I did. I lived on a farm, remember? How else would I know what a hippie was supposed to look like?

"Who do you think they were?" I asked.

"We both know who they are, Tony. FBI. Federal Bureau of Idiots. Takin' pictures and takin' names. The best our nation has to offer. It's what those guys do. That's their job. We're not supposed to notice them."

"Who do you think they're looking for?" I smiled for the first time all day. "Anybody we know?"

"You mean maybe the guy who is sound asleep under your bed right now, one Mr. Steve the Freak?"

"I have no idea who you're talking about. I don't know anyone by that name. I don't know nol thin'. I don't hear nothin'. I just mind my own business. That's my story and I'm stickin' to it, copper," I said. If Steve knew what was good for him, he'd be hiding under my bed right now, with a flashlight and a Mr. Natural comic book.

I heard a 35mm camera being cocked and looked up in time to see a big guy firing one frame after another with a black camera that said NIKON over the lens.

"News photographers," said Bob. They're everywhere. They're like carpenter ants in the barn floor. You know, I think you ought to cheer up. The way I see it, Mr. Vitelli, you just caught a huge break." Bob offered me a cigarette. I pulled one out of the pack and he lit it for me. "Now you don't have to get married. You didn't want to get married anyway. Now you don't have to. You should be happy."

"I would have married her. I wanted to." My voice sounded far away, like some other guy's. Some confused, worried guy, just like me.

"No nineteen year old wants to get married."

"I did."

"That's because you're insane. Besides, maybe she's not pregnant. She doesn't look pregnant to me. I saw her on stage just now. Actually, she looked kind of unbelievable. If all pregnant girls looked like that, more of them would be pregnant, if you see what I'm saying."

"Maybe it's a small baby," I said. "I was only five pounds when I was born. I'm still the shortest guy in my family. Maybe it's a little baby."

"You still don't even know if you're the father. Of a baby you don't know she's having. Tony, you've got to move on. Snap out of it, man. You must be blind. Melissa doesn't deserve this kind of devotion." Blind? The whole reason I was in this mess was because I wasn't blind. Didn't he remember what Melissa looked like?

Gordon ran back, again out of breath. His extra forty pounds didn't make him much of a track star. "Tony," he tried again.

Bob ignored him. "Besides, whatever happened to Clarence? I thought the baby—you know, the baby she's not having—that baby— was supposed to be his."

"Tony, Clarence is…" insisted Gordon.

"It's not his baby. It's mine. I'm the fa…"

"TONY!" bellowed Gordon.

Bob and I shut up. "What?" I asked quietly.

"If you want to know if Clarence is the father of this imaginary baby, *go ask him yourself! He's in the building!*"

I stood there with my mouth open. Before I could reply, a loud crack echoed out of the field house doors. Kids charged out holding their hands over their ears. Someone had set off a cherry bomb inside the building. Dazed kids swarmed out in all directions. Someone shouted orders at us with a bullhorn. Crowds were pouring out of the building. Firecrackers went off all around us.

Bob reached out and took me by the arm. "Party's over. Time to go."

Chapter 55

No more folk singing, no passing of the wine skin or a joint. People were scattering in all directions, yelling and holding their arms over their faces. The General bellowed at us over the noise of the firecrackers and car horns.

Bob unscrewed the top to the mayonnaise jar and began to smear himself with the disgusting contents. Would the stinky stuff actually repel tear gas? He handed the jar to me. Things started to happen quickly.

"They *are* just firecrackers, aren't they, Bob?" I asked, pulling myself to my feet. I scooped out some of the orange goop and slathered it on my arms and face. It stank, like a rancid egg salad sandwich. Maybe we should have refrigerated the stuff.

"What else would they be? Gunshots?"

"Yeah. Gunshots. What if they're gunshots?"

"Then we're screwed, Tony. The orange crap isn't going to stop bullets."

Why was I even here? I wanted to find Melissa, and I did that. What did it get me? A big fat nothing. No answers to any of my questions. We didn't get to talk. Not really. I talked, and pretty much all she said was "no." I didn't even get to see her face when she said it. Now some asshole was yelling at me through a bullhorn, soon I'd be covered in stinky, sticky shit, and maybe I'd get myself shot by the end of the day. The whole world had gone nuts. Steve the Freak had the right idea: hide in a rabbit hole till the shouting was over. But something, someplace inside me insisted that I had to see this through; that this was bigger than all of that. That this was important.

Bob and Gordon had joined the crowd of people moving in the direction of the smoke and noise. Wait! We were all moving in the wrong direction! This didn't make sense. You're supposed to run away from danger, not toward it! A dog or a cat knows that. Hell, a clam or a barnacle knows that. Aren't human beings supposed to be smarter than frigging barnacles? My brain screamed, *Run down the hill!* but my legs ran in the other direction, the way everyone else was running.

Our destination appeared to be the big open field at the end of the street, the Agriculture Quad. The idiot with the bullhorn—the General—was bellowing at us, I could understand maybe every third word. I had no idea what I was supposed to do. He used the bullhorn like a cattle prod, herding us in the direction of the smoke and noise. He pelted us with commands, screamed over the confusion. I stood at the edge of the chaos. I couldn't decide if I was thrilled or horrified. Most of us had never experienced anything like it. I hadn't, anyway. We weren't combat veterans! We were students! It wouldn't take much for a full-blown riot to explode.

From far ahead came the sounds of angry voices and the rumble of truck engines. More popping of fire crackers. Then a deep thud of something larger, a real explosive, not fireworks, something military-sized. What was that? Was it them or us? A cloud of thick white smoke obscured the crowd. The cloud was rolling toward me and I couldn't turn around; we were right in its way.

"What happened?" I yelled to Gordon. "Which way are we supposed to go? Is that smoke? Tear gas? What?"

"It's smoke. The tear gas comes later. They use smoke to confuse us, so we can't see the guy in charge. They want to separate us from our leader."

"We have a *leader*?" I shouted back. I was surprised to hear that someone was directing this mess. "Someone's actually in charge of this? Who the hell is our leader?"

Gordon was an old pro at civil insurrections, A whiff of tear gas had made him a battle hardened veteran. "The General! Gary Borack. The guy with all the photographers following him."

The smoke passed over us and the white haze made it hard to see what was going on. It smelled like a chemistry experiment just before the teacher opened the windows. Someone bumped into me and I fell to one knee. When I tried to stand up a bunch of kids pushed past me, in a hurry to get anyplace but where we were. A jolt of claustrophobia hit me, like I had felt in the crowd in the field house. *Get a grip. Now is not the time to freak out.* Being a revolutionary was not a good occupation for me. I got to my feet and watched as the smoke drifted away. The scene was absolute mayhem. If my father had seen this he would have had a frigging heart attack.

"Join arms! Join arms! Block the street!" The General barked orders at us from somewhere in the crowd. People swarmed in the direction of the shrill commands. Another smoke bomb went off and an acrid white cloud obscured the dozens of protesters who lined up three deep across the entrance to the Ag Quad. "Link arms! Make a human wall!" yelled the amplified voice. A crowd of kids swarmed in one direction, then turned in another direction like a school of fish chased by a shark.

Flashing blue, red and white lights of a campus patrol car flickered in the smoke. A different amplified voice crackled. *"Move away! You are trespassing. Move away. Go home. Get out of the street!"* The cop car slowed to a crawl as a dozen angry forms clustered around it in the swirling white haze. The high pitched squeal of the siren blasted through the crowd.

A voice screamed. "She's fallen! Stop the car!" I squinted into the smoke to see who had gone down. The cop car continued its slow advance, directly into the packed crowd. Someone bent over and grabbed for the prone figure and pulled her out of the path of the car. The crowd piled in tighter, as if sheer numbers could overpower an automobile. More kids yelled for it to stop. Someone banged his fist on the roof, another banged on the hood. *"Move back!"* came the response from the speaker. The crowd, now ten deep, pounded on the roof, hood and trunk with their hands, then with boards and rocks, beating out an angry metallic drumbeat. The General pointed his bullhorn at the cop car.

"Get out of the car! Leave the car!" he bellowed. The police car began to rock up and down, then back and forth, its springs and shocks squealing and groaning like a huge injured animal. It was entirely engulfed by people, alternately pushing down and pulling up and rocking side to side. "Get out of the car!" yelled the General. Someone battered on the driver's side window with a rock until it shattered into a million tiny bits of glass. The door flew open and two men in blue uniforms were pulled from the car. Like the Guardsmen, they were hardly older than me, and they looked just as scared. Big handguns were strapped to their belts. A

dozen beefy guys—big as football players—pushed up on the passenger's side till it lifted off the ground. Then a dozen more pushed up on the frame until the cop car stood on its side. A puddle of liquid—gasoline, streamed out of the upended car. A roar of approval rose from the crowd. The roar turned to screams as a bright flash of yellow pierced the smoke.

Fire!

"Get back!" yelled Borack, and the swarm moved in one mass knocking people over and leaving behind a field of abandoned backpacks, bandanas, red flags and signs.

The loud blast of a siren announced the arrival of a firetruck—a huge pumper. People obediently cleared out of its way. Thank God! The firemen were here. The firemen were the good guys! This was the first thing the other side did that had made sense. Six firefighters, in yellow coats and helmets, hung onto the sides of the truck. The firetruck rumbled into position halfway between the burning car and the rest of us. Then something happened which I just could not believe.

"Wait a minute!" I yelled to Gordon. "The fire is over there! Why did the truck stop here? What the hell are they doing?"

"Welcome to the U-Nazi States of Ameri..." That's all I heard. A tremendous whooshing preceded a blast of cold water. It hit me hard in the chest, blowing me off my feet, and throwing me face down into the mud. This was insanity! When I was four years old I wanted to BE a firefighter! I wanted to wear the yellow coat and helmet and carry children out of burning buildings! Now, the firemen were trying to kill me! None of this made sense.

"Pull back! Regroup! Follow me!" barked the bullhorn. Gordon reached down and pulled me to my feet, the mud sucking at my knees and shoes.

"They don't give a shit about us. This is what we've been talking about, Tony. Do you get it yet?"

Chapter 56

This fight had two sides. I understood that now. Them and Us. I watched the throngs of people slogging through the mud, headed away, headed down the hill, just as the fire truck blasted us again. The water cannon atop the truck—a thing designed to put out fires and save lives—blasted unarmed, retreating students for the second time. A girl with long dark hair darted by me. It wasn't Melissa. I was on my own. I couldn't surrender even if I wanted to.

I didn't want to. "They don't care whether we live or die," I said to Bob.

"Good boy, Tony. Now you understand."

A deep *whomp* was followed by a whistling, hissing sound, and Bob grabbed my arm. "Now they start with the tear gas. They're playing for keeps. Put on your goggles and bandana. It's going to be a bitch."

I reached for my knapsack. It wasn't there! I frantically twisted side to side grabbing the air for it. I had dropped it in the mud, and with it my bandana, goggles and towel. I might just as well have been naked. Tony Vitelli, in the buff, versus the United States Army. The gas dropped down on us like a trail of fireworks, each spark dragging a plume of pale vapor. My eyes burned as if glowing embers had blown into them. I couldn't even squint. I threw my arms out like a blind man, and shouted the only thing I could think of: "I can't see!"

Gordon grabbed my arm and guided me out of the gas. Both of us began to cough, a dry hacking from deep in our lungs.

It didn't work! The useless, stupid orange goop didn't work. People around us began to panic. For the first time in my life I couldn't fill my lungs. Even when I was a little kid, learning to swim, I was never more than a few seconds away from fresh air. But now I couldn't breathe. I doubled over, hacking and wheezing, trying to puke the pain and fear out of my body with one horrible inhuman roar after another. I was hurt. I was furious. My lungs ached to scream obscenities, but I couldn't even speak. Instead I stumbled in whatever direction Bob steered me, bouncing and bumping into bodies. Everyone pushed in different directions. I had no idea which way was the way out.

I tried to open my eyes. The hosing had washed some of the tear gas from my face, and I could squint through the burning. My vision slowly cleared until I could see...a battlefield. The retreating army—us—was a vast tangle of denim and tie-dyed shirts, long hair and ponytails. Thank God my father couldn't see this. This would kill him. A jail cell is the safest place for him today.

"Pull back!" squawked the megaphone. "We meet at the Stump! Go to the Stump." The huge tree stump, center stage of all radical diatribes and political haranguing, was a full block away, down the hill, out of the gas cloud, away from the burning cop car. Bob handed me something soft and wet. A cold wet towel! Thank God. Just what I needed. His backpack, loaded with supplies, was still intact. I grabbed the towel and buried my face in it, the best present anyone could have given me.

I could just see the General, followed by a bunch of people in baggy jackets, holding cameras, slogging past me on their way to the Stump.

Gary Borack, the most radical guy on campus, a guy who I had always thought was a lunatic, actually began to make sense. Bob grabbed my arm. "Can you see? Tony, can you breathe?"

I nodded my head. "Why would they do that?" I wheezed. "We're unarmed! Why would they do that?"

"Oh, they have plenty of good reasons," said Bob. "For one thing, you've got long hair. They don't like that." He released my arm and disappeared into the crowd. I was on my own again. Two guys hoisted Borack to the top of the five foot high tree stump. He towered over us like a statue on a pedestal. For the first time, I was relieved to see the General and his bullhorn. Somehow, for some reason, I felt safe. Or safer, anyway. What would have happened to us without him?

Then, all at once, I got it. He was on our side and I was on his side. I had seen with my own burning eyes how careless and abusive the other side could be— the police, the guardsmen, even the firemen! The

General put the bullhorn to his lips and threw his right arm high in the air. *"See this?"* He thrust out two fingers—the peace sign. *"We're DONE with THIS!"* Now he defiantly waved one finger—his middle finger. *"Power to the people!"*

"Power to the people!" I yelled, my voice throttled with pain.

"You have seen what they are like! Now you've seen what they can do! They don't care whether we live or die! How does it feel? They think they can do whatever they want with us. Are they right?"

"NO!" I yelled, along with a hundred other voices.

I pushed my face into the towel and sucked in some cool moist air. I needed a break from the yelling. Someone tugged at my shoulder.

"Off the pigs!" yelled the General.

"Off the pigs!" I repeated from under the towel. Yeah. Off the freaking pigs.

All around me I could hear the clicking of camera shutters. "Over here! Look up!" Yelled the photographers. None of them yelled *Smile!* It wouldn't have helped. It would be a long time before anyone felt like smiling. A tall guy in a jacket covered with pockets pointed a big lens at me and called out "Stick your tongue out at me! Shake your fist!"

I looked away. I wouldn't give him the satisfaction. "Bite me!" I yelled. "Go screw yourself!"

"Power to the people! Say It!" demanded the General. He made an angry fist, and shook it. *"Do it!"* he shouted.

I threw my fist into the air just as someone's hand reached for mine. I twisted my shoulder and grabbed for it. "Do it!" I yelled to the guy next to me, my voice hoarse from the screaming. I held his arm high in the air, then released it, as I gave the whole world the finger.

"Tony!" the man said.

"Look over here!" yelled a photographer.

"Tony!" the man said again. I turned and forced my eyes open. *Click! Click! Click!* went a hundred cameras.

"DAD!"

Chapter 57

I ached all over. I stretched out in the worn vinyl booth at the Royal Palm and put my feet on the bench seat across from me. Everything hurt. At least I was safe. I was also more or less clean, thanks to half a dispenser load of paper towels and most of the soap in the soap squirter. My dad was blowing through the other half of the towels, as I rested my aching knees and burning eyes and throat. The blessed quiet, and the cold beer, the darkness of the bar, were just what I needed.

We had hurried through the "What the hell are you doing here?" followed by the "I should ask you the same thing!" crap. Neither of us felt like pursuing the argument much further without some nourishment. When you go looking for food with my father, Lou, you generally end up with pizza and beer, which was just fine with me. A fancy joint would have thrown us out on our ears looking and smelling the way we did. The fact that we could just sit down at one of the beat up tables might have had something to do with the extra five dollar bill Lou laid on the bar when he ordered the pitcher of Genesee. He wasn't known to be a big tipper, but most people didn't think he was stupid either.

We had started with the beer. The first few glasses went down in silence. Neither of us had the energy to jump into the argument we knew was coming. We started with a few explanations. Little by little I made sense of the series of events that had brought us to the Royal Palm.

I had been gassed, hosed, splattered with mud and harangued for most of the day. My father had been sprung from jail—on a Saturday, two days early—by none other than Stovertown's own attorney, a guy by the name of Barry Mandelburg. My mom had found him with the help of the information operator within minutes of my phone call. Lou said she picked him out of a field of, I think, three lawyers, because his name sounded Jewish. Also, Mandelburg sounded like mandel bread, which my mom was crazy about. If she had been looking for an Italian lawyer, I'm sure anyone named Biscotti would have gotten the call. Just by coincidence, the legal fee and associated expenses to get my dad out of the clink came to almost exactly the $900 figure I had given her. Counsel for the Defense took Diner's Club over the phone. It didn't hurt that he was the sheriff's brother. So Officer Fascist Pig's real name was Officer Mandelburg. I never would have guessed.

When they gave him his car back, my dad drove directly to Ithaca. Steve the Freak found him knocking at the dorm door, holding a scrap of paper torn from my one and only letter this semester, which gave him my new room's address. I wanted to be sure he knew where to send my birthday check. So: he had met Steve, he had seen the room. He had seen the poster that said "Johnson, pull out like your father should have!" He had driven 150 miles on an empty stomach with not even a bottle of beer to keep him company. He'd been teargassed and hosed, and on top of everything, he'd had his picture taken saluting Gary Borack—one of the best known commie pinko faggots of all time—with a clenched fist.

It was Lou's turn to use the luxurious and well-appointed comfort facility at the Palm. He had been in the crapper long enough to have taken a shower, had his hair cut and been fitted for a tux. I was in no hurry to see him, but I knew we couldn't put off our "little talk" for too much longer. There wasn't much left to hide from him. He couldn't have walked into my life on a worse day. There was no point in pretending I was something that he could easily see I wasn't. He didn't look too good himself. This went two ways. Neither of us had a real strong moral position…this could be a real interesting little talk.

I knew he would come out of the bathroom, sit down and start in on me. He'd ask me what I thought I was trying to accomplish going to a protest march that he told me to stay away from. Did I have any idea how stupid I looked? Did I know how easily I could have been killed? When was I going to ever listen to him and not treat him like the dumbest moron on the planet? I had heard it all before. I just didn't have the heart for it. It had been a tough day for both of us. I had known it would be a bastard of a day, I just didn't know how bad it could be. A fight was something I couldn't deal with right now.

I could read the time on the clock above the bar. The clock had a cracked face with a dent in it the size of a pool ball. How many more minutes did I have to live?

Chapter 58

Igor, the bartender, grunted something I couldn't understand and dropped the pizza platter unceremoniously on the table. I grunted something that sounded like, "Thanks." He never looked at my face. I thought that he might recognize me from the night he threw me out because of my crappy pool playing. Even if he did, I doubted that he would have said anything. Probably ninety five percent of the regulars at the Palm had been thrown out at one time or another. That was just the kind of place it was.

My dad emerged from the men's room and slid into the booth, smelling like he had just bathed with industrial hand soap. He pulled a slice from the pie, took a bite and drained half his beer glass in silence. I did the same. It was the first thing I had eaten all day.

"I'll tell you one thing," said Lou. He held up the slice of sausage and pepperoni. It was folded down the middle like a paper airplane, the bottom crust was burned here and there to crispy perfection. "They make damn good pizza in this town."

"Yep," I replied. "Great pizza, great bagels and great Indian food."

"Why do you think that is?"

"Half the kids are Italians from the City, half are Jews from the Island. And the other half are really smart kids from countries you never heard of. Mostly India."

He smiled at my attempt at a joke. "When did you become a math major?"

"I'm still an English major, Dad."

"I guess you are, until they throw your ass out of here, Tony."

Well, that didn't take long. He went from nibbling on a slice of pizza to gnawing at my throat in one minute flat. A new record, even for him. "And they will throw you out, you know. Don't kid yourself. Then what will you be? Tell me that."

I managed a lame smile. "Then I'll be homeless, unemployed and hungry."

"And you'll come knocking on Mom and Dad's door. Forget it. We don't want you. Don't come home."

I dropped the lame smile bit. I drained my mug of Genesee and set the glass back on the table, all without looking at him. "Maybe you don't want me, but how about Mom? Are you sure that's what Mom wants?"

"Your mother wants what I want."

"Oh yeah," I said. "Of course. It's always been that way. And I guess…"

"It's always going to be that way," finished my dad. "I don't like the flip tone of your voice, kid. Is that what they teach you here? Disrespect?" He finished his beer and refilled both glasses. He was on number three, one ahead of me.

"They teach us to question authority, Dad, not disrespect it."

"Oh, for the love of God, Tony, give me a break."

"Why are you even here, Dad? What did you think this would accomplish? What did you expect to see?"

"Just what I'm seeing. I wanted to see for myself just what you've done with your life. I wanted to see what your mother and I bought for our six thousand bucks a year. And I have to tell you, Son, I don't like what I'm seeing. I'm pretty disappointed." No surprise there.

"I'm real sorry I let you down," I said. I didn't sound very sorry.

"There's that tone again, Tony. Can't you say anything without sounding like a snot-nosed kid?"

"Change the subject, Dad. Maybe that will help."

He drained half the beer. "All right. Let's try this. When am I going to meet that beautiful girlfriend of yours? Your mom says you're crazy about her, what's her name…Maria?"

"Melissa."

"Yeah. Beautiful Melissa. Are you guys still together?"

"Nope. She took off a couple months ago."

"You've got a long string of success stories, don't you, Tony? One home run after another."

"Why don't we talk about your DWI, Dad? That should give us a few laughs. I hope you're not planning on driving back to the Island tonight."

"Ooh, listen to you. You have a couple beers and think you're a tough guy, huh? You wanna pick on the old man, is that it? If you weren't my own kid, you and I would go round and round over a remark like that."

"I'm not a kid anymore, Dad. You think you can say anything you want to me but I gotta keep my mouth shut and call you 'Sir,' is that right? You can't. Those days are over." I sat back in the booth and crossed my arms, trying to look tough, grown up, anything but the nervous wreck I was.

"You're not a kid, huh? Well, what are you, Tony? What are you?"

I answered quickly, without thinking. If I had, I wouldn't have said what I did.

"I'm a man, Dad. Just like you. I'm not afraid of you." I said it quietly, like I was explaining a simple fact that everyone knew. Everyone but me. He raised his eyebrows and frowned. But he didn't look real surprised.

"You're not afraid of me," he repeated back to me. "How about that?" He looked me right in the eyes like he had Superman's X-ray vision. I stared right back. I tried to read his expression so I could duck out of the way when he threw the first punch. I could feel the rush of adrenaline but I stayed perfectly still. He just held my gaze, and little by little something like a smile crawled over his face. I couldn't read him.

Lou nodded. "Good. It's about time you grew some cogliones. If you're not going to take it anymore, I guess there's no use talking to you like that. Good. I won't do it anymore." What did he just say? Did he say, 'Good, I won't do it anymore?' He held out his hand. "Now maybe we can have that man-to-man talk, Son."

I looked at his outstretched hand as if it was some strange growth that had attached itself to his arm. "What's that for?" I asked.

"It's my hand. You're supposed to shake it. Like men do. You've seen that in the movies. Right, Sarge?" He called me Sarge! That meant the argument was over…and I had *won*.

I slowly raised my own hand and took his. It wasn't the first time I had shaken my dad's hand, but I hadn't done it since I was a kid. I was surprised at how large and powerful it felt. He squeezed mine just hard enough to tell me there were real muscles behind the grip, and I did the same.

He slid out of the booth and stood up. "I gotta see a man about a horse. I'll get another pitcher." What had just happened? I spoke my mind and I'm still alive. And he's getting another pitcher. Wow.

His pack of Marlboros lay next to his empty mug. Boy, what I wouldn't give for a few drags right now. Even though my throat and lungs still burned from the tear gas, I longed for a cigarette. But my father had no idea that I smoked. Did that even matter anymore?

Lou returned and slid back into his side of the booth. He leaned back in the cracked vinyl and picked up the pack of Marlboros. He tapped one out and reached for the matches. I followed his every move with my eyes.

"What are you looking at my cigs for? Don't tell me. Let me guess. You're a smoker now? Jesus, Tony, is there anything you haven't screwed up? Here." He swung the open end of the pack to face me. "Take a damn cigarette."

I didn't move. I looked away. He moved his head, ducking, until I had to look him squarely in the eyes. "Take one, Tony. Be honest with me for once. What the hell, huh? We're talking man-to-man, remember?" I took a Marlboro. He handed me his cigarette as a light. "How much do you smoke, Son?"

"Not much," I said, exhaling. "Sometimes when I'm drinking beer."

"Keep it that way."

"So what do you want to talk about, Dad?"

"Let's talk about this: What are you going to do when they throw you out of here? You can't come home. You're not a kid anymore. Are you going to look for a job?"

"Of course I'm going to look for a job. I don't expect you're going to send me a check every week."

"You're goddamn right I'm not. What kind of jobs are out there for a college dropout English major? What are you planning to be? The poet laureate of Haight Ashbury? Don't you think they have a few of those?"

"The university has a summer jobs program, Dad, and I'm..."

"Yeah, right. Get serious. How long do you think you'll last before they draft your ass? A few weeks? You'll be doing pushups in Georgia by the fourth of July."

"Isn't that what you wanted? Didn't you say the only real man is a fighting man? The only real man is a soldier. Remember that?" My father sat back and glared at me, as if I had caught him committing a crime. Then he shook his head slowly and looked up.

"What are you? On LSD? I never said that. Maybe I did…but I didn't mean it. Not like that, Tony. Not like that. Every father wants his kid to live to have a family of his own. No father wants to lose his kid in a war. Especially this war." Another surprise! It was the first time my dad even hinted that the Vietnam War might not be the very best war ever.

"You said that you raised me to do my duty, to serve my country." I scanned his face for disagreement. "You said that word for word."

"To serve your country? Yes! That's what Americans do. But we don't have to die to do it, Tony. There are lots of ways to serve your country that don't involve getting shot. There's no law that says you have to take a bullet to be a patriot."

"Maybe I'm confusing you with someone else." I took another puff and refilled my glass. This was actually going pretty well. We seemed to be getting somewhere. In fact, I was ahead.

"Okay, here's the thing, Tony. This is what I want to say to you. This is why I came up here. The writing is on the wall. You're about to get thrown out of college. You need a plan."

My dad lit another cigarette and waited for me to consider the words "You need a plan." And what might that be? I dreaded the answer. I said the only thing I could think of.

"I'm not getting thrown out."

"Who did you hear that from? The Easter Bunny? What, they got a dean's list here for someone with one C, three Ds and an F?" He knew my grades better than I did. Bullshitting him was going to get me nowhere.

"Okay, what do you think I should do?" I asked. "Maybe you have a better idea."

"You're damn right." He smacked the table with his glass like was arguing with my mom. "You'll enlist." I dropped my cigarette. I coughed.

"Enlist?" You mean volunteer? Why the hell would I want to do that?"

"Listen to me, you dope. When they draft you, they'll give you six weeks of training and stick a rifle in your hands. You'll be slogging through a rice paddy before you know what hit you. If you enlist, maybe you'll get a chance to finish your education. Maybe they'll give you a job working for that newspaper, the army paper. *Stars and Stripes*. Maybe you can make propaganda movies or write speeches or something."

"Really? They have jobs like that in the army?"

"Of course! There are plenty of jobs for English majors in the military. But not for draftees. If you're drafted there is only one job you get. Target. Here, listen to this. Your buddy Jerry Harrison enlisted. You two kids used to play army together."

"Jerry enlisted, huh? That sounds about right. He always wanted to carry a gun and tell people what to do."

"He just got out of communications school. He's going to be a non-com." I nodded as if I had the faintest idea what that might be. "They're going to make him an officer. More money, maybe a desk job. His dad is worried sick about him, Tony. I see Mr. Harrison every day in the office and the guy can't talk about anything else. But if Jerry had been drafted he'd be in combat right now. Look, Son, don't take this the wrong way. I'm not trying to insult you. But you're a lover. Not a fighter. You're a nice guy. Too nice. Those bastards will be all over you as soon as you step into the jungle. You won't last a week."

"Thanks a lot. You have a lot of faith in me, Dad."

"I'm not trying to hurt your feelings, Tony, I'm trying to save your damn life. Combat isn't for everyone. All the training in the world isn't going to make you a killer. You're a great kid, but the jungles of Vietnam are not the place for you. I'm telling it like it is, Tony."

"What if I do enlist and they don't have a job like that? What happens then? Can I change my mind?"

"Yeah, right? Oh sure. You just go up to the sergeant and say, 'Excuse me, Mr. Sergeant, my dad promised me that I could have a desk job, so I guess I'll just be on my way." He belched quietly, took a drag, and finished the beer. He poured a fresh one from the new pitcher. That made number five. "I don't think that's going to work, Tony. If you're in the army then you're in the army, one way or another. But your chances of avoiding combat are a hell of a lot better if you enlist and get special training. Maybe the war would be over by the time you're finished."

"I could always be a conscientious objector. A couple of my friends had to do that."

"Really. And what are they doing these days?" I tried to invent something that sounded better than the truth.

"Emptying bed pans in a veteran's hospital."

He shook his head as if I had told him they were hard at work licking out septic tanks. "Oh, there's great money in that, I bet. I'm sure their moms and dads are proud of them, huh?"

"Maybe I'll go to Canada."

"Canada? Forget it. They don't want you in Canada. You don't even know where Canada is. If you go up there, stay there, cause they'll jail your ass the minute you come back. Take my word for it, Son, enlist. You're out of options."

"There's one other thing I could do."

"I'm all ears."

"I could…stay in school." That was a real stretch but it was all I could think of.

"Let's see," Lou began, "You have a C, three Ds and an F. Just how do you figure to turn that around?"

"I just have to change one grade. Just one. If I change the F into an A, I'm golden."

My father tried hard not to laugh. "Is that all? No problem then. How do you figure you're going to do that, pray tell?"

The conversation suddenly slowed to a stop. Lou tapped his finger on the table like a ticking clock. "Huh? How?" He had a point. I was about to flunk my 'gut' art history class, Cubes and Boobs. The final paper in that class was due bright and early on Monday. I hadn't cracked a book all semester. I had attended the first two lectures. Just the first two. "I don't know yet, Dad. I have all day tomorrow to figure that out."

"How about this, Sarge. On the slim chance that you can't figure out how to turn an F into an A on one day's notice, and they do throw you out of school, I want you to promise me that you'll enlist. I'll call my old army buddies and maybe I can help get you into a school or something. Can you promise me that?"

"You want me to *promise to enlist?*"

He nodded. I saw no way to wiggle out of it. He wanted an answer, yes or no. "If you flunk out, you'll enlist. That simple. Can we agree on that?" He wasn't letting go. I could see it in his eyes.

"Sure. If I flunk out. I promise."

Any other day, the most insignificant reason to enlist in the army would have been because I promised my father. I promised my father whatever he wanted to hear, just to make my life run a little smoother. I'd been making promises I had no intention of keeping since I was old enough to talk. But this one felt different. It felt a little creepy to make a promise like that to my father now. Something had changed.

Chapter 59

We had been drinking and eating pizza and philosophizing for about three hours when we staggered back out onto the street. On the way out the door my dad offered Igor twenty bucks for the painting of the dogs playing poker which hung over the pool table, but Igor politely declined, saying, "That's the third offer I got today."

No way was Lou going to drive back to the Island with two pitchers of beer in his gut. The question never came up, thank God. I guess real men don't let each other get behind the wheel when they're shit-faced. Especially if one of them just got out of jail for a DWI. I was trying to work myself up for one more big argument, even grabbing the keys if I had to, but it wasn't necessary. Dad was ten beers into it when he announced last call, and went to see a man about another horse. He was ten to my seven, but about the only difference between us that I could tell was that he had to see about a lot more horses than I did. I figure he had a one-can bladder. He stopped by the bar, cashed two dollar bills into dimes, and got a few hotel suggestions from our gracious host Igor. Ten minutes later he was back at the table with the bad news.

"There isn't an empty room between here and Binghamton. That little party you guys threw this afternoon attracted a lot of outsiders, I guess. Every news reporter, photographer and communist organizer in the state is in town. I'm bunking with you tonight, Tony."

This was not what I wanted to hear. I already had one illegal roommate, someone who I doubted very much would get along with Lou, and there were only two actual beds in the room. I didn't think that Gordon would feel obligated to give up his up for my father. I was also sure that Lou would never accept the offer to use mine. I was so sure of this I said something stupid, like "You can sleep in my bed, of course, Dad," and he responded instantly with something along the lines of, "Good, I will."

I expected that my dad, a World War Two vet and army reservist, wouldn't have had much to talk about with a raving left-wing politico son of a Jewish socialist from Brooklyn and a long haired, pot smoking, draft dodger whose sense of humor resembled the Cheshire Cat from *Alice in Wonderland*. But I guessed wrong. Gordon and Steve proved up to the challenge and were more than worthy adversaries, and the three of them argued and baited each other far into the night. Eventually, I curled up on Steve's rug, earplugs jammed deep, pillow over my face, and tried to figure out how the hell I was going to get an A in Cubes and Boobs. I had given my old man my word that I would enlist, and it scared the crap out of me that I'd actually have to do that. I drifted in and out of sleep, and at one point I dreamed that I saw the three of them passing the bong. Absurd.

Lou was up and out first thing in the morning. Steve and Gordon were up as well to see him off. I practically shit when the three of them engaged in a frigging joint bear hug. My dad had parked right outside the dorm, and when he drove away he beeped out *Shave and a Haircut* on the car horn. "You've got a great dad," said Steve. "He's a riot."

"He can hold it in longer than anybody I've ever seen," said Gordon.

"Hold what in? What are you talking about?"

Steve and Gordon slapped their right hands together. Steve was doing his famous giggle.

Neither answered me.

Gordon said, "Lou says you're going to enlist. We can't wait to see you in a crew cut. You're gonna knock 'em dead at Fort Benning. He said you promised him. You can't let him down, Tony. It'd break his heart."

"And then he'd break your legs," added Steve.

"He said that?"

"Not in so many words, but that's the feeling I got. You sold him short, Tony. He's a riot."

I still had a whole day to figure out how to turn and F into an A in my art course and avoid the whole enlistment thing entirely. It was time to get to work.

Two hours later I was in the Art School Library, paging through a picture book on Cubism. I had no time to read the assigned textbook. Whatever I was going to learn in the class would have to happen by way of "a picture is worth a thousand words." The real question was whether or not a picture was worth the six thousand bucks I was about to blow out my ass if I flunked out of my freshman year. I had until nine AM the following day to write one of my scholarly sounding but largely bullshit papers that answered the burning question, "What is Cubism?" That was one thing I could do really well. I could churn out horse hockey with the best of them. That's how I got into Cornell in the first place.

"Yes," I said to myself, paging through the dozens of photographs of paintings and Cubist sculpture. "Just what in frigging hell is Cubism?" I spent an hour poring over pictures of angular apples and pears with edges so sharp they looked like the pieces of fruit would be more likely to bite you than you would be to bite the fruit. Oddly proportioned women draped on oddly shaped beds shared the pages with guitars and violins that could only be played by a double-jointed octopus. No words came to me. I had no idea whatsoever what constituted Cubism. But I knew it when I saw it. That should count for something.

Yes! Yes! That was going to save my ass.

Then I was back in the dorm room inspecting the wreck of my beautiful twelve-string guitar. It was a damn good thing that Lou never asked me to play it, or even to see it. I had a response ready if that had happened. "Sure," I planned to say. "I just learned *Eve of Destruction.*" My dad would frigging jump off a damn bridge to avoid hearing that song. But the subject never came up, and I never had to open the casket and reveal the horrific mutilated body of my poor guitar. The sad remains, I knew, were my only hope of passing the art course—which would keep me in school, thereby avoiding the draft which meant I wouldn't get shipped over to Vietnam, where I would most certainly be immediately shot and perish before my twenty-first birthday.

It's funny how things work out sometimes. You just can't plan this stuff in advance.

I needed tools. I knew who had them.

Bob and I stood over the locked toolbox in the bed of his beat up Ford F-250. It must have been one the first 250s made, maybe when they called them Ford F-240s or maybe it was even a Ford F-1. The box sprung open and revealed its treasures in the blazing spring sunlight. Along with the wrenches and sockets and screwdrivers were the very hammer, saws and bottle of Elmer's Glue I needed. The bed of the truck was littered with bits and pieces of boards.

"Do you have any black paint?" I asked.

"As it happens," said Bob, "I do. I have a can of flat black I used for those STOP THE DRAFT posters. Not much."

"I just need a little."

"Answer a question for me first, Tony. Then you can use the tools and the paint. But I need to know something."

"Yeah, what?"

"Yesterday, you never tried to find Clarence. Gordon told you he was in the building and you didn't do anything about it. How come?"

"Jeez, Bob, that was right before all the craziness, remember? What's-his-name was yelling at us with the bullhorn and…"

"Yeah, yeah, but that's not why. I don't think you want to know where he is. Do you?" I paused. He had me. The last thing I wanted was a confrontation with Clarence.

"What's the point? He's only going to lie to me. He hates my guts. I'd just as soon he stayed lost."

"But the reason you don't want to talk to Clarence is because he has the answer to the thing you most want to know in the whole world. You know what that is?"

The thing I most wanted to know in the whole world? What could that be? There were so many things I wanted to know. Most of them had to do with Melissa. "You mean whether he's the father of Melissa's baby?"

"Melissa's not pregnant. She told you that, remember? What else do you want to know?"

"How to find her."

"Right. And you don't really want Clarence to answer that question, do you?"

"Why not?"

"Because, you jerk, Melissa's living with Clarence. Duh. How is it that you can remember to breathe, Tony? You amaze me."

Chapter 60

"Are you going to talk to Clarence or am I wasting my breath here?"

I carefully lifted the remains of my precious guitar from the case. It was the first chance I had to examine it since I had stepped on it—no, I had stepped *through* it. The damage was worse than I thought. The poor thing would never live again.

"Yoo hoo. Hey, Tony, I'm talking to you here, boy."

"I can hear you. Yes, I'm going to go and talk to Clarence."

"When?"

"First things first. I only have a few hours to do this. Are you going to help me or what?"

"I take it this is the first time you've used tools. That thing right there is called a hammer."

"Yeah, I know what a hammer is. I'm bringing that with me when I talk to Clarence."

Bob stopped smiling. "That's a really bad idea, Tony. What happened to you the last time you pulled that crap with him?"

"Maybe I'll bring a baseball bat."

"Okay. Forget I said anything. The world would be better off if the two of you never saw each other again." He backed away from me, folded his arms across his chest and frowned. I needed his help to get this crazy thing finished in time so I changed the subject. "Don't worry, Bob, it'll be fine."

The wide neck of the guitar was broken completely off the body and the whole front of the sound box was smashed in with a hole that pretty accurately resembled the outline of my right shoe. It would cost far more to fix the thing than to replace it. "Hand me a saw," I said.

Bob selected a hand saw from the pile of tools we had carried into my room. "Here. Don't cut yourself." The door to the hallway opened and CJ wandered in without knocking. I was always surprised to see CJ, as none of us thought he would make it to the end of the semester. He was always surprised to see me, for the same reason.

"Gordon told me you were an artist today. This I gotta see." He looked at the victim. "Whoa. What happened there? Did you take out your frustrations on the guitar?"

"I stepped on it," I said.

"Best thing that ever happened to it," said CJ.

"It was a gift from my dad. It was a great guitar. Pretty expensive."

"Like hell it was," he said. "Did your dad tell you that? I worked last summer in a music store. That's a Stella. They're infamous. We sold that model for about sixty bucks. People kept bringing them back because they wouldn't stay in tune. Those things are crap. You're not going to try to fix it are you? Give it a decent burial. Or burn it."

Sixty bucks? My great super-duper twelve-string guitar cost all of sixty bucks? I remember Lou telling me it was like three hundred. No wonder the damn thing was so hard to play. It wasn't my lack of talent at all; it was the guitar all along.

I carefully began to cut the broken end of the neck until I ran into a steel rod someone had hidden in there. Then I just broke the damn thing in two pieces.

"Nice," said Bob. "You've got a real knack for this."

"Now I need some big nails."

"Don't use nails, Tony. Drill it and use a screw. Nails will split the wood."

"I'm in a hurry. I don't have time for a screw."

CJ shook his head. "You're the first guy I've ever heard say he didn't have time for a screw."

I actually had a plan. I would cut the guitar into pieces, then simply rearrange them until it looked like something Picasso could have made. The completed sculpture would be an inspired work of genius. This would be that walk in the park everyone wants to go on. *Don't over-think this*, I said to myself. *Go with your gut. Less is more.* That was something my high school creative writing teacher used to tell me all the time.

Little by little, the demolished twelve-string guitar changed into a sculpture. The neck launched from the body at a jaunty angle and a random collection of strings hung loosely from the tuning pegs. I glued the back of the guitar to the front, so you could see both sides at the same time. I neatly sawed away the remains of the sound hole. Hole removal was itself an interesting concept. Wherever the guitar had curved, now it was angular, pieced together like a child's puzzle.

While I worked, other kids from the dorm came to check it out. They either stared at my creation as if it had crawled from its mother's belly during a thunderstorm, or they just broke out laughing. It didn't matter. I knew I was golden.

"Are you kidding me?" they asked.

"Don't worry. It will be fine."

"I thought you were an English major, but now I see you're a real artist," said Bob. "A bullshit artist."

"You think bullshit comes easily?" I asked him. "It's an art in itself." I pounded in the last few nails and the wood began to split, just as Bob had predicted.

"Slow down, Tony. You're making art, remember? Not junk."

"There's a difference?" I laughed. I doubted that my fat, wheezing art professor would think that was as funny as I did.

"Good. Done," I finally said. "Time to paint." I only had one color, flat black, and I sloshed it all over the base and the wooden supports which I had made from the scraps in Bob's truck. The supports sort of faded into the background and disappeared. The end result bore both a strong, as well as a vague, resemblance to a guitar suspended in space. As far as I was concerned, its picture belonged on page one of the book I had holed up with in the library. But what I thought didn't really matter. What mattered was what my professor thought.

Chapter 61

When the paint dried—more or less—I was on my way up the hill. My art teacher was the only one who had office hours on Sunday evening. I knew this because of a sign thumb-tacked to the office door, next to another sign which read "Final papers not received by nine AM Monday morning will receive an F." Next to that was a larger one which read, "Contrary to VERY popular belief, the university is not closing down because of the Paci-Fest disturbance, and life, unfortunately for many of you, GOES ON." Next to that sign was the one I was looking for, the subject of the term paper: *What is Cubism?*

I was out of breath, as usual, when I returned to my instructor's basement office with my highly modified and nearly unrecognizable twelve-string guitar. As soon as the paint dried I had wrapped it up in an issue of *The Cornell Sun,* and raced up the hill.

The office door was half open. But the art teacher I remember from the beginning of the semester was not there. Instead, a tall blond girl, who looked about my age, sat quietly at the desk, reading *Trout Fishing in America.* Her long hair, tied in a ponytail, peeked out of the back of a Mets ball cap. She was sipping from a Minnie Mouse coffee cup. Who was this lovely person? Probably a graduate student. This was a huge problem. It was the right office. Where was my art teacher? Was this hot chick the teaching assistant? I had to make a quick decision and there would be no turning back.

I tapped twice on the open door, and entered at, "Come in!" Without speaking, I placed the oddly shaped, newspaper covered bundle on the desk.

"What is this?" she asked. She put down her coffee cup and rolled her chair back to give the package plenty of room. I don't think she thought it was a bomb, as neither of us immediately ran out of the room.

"This is my final paper for Cubes and...the Cubism course."

"And who are you?" Here we go. Don't look back. This is the real "pass/fail" point.

"I'm one of your students. I'm Tony Vitelli." I stopped myself from asking, "Who are you?" That would put a cannon ball through the canoe for sure.

She looked at a notebook on her desk. "You're registered for the class, but I've never seen you before."

"I usually sit in the back," I said. "And I've been sick."

She looked at me over the top of her glasses. "Of course you have." She looked down at the bundle. "Obviously, this isn't a paper." She smiled at me. I smiled back. Damn. She was cute. A long sleeve white shirt over blue jeans. Blue eyes. Simple and classic.

"The assignment was to answer the question." I said. "The question was 'What is Cubism?'"

"And this is?"

"Cubism."

"Oh, is that right? Let's take a look, shall we?" She slowly tore away the newspaper, starting at the neck which stuck out at an outrageous angle. There was no way anyone could have guessed what was in the package. She smiled immediately on seeing the tuners and the strings. Then she shredded the rest of the paper and held up my creation. I hoped she didn't notice the black paint all over her hands.

"This is Cubism, huh?"

"Yes," I said, with as much conviction as I could gather.

She held it at eye level, slowly turning it around as if it dangled on a string. She held it arm's length, and cocked her head to one side. Then she chuckled and nodded her head. She took off her glasses and laid them on her desk. "Well. Yes it is. Mr. Vitelli. I think you nailed it."

I smiled back. "I certainly did."

"You made this?"

"Just now, in fact," Damn, she was cute.

"It's remarkable. I take it you pulled this out of thin air..."

"More like out of my ass, so to speak. Do you like it?"

She laughed. "I do. I love it. I'll give you a B. For 'balls.' How's that?"

That would be B for busted. A B wouldn't work. I made the basset hound face that always worked on my mother. "How about an A, for 'ass?' I need an A to stay in school. If I flunk out…"

"Then you'd get a D, for drafted, is that right?"

"Right. I get drafted."

"Those are big stakes, Mr. Vitelli. You're quite the gambler. Did you ever think that art could suddenly become so important to you?"

"I'm as surprised as you are, uh, uh…"

She held out her hand. "I'm Barbara Powell. I don't think we've met. I've been your instructor for most of this semester. I took over when Professor Duncan got sick. Surely you remember that? Right?"

"Of course. Yes." I said. "That was tragic. Tragic indeed. It's great to meet you…" I looked at her right hand…or was it the left hand? Neither hand had a ring on any of the fingers. "Miss Powell."

"Tell me," she asked, "did you learn anything from my class?"

"More than you know, Miss Powell." Damn, damn, damn! Why hadn't I noticed her before? I would have gone to class. I would have gone just to stare at her for forty-five minutes three times a week.

"Call me Barbara. Can I put this in the freshman art show for you?

"Be my guest, Barbara. Please call me Tony."

"Well, Tony, today is your lucky day. You caught me in a good mood. And this is really quite remarkable. It's worth an A. Congratulations."

I would live another day. I was learning a lot at Cornell. Imagine what I would have learned if I had gone to class!

the past. You dig that up now and you might get hurt. Be smart. Walk away from this. Look, Melissa is *living* with him, Tony. Whatever happened is her business. She's a big girl. She knows what she's doing. Stay out of it."

"Just give me a ride down there, okay? How is that gonna hurt?"

"That could hurt in a whole bunch of ways, Tony. You should think about that. You got dumped. It happens. Find another girl. Don't be a dope."

"I don't want another girl. I want Melissa."

"Tony, no one needs a girlfriend more than you. You have to get out there and meet someone new. You need to meet another girl while you still can. Use it before you lose it, buddy. She's just one girl in a town full of them."

He just didn't get it. To Bob, the words "Melissa" and "girl" were interchangeable. He had no idea how wrong that was. "Bob, you're forcing me to make up one of your damn farm sayings."

"This ought to be good. Go for it, pal."

This proved to be harder than I thought. What would make sense to him? *Farm…animals…*okay, I thought. Try this: "I can't get a new cow into the barn until I get the old one out of the barn door." Bob grimaced as if I had just farted.

"That's awful. Is that the best you can do? Tony, I have to ask you, why are you so all of a sudden hell-bent on facing off with Clarence Carter anyway? Aren't you the guy who holds the all-time record for taking the easy way out? You're supposed to run away from danger, pal, not into it." That was exactly what I did at Paci-Fest, I recalled. I should have learned something from the experience.

"Yeah, well things have changed, like you said. You know what, Bob? I'm a *man* now. What do you think of that?"

"Oh, good lord, who told you something nuts like that, Tony?"

"My father. That's who."

Bob's ancient rattle-trap pickup wheezed and shuddered to a stop in front of a weathered wood frame building that looked like it would burst into flames on a sunny day. The three story building had a dozen mailboxes lined up on a wide front porch that hadn't seen a paint job since the Truman administration. A black student, wearing a red sweatshirt with the sleeves cut off, sat in a lawn chair reading a thick textbook. From someplace inside the house came the thumping of muffled bass. The neighborhood was a gloomy place. The big old house stood at the end of a long street which gradually changed from residences to garages and warehouses, then to neglected worn buildings. No sign identified the house. If this was the Afro American Co-op, they weren't anxious to advertise that fact. I had never heard of it.

"Keep going," I said to Bob. "This can't be the place."

"This is the place. Get out of the truck. Don't chicken out. After all, you're a man, right?"

"Come back for me in a half hour," I called after him.

"The hell you say. I'm going to Wendy's house. Walk, Tony. If you still can."

I climbed the stairs to the porch. I went immediately to the twelve mailboxes. The three story Victorian house, built sometime in the last century, had been a residence for one family. Now it was carved into twelve rooms. None of the mailboxes said Clarence Carter. None of them were listed as Melissa Kolaski either. Clarence must have given Bob the wrong address. I was about to turn and leave when the kid in the lawn chair spoke.

"Can I help you?" From the sound of it, that was the very last thing he wanted to do. He'd never make it in the hotel business.

"I'm looking for Clarence Carter. Does he live here?"

"Who are you? Who told you he lived here?"

"I'm his old roommate. From school."

The kid looked up from his book and studied me carefully. "He's not a student. Who told you he lived here?" he asked again. The tone, which had not been friendly to begin with, now sounded very much unfriendly. I didn't need to explain myself to this guy. This was none of his business.

"He knows I want to talk to him. He told Bob Crawford I could find him here." The kid looked me up and down as if maybe I was the first white person to stand on the porch. "Actually," I said, "forget it. I'm really looking for Melissa Kolaski. I guess she doesn't live here either, huh?" Melissa's name acted like some sort of mystical password and the kid relaxed a little.

"Clarence should be back any minute. Have a seat." Even though there was an empty chair next to his, he pointed to another one, about as far down the porch as you could get.

"That's okay. I'll stand."

I didn't have to wait long. Clarence rounded the corner and walked up the driveway before I had a chance to engage my host in another round of conversation. I saw Clarence before he saw me. I could recognize him anywhere. He walked ramrod straight, and wore ironed black dress slacks and a white shirt, like he had when he first arrived in Ithaca. He carried a briefcase. He looked like an office worker or a business man, out of place, on the porch of the Afro Co-op. He climbed the stairs to the porch before he acknowledged me. He didn't extend his hand, didn't smile. I didn't either. The kid in the lawn chair watched the display as if we were two exotic birds, facing off in a biology movie.

"Mr. Vitelli. Bob Crawford said you've been looking for me. Here I am. What can I do for you?"

"I'm looking for Melissa."

"I'm disappointed. I understood that you were looking for me."

"Where is Melissa?" I was sure he was going to slap me down, like he did before, and say something like, 'She's not my responsibility,' or some other crap like that. He didn't.

"She is still at work."

"Does she live here?"

"Yes. We both live here."

"Bob was right. You guys live together."

"That is an assumption on your part. We both live in this building. We do not live 'together.' Is that what you are worried about?"

The guy in the lawn chair looked up and grinned at Clarence. "Why don't you two love birds get a room?"

Chapter 63

There are plenty of places I haven't felt welcome. The inside of the Clarence's residence was right at the top of the list. He pushed open the battered screen door and held it open with his brief case. "After you," he told me. The house was warm and damp and smelled of cigarettes and musty, overstuffed furniture. The door opened to what had originally been a formal sitting room. Now it was occupied by a black and white television set, a couch and a card table covered with piles of leaflets and political literature. I followed Clarence into the adjoining room, which had once been the dining room. Another table, boxes of more leaflets. He pulled out two chairs.

"Sit. We have some unfinished business, do we not?"

"Do we?" I asked. *You're goddamn right we do,* I thought.

"I believe you have something you want to ask me."

"I have a lot of things I want to ask you. Are you going to answer me?"

"Why not? I have nothing to hide."

I threw back my shoulders and threw out my chest as if I were a small bird trying to scare away a hawk, but I remembered that hadn't worked for me the last time I tried it. I said "You and Melissa don't live together?"

"If that question is really, 'Do you share a bed?' the answer is no, we do not live together."

I had more questions. Could I believe the answers? I tried to piece together a convincing way of asking the next question. I would lead up to the big one.

"What was the deal with the apples and the machete? Why were you trying to kill me?"

Clarence did something I had never seen or heard before. He laughed out loud. He sounded like a villain in a cartoon. If he had had a mustache he would have twisted it.

"Why was I trying to kill you? I don't kill things. Especially people. I am a vegetarian. I am a follower of the Koran. I was helping you. I wanted to help you do the very thing you should have done on your first day at school. I wasn't trying to kill you."

"Yeah? What were you trying to 'help' me do, Clarence?"

"To get your room changed, of course. You couldn't stand being in the same room with me. You didn't have the nerve to change your room and you needed some help with that. You didn't want everyone to think that you didn't like black people. I was trying to make you do the very thing that you wanted so badly. I did you a favor."

"If that's how you felt, why didn't you get the room changed yourself?"

"I didn't need to." He smiled at me, as if somehow I had missed something that was obvious to everyone else. "You didn't bother me."

"Oh, bullshit."

He smiled again. "I hardly noticed you."

I stopped the words 'fuck you' from spraying out of my mouth just in time. Here we go again. I am too insignificant to bother with. Just a bug beneath his feet.

He stopped smiling. He leaned back and crossed his long legs. Then he crossed his arms.

"But that is not what you want to know, is it? You have another question."

"Oh yeah? What's my other question, Clarence?"

"You want to know if I raped your girlfriend. Am I right?"

"Did you?"

"In a word...no. I did not."

"You took her on a date."

"I'm sorry. This must be another example of 'cultural differences.' Perhaps I don't understand what white folks do when they go on dates. This may come as a shock to you. Black men do not feel compelled to force themselves on every woman they see. To say that it was a date is something of an exaggeration. I met her in a bar downtown. I bought her a beer. I had one myself."

"I thought you said you were a Muslim."

"I am. I am also an American. I live in the United States. I'm not a fanatic. I choose to drink alcohol on occasion. There is no law against it. The Koran does not forbid it. You've read the Koran, I assume. No? I am shocked." The sarcasm dripped off his face like drool on a Saint Bernard. There was nothing about this guy I liked. When I didn't respond, he continued. "We talked. We danced. I would hardly call it a date. Melissa told me you were aware of our meeting. Tell me, what is your problem?"

"My problem is that I think you raped her."

"And why do you think that?"

"She left me a call for help and now she's pregnant."

"She is not pregnant. That is not a story that is mine to tell. You can discuss that with Melissa. I can only tell you this: We sat and talked. I liked Melissa. I still do. She was in one of my classes before I left school. She is a bright, concerned woman. She can think for herself. The bar was crowded. We sat and talked about the movement. She excused herself. I waited but she did not return. Finally I left."

"I don't believe you."

"I'm not concerned whether you believe me or not. I left school to work full time as an organizer for the movement. I didn't see Melissa for over a month. When she returned, she found me...I did not seek her. She needed a place to live and I found her a room here. We both work for the movement."

"What happened that night? If you didn't do it, who did?"

"I'll say this one more time, and then I think it would be best if you would leave. Melissa's life is her own business. I do not speak for her. We are not lovers. We are friends."

"Yeah, sure you are," I said.

Clarence's expression changed, as if he had reached the end of his patience with the bug crawling across the floor, as if the next move he made would be to squash it beneath his shoe. He stood up. I had forgotten how big he was. I looked up at him. "I think you are more than friends," I said. "Way more."

"Then you would be wrong. I like Melissa. It's not my business to pry into her private affairs. She is a beautiful woman with a quality I find very rare in the white people I have met in this town. She is 'friendly,' a trait which you do not share. Just because I will sit and drink a beer with a woman does not mean I have to have sex with her. I do not have sex with white women."

"Imagine that," I said. "Why not?"

"Because they are *white*. My woman is a black woman. She is a soul sister. My woman will always *be* a soul sister. I have nothing to prove to white people. This does not mean I hate them."

"But you do hate us!" When I said this, Clarence lost it. His neutral expression and calm voice became sharp and intense.

"It is you who hate black people! We shared a room for half the year and you barely said a word to me. How you feel about us is evident in everything you say and do. Perhaps that is why your girlfriend ..." he didn't finish the sentence.

"Why did she come to you for help? Why didn't she come to me?"

"As I've said, that is a question you will have to ask Melissa. I am sure she will be happy to explain."

I had plenty to think about on the long walk back up the hill to Collegetown. Bob had said "No one needs a girlfriend more than you do." How did he know that? And why did that feel like the truth? I had always had trouble talking to girls. Now, I felt paralyzed by the whole prospect of even starting a conversation. What would happen next? The same old shit! I'd ask her out, she'd probably turn me down. If we did go on a date, all I'd do was compare her to Melissa. I'd take her out, we'd date...then just when I decided that I really liked her...she'd dump me. But the chances of even getting a date were slim. Girls avoided me like I had cholera. Facts were facts. I was alone.

I remembered what Lorraine had said about that. "You get used to it." When?

Chapter 64

It had been weeks since I had checked the lobby mailboxes in McFadden Hall for a letter. The lobby was the long way into the room. The window was a lot faster. I had gotten into the habit of checking for mail three times a day, in case Melissa answered one of the letters I had sent as I searched for her. But that gradually dropped to once or twice a week, and then it stopped entirely. No one else sent me mail except for my mom. My dad hadn't even called.

It was close to my birthday. Maybe there would be a surprise for me. I found a large, flat envelope in the box. The address said simply "Vitelli, Rm 101, McFadden Hall" and had no return address, and no stamp. It was the only thing I had received since getting my academic warning notice.

It was about noon, so Steve was just pulling himself off the floor and attempting to stand up. He saw the envelope in my hand.

"Birthday card?" he asked. "Is it cash? Because you owe me money."

"Nice try." I slid a single card out of the envelope. It was a rectangular piece of heavy paper, about the size of a paperback book, printed in bright red ink, with some stuff filled in with a black marker. I think they used the same color ink to print the warning notices. Then I realized what it was.

"That looks official," said Steve. "Whaddya got now? A pink slip? Are you outta here?"

I read from the card out loud. "It's some kind of award. 'Cornell Spring Art Show. Title: Cubism. Media: Sculpture, three dimensional, Found Object.'"

"Really?" said Steve. "They gave you an award for that?"

"Wait, there's more. 'Artist: Anthony Vitelli.' Wow. Check that out. I'm an artist! 'Sponsor: Barbara Powell.'" I turned it so Steve could see the big words HONORABLE MENTION written diagonally across the card in red marker. There was also a gold sticker on it. *A sticker? They still use those?*

"How did you meet Barbara Powell?" asked Steve.

"How did *I* meet her? How did *you* meet her? You're not even a student here."

"I've taken a few of her classes. Water color and oils."

"How can you take classes?"

"I just walk in and sit down. I don't know why people think this college is expensive. Aren't you happy about getting an award?"

"Yeah," I said. "Big deal." I dropped the card on my dresser in a pile that included my warning notice and a check marked *Returned: Insufficient Funds.* It would take more than a piece of paper to cheer me up. The little rush had faded as fast as it had arrived. Once again, I felt like I had been waiting all day for a bus which didn't run anymore. Even Steve could see that.

"You don't look too happy, Tony. What's your problem?"

"Sorry. But you're the last person who can help me."

"Try me. I'm a doctor, you know."

"You're a doctor, huh?"

"I'm the *Doctor of Love.*"

"You...the Doctor of Love? And I thought the world was in trouble before."

"No, really. I can help. Tell me your symptoms."

"You're a homo, Steve."

"You don't know that for sure. Go ahead, tell the doctor your symptoms and I'll diagnose you." He sat down at my desk, picked up a piece of paper and a pen, and looked over the top of his granny glasses as if he expected me to spill my guts. What the hell, why not?

"Okay, Doc. I'm bored, I'm..."

"Wait a sec. Do you have an appointment?"

"Oh, for crap's sake. Never mind."

Steve put down the pen. "Okay, you're bored. What else?"

I thought for a few seconds. Steve was right. I was definitely messed up. "I'm bored and I'm angry. I'm frustrated. And I'm frigging lonely."

"Mm hmm." He hadn't written anything.

"Aren't you going to take this down?"

"I don't need to. I have a photographic memory. Let me see. You're lonely. Are you horny?"

"I'm always horny."

"Drop your pants so I can examine you."

"Not in a million years. So what's wrong with me, Doc? What do I got? Is it fatal?"

"I believe you have an advanced case of *heartsickness.*"

Did I really need Steve to tell me that? Was it so obvious? "Let me have it straight, Doc. Can it be cured? Can you write me a prescription?"

"I don't need to. You already have one. It's on your dresser." I examined the pile of papers. What would qualify as a prescription? I picked up the card that said "Honorable Mention" in letters so big I could read them with my eyes closed.

"She's cute, Tony. Do you like her?"

"How could anyone *not* like her?"

"Then there is hope for you. I suggest you seek treatment as soon as possible so you can live a normal life."

I read the card again, stopping at her signature. It was graceful and light, even friendly. How can a signature be friendly? "Thanks, Doc. I'll scurry over to the drug store and see if I can pick this up."

"Make another appointment for next week. And Mr. Vitelli? *Now* you owe me *more* money."

"Send the bill to my insurance company," I said as hoisted myself up on the window sill, headed to Franklin Hall.

Chapter 65

The basement of Franklin Hall was a maze of corridors that intersected each other. Evenly spaced solid oak doors all with transom windows above them, held open by metal rods. The spaces between the offices were covered in cork bulletin boards, with very little cork showing. Posters for research grant opportunities, job placement lists and recruiting posters for grad schools all over the world shared space with test results and calendars with the exam days circled. Most of the stuff on the bulletin boards no longer applied, and would soon be removed by maintenance people. Classes had ended a week earlier. In the hallway were two other students, both Indian, one in a turban, and both of them looked like they had been lost in the New York subway system for the past week.

Barbara Powell's door was closed but the Simon and Garfunkel song *At the Zoo* leaked out of the open transom window. It was now or never. What did I have to lose? All she could say was no. It wasn't against the law, after all. I tapped quietly.

"Who's that knocking at my door? said the fair young maiden." Her voice lilted as if singing the words, but the tune—if it could be called a tune—wasn't familiar. That's odd. I thought everybody knew that tune. Still, I was sure that this was the opening verse to a limerick concerning a favorite hero of mine, Barnacle Bill the Sailor. There weren't many girls I knew who could, or would, quote a Barnacle Bill limerick.

I pushed the door open and stuck in my head. Her desk was covered in lengthy, well researched and most likely boring papers that grappled with the weighty question of the meaning of art. She was gathering them in piles. All of them displayed big red letters scrawled across the titles. Lots of Bs. More Cs, a few Ds, even an F or two. From what I could see, only one A had been awarded. Mine. On the chair, where I planned to sit, was the winning entry, a striking sculpture of a guitar, unceremoniously plopped upside down. I strode into the office and announced, "It is I, Tony Vitelli." The only thing missing was the trumpet fanfare.

She wore white shorts and a plaid western style shirt with snap buttons. The blond ponytail was now a bun, tied off behind her head. This, I realized, was her summer wardrobe and students were not expected.

"Mr. Vitelli again! What preposterous surprise have you brought me today? It's not even office hours." She surprised me with a smile that lit up the drab office. She sounded happy to see me. This was a good sign.

"It's Tony, remember? I'm supposed to call you Barbara. I'm not here on official school business so I didn't worry too much about the office hours thing."

"Of course, Tony. I need a break from this crap. I'll indulge you. What did bring you to these hallowed hallways?"

"I was just thinking...since I'm not a student of yours anymore..."

"Oh, no." She actually looked concerned. She took off her glasses. Either they were just for reading, or maybe she thought she was more attractive without them. She was, but not by much.

"Did you flunk out after all? I'm so sorry. I did what I could."

"No. No, I'm still in school. I'm just not your student anymore. The semester has ended. Grades are in. So I'm not your student now."

"And why is this important, if I may ask?"

"It's Friday afternoon on a beautiful spring day." I stepped boldly out on the plank, high above the ocean, and I planned to walk to the very end without a blindfold. I had even practiced. With all the bravado I could put together, I stammered through, "Are you busy this evening?" I sounded exactly like her little brother asking the same question. If she had a little brother.

She burst out laughing, then immediately covered her mouth with her hand as if that could wipe away the last few seconds. Then she raised her eyebrows and frowned, just a little bit. She was making some kind of a face, just for me. Adorable.

"Are you asking me out?"

"Would you go out with me if I was?"

"Oh, no, you don't. I'm not going to play that game with you. You go first."

"All right. Would you like to go downtown with me tonight and listen to a band, maybe have a few beers—do anything but talk about art?" That part went a little easier.

"Well. Tony, that is refreshingly honest. Actually pretty tempting. But what makes you think I'm not in a relationship? What about my boyfriend or my husband? Maybe I'm married."

"You're not married, Barbara. You said so yourself. You're a fair young maiden."

"But you're sure I don't have a boyfriend. That's not very flattering, Tony. What makes you so positive?"

"I'm a gambler, remember? I'm rolling the dice here." I couldn't read her face. She was almost, but not quite, smiling. Come on, throw me a bone. This wasn't a poker game. Or maybe it was. "Do you know what a gorgeous day it is? You can't even see outside, Barbara. You don't have a window. I'm offering you fresh air and freedom. How can you turn down such a wonderful invitation?"

"Surprisingly enough," she said, "I'm between, uh, companions at the moment. But I don't make a habit of dating my students, whether it's allowed or not."

"We don't have to call it a date," I said. Hey, it worked for Clarence.

"Tell me something, Tony. It's pretty clear you're not an art student as you don't know jack shit about it." I did what I could to not laugh but at the word 'shit' I made a noise that sounded like a cross between a snort and a cough. "So what is your actual major, if you don't mind my asking?"

"English. I am a genuine, certified English major with all rights and privileges thereto."

"Thereof," she corrected me.

"Thereto," I said again. Soon I would be over my head. This was either going to work or I would burst into flames and be reduced to a cinder.

"Okay, have it your way. Thereto. So you're an English major. I should have known. I've met a few of those. So you're basically a bullshitter, then."

"Nothing basic about it. I'm highly skilled."

"I believe you. Are you bullshitting me now?"

Whoa! I didn't expect that. "No," I said, with a lot less swagger. "You're pretty good at this gambling thing you've got going on. But I'm a lot older than you."

"Oh, you are not," I interrupted her. "We're almost the same age."

"That's very flattering but you can turn off the charm. You're a freshman and I'm a second year grad student. That makes me five years older than you. That's pretty significant, don't you think?"

"Wait," I said. *Think! Think!* "There is something you don't know about me. Two things, actually. First, I'm not a freshman anymore. Now I'm a sophomore."

"That doesn't change much. What's the second thing?"

Say it! Tell her! "And I was left back in first grade. So that's a three year difference. I don't usually tell people that."

"You were left back? And yet here you are, studying at...or should I say 'skating,' at a highly competitive college. Why were you left back? Did they tell you?"

"Oh, they certainly did. I know the reason, exactly, word for word. My father reminds me every few weeks. I was, uh, 'an under-achiever.' Also 'disruptive.' They said I 'wasn't ready.'" I smiled like the whole world envied me for being disruptive and not ready.

"Imagine that. 'Not ready.' They had you all figured out at the tender age of six."

But that was years ago. Now things were different! Should I say it out loud? Should I say "Now I'm ready! Right now!" No. I should just shut up. I was ahead. So I just kept smiling, as if God himself had told me, "Say cheese!" That kind of smile.

Barbara smiled too, as if she had heard the same celestial command.

"As long as we're revealing big truths about ourselves, my young friend...Tony..."

"Not so young," I said.

"I should tell you one of mine," she continued. "I skipped a grade. I went from second directly into fourth. What do you think of that?"

Holy crap! Score! "That means you've just got two years on me. Two. That's pretty *IN*significant, don't you think?"

"And yet," she said, "I still feel older than you."

"You sure don't look older than me. You look like we're the same age. You look great. I love the way you look."

"Oh, you're killing me, Tony."

"So you'll go out with me?"

"Maybe. But not tonight. When you're a little...older. Ask me again later."

"But no matter when I ask you, you'll still be older than me!"

"I'm sure you'll figure it out." Then she smiled again. What the hell was she talking about? Even if she was just two years older than me, in four or five years she'd still be two years older than me... didn't she realize that?

When I left she was still smiling. I wanted to keep talking but I knew that was a bad idea. I'd eventually say something flat-out stupid. Fair young maiden, huh?

Chapter 66

Steve and I had half the posters removed from the walls and piled on Gordon's bed when we stopped. The removal of nearly thirty pieces of paper, each with an S or a D made from a thousand computer printed characters, required the use of a sturdy chair. Neither of us trusted the battered piece of standard-issue university furniture, so the SDS signs which circled the room an inch below the ceiling would be the last to go. We were moving out. Gordon, Bob, Steve the Freak and I had found an apartment.

Actually, it was Gordon who had found it. With the semester ending, the university wanted their dorm room back and we were getting the boot. The new apartment had been in front of our eyes the whole time. More like above our eyes: a three bedroom occupied the second floor over our favorite hangout, The Royal Palm. The place stank of beer and you could hear every bass note from the jukebox, but the price was right and commuting time to get a beer or a pizza was pretty much zero. It also had a great walk-in closet, perfect to hide our resident draft dodger. Three and a half bedrooms for the price of three. Perfect.

Steve had avoided detection from the university and the local police for the entire year. It had been so long since anyone came looking for him that we assumed that no one gave a crap about him anymore. If he had been the type of guy to get depressed he would have been sad about that.

Gordon and Bob had left a few minutes before with a load of books and Gordon's beer can collection. It was Steve's and my job to remove the original hand drawn political cartoons, all signed "The Freak." Then we would round up all the great Marxist sayings and somehow get the giant portrait of Mao Tse Dung off the wall without ripping him. Pieces of paper were strewn everywhere. We had to be out of the dorms by the next day or the Campus Pigs would move us, free of charge. We didn't want that. Four copies of a *Demand to Vacate* notice had accumulated on the door. A new one appeared each day.

Steve rolled up the frayed sleeping bag that he had made out of the frayed army blanket. "Now that you get to stay in school and you don't have to move to Canada, what are you going to do this summer, Tony? Get a job? Join the army? Chase your old girlfriend, like usual?"

Not another "What are you going to do this summer?" question. I sighed. I really had only one objective clearly in my head. Before I did anything else, I had to find Melissa and talk to her. If there was a chance I could get her back, I'd do it. But that's not what I told him. We had been down that bumpy road a million times and we were both bored with it.

I was about to launch into a lengthy and fictional explanation of some elaborate plans for the summer, but no one could do that as well as Steve, not even me. "I applied for a summer job with the college," I said simply. "In the language lab, changing tapes for the summer students. My mom wants me to come home. Maybe I'll become a pool shark like Bob. Also, I'm out of money."

"Me too," said Steve.

"You're always out of money. You're the guy who eats three hot dogs while waiting in the cafeteria line. Are you going back to Nebraska to see your family?"

"Oh, I can't do that. I'm public enemy number one in Nebraska, remember? The draft board is going door to door with my picture. They'll string me up the minute I cross the state line."

A car door slammed and I looked up. They didn't allow parking in front of the dorm. My dad hadn't paid attention to the Tow Away Zone sign, either. He got lucky. Most people found out the hard way that they weren't kidding. A white car had pulled in front of the building. It was so plain and ordinary that even when you looked directly at it you could barely see it. The driver just pulled it onto the shoulder, forcing other cars to go around him. Like he owned the road. Who in hell would drive something so ugly and be so arrogant about it?

Two guys in black suits and white shirts got out of the car. They had identical haircuts, something in the no-man's land between a crew cut and the crappy haircut your mother made me get before school started. The big guy carried a battered leather briefcase. They each had on shiny black shoes with thick rubber soles. Cop shoes. My brother-in-law had a pair like that, so he could sneak up on the bad guys. The short one looked directly through the windows, directly at me.

"Cheese it," I said as calmly as I could. "The cops."

"Cops?" echoed Steve.

"Yeah. Two ugly dudes in dark suits are headed into the building. They look more like cops than Joe Friday and what's his name, the other guy, the Dragnet guys."

"Oh, crap. Where should I go? Do I have time to get out of the building?"

"Get in the closet."

I could hear the door to the corridor open and the sound of two people in the hallway, headed in our direction, stopping to examine each door. I jumped up from the bed and kicked the bong under it. There was no time to clean up or hide anything else. The door to the closet closed softly just as the knock came.

"Who is it?" I sang it, even though my heart, once again, was pounding. It was a familiar feeling. This whole damn year I had felt my heart pounding, felt the heat soak into my ears, felt my mouth dry up. I hated that feeling.

"Mr. Vitelli? Please open the door. Federal agents."

No kidding. "Just a minute!" I called, as casually as if somebody yelled "Federal Agents" through my door several times a day.

"May we come in?" It wasn't so much a question as an oddly worded command. As if he should have rearranged the words to something like, "We may come in." Or just "We come in." I took a deep breath and opened the door.

The men stood so close together that if I hadn't seen them getting out of the car I might have thought they were Siamese twins. In unison—like they had spent the afternoon practicing—they held out brown leather wallets and flapped them open to display gleaming gold badges and photo ID cards just like on TV. Except on TV they were in black and white, at least in my house. I had never seen a real FBI badge before so I didn't know what to look at first. In the TV shows, they just hold their wallets up and drop them open like they were exposing their

217

The brand new issue. It couldn't have been on the stands more than an hour. There on the cover was the General—Gary Borack—standing on the Stump in front of Willard Straight Hall, yelling at the crowds of kids. And there, right in the foreground, face to the camera, stood me, in all my long haired glory, soaked from a fire hose and covered with dirt, as if I had survived a fierce battle, as if I was Borack's chief lieutenant, ready to charge the enemy.

But that's not what stopped my heart. My fist was raised in a commie salute. I was holding the unwilling hand of the poor guy standing next to me. That guy was my decorated army veteran, dear old Dad. This would kill him. Wait till he goes into the office tomorrow. Everyone in the world probably thinks he's a pinko.

"Is this you, Mr. Vitelli?" asked Agent Hagburg.

I managed to sputter out, "There are a lot of guys who look like me around here...long hair isn't that rare in Ithaca, you know."

"Son, this will go a lot faster if you cooperate and don't insult our intelligence." So now I'm *son*. "Yes, this is you. Yes, you were at the demonstration. Okay? We all agree on that? Or do you need to see more proof? Isn't the shirt you are wearing—right now—the same shirt that you have on in this picture? Or what, maybe I'm blind."

I looked at the magazine cover and I got a rush. It took me a second to catch my breath! I was on the cover of LIFE! I mean, *we* were on the cover of LIFE! Me and my dad! We were famous!

"Can you please answer me, Mr. Vitelli?

I didn't like this guy. Until he arrested me for something I'd have to give him a little of the grief that a famous guy who's on LIFE magazine gives to people he doesn't like. The blood came rushing into my ears again. It sounded like Niagara Falls in my head. My pulse was slamming along, as usual, and every piece of me, every organ, every muscle, had decided, "Hell no, we won't go!" This jerk...I was about to give some shit to this jerk.

I answered him with a distinct defiant edge to my voice—that snot-nosed thing my dad loved so much, that I was so good at. "The last time I checked, it wasn't a crime to attend a peace rally. Yeah, that's me. Is that against the law all of a sudden?"

Lard-Ass smirked. "No, Tony, it's not against the law. The right to assemble is protected by the Constitution. But it *is* against the law to harbor a fugitive from justice or withhold information in a lawful investigation."

"What was your name again?"

"Agent Leroy Hagburg."

"Well, *Leroy*," I said, "then I haven't broken any laws, have I? Are we done here?"

"No, *Tony*, we're not done. We're just getting started."

Agent whatever-his-name-was—Agent Dick Head, the other guy, was now carefully examining every anti-war poster, one at a time. He was especially interested in one of Steve's cartoons—a row of bodies hanging from tree limbs, marked CIA, Police, FBI, DEA.

"We know you were very busy at the protest demonstration. We'd like to talk to you about that. We're trying to find someone."

"He must be a big, bad criminal if the mighty FBI is after him."

"Bad enough. The Selective Service would like to chat with him. He's been very busy as well."

"You guys have nothing more important to do than go looking for every guy who doesn't want to fight in an illegal war?"

"It's not our job to decide on the legality of war, Mr. Vitelli. We do not go looking for every draft dodger. Sooner or later justice will catch up to those guys, even if it takes years."

Agent Dick Head said, "We don't give a rat's patootie about that. We get involved when it gets serious. We're looking for the bad guys. The real criminals."

I could hear Steve say "YES!" in the closet. It was more a message sent by mental telepathy. Nothing could have made him happier than to be described as a real criminal by none other than

a duly appointed agent of the FBI. I knew he was on the verge of laughter. I hoped he didn't blow it. It was hard enough for me to not laugh. If anybody in the whole world could *not* be described as dangerous it was the Freak.

I shrugged. "If you're looking for public enemy number one, I'll drop everything and do whatever I can to help. Any good American would, right? So tell me, who are you looking for?"

"I have his photograph right here. We think you know him well, Tony; we think you two are great friends." He pulled an 8x10 photo out of the folder but didn't show it to me. He wanted to let the suspense build up. He wanted to see my shocked reaction. I would deny him that. I would gaze at the picture with disinterest—boredom, even, and say, "Oh, him."

I hoped it was a good picture. I hoped Steve had brushed his long red hair and his wire rim glasses were on properly and not perched on the end of his nose, which made him look like a mad scientist in a horror movie. I hoped he was smiling so he looked smarter and less homeless. I hoped he had on a clean T-shirt.

"Well, Leroy," I said finally, "are you going to show me the picture?" He turned it over and held it up with two hands.

It was a photo of an intense, tall black man in a fez.

Agent Leroy Lard-Ass Hagburg appeared satisfied by my genuine reaction, as if I had managed the very expression he was going for. "Once again, Tony," he said, "I believe you know this man well." He pulled another photo from the folder: Clarence outside our old dorm.

"I don't know that guy," I blurted.

"I'm really disappointed you said that, Tony. Now I'll have to think everything you tell me is a lie. That will just slow things down. Yes, you know that guy. We both know this is a picture of Clarence Carter. Yeah? Can we move on? You might want to remember that agents don't work for the FBI because they are the dumbest motherfuckers on the planet." That distinction, I knew, belonged to me. Bob told me so himself.

"We happen to know you and Mr. Carter were roommates for five months before he skipped town and you moved out of the room. That's quite a coincidence, don't you think? Both of you splitting within a week of each other? We know quite a bit about you."

"Really? What else do you know?"

"We know that you two spent some time practicing your knife skills on the furniture. It looked like someone worked your dresser over with an ax, son."

"Machete," I said. Like an idiot.

"Oh, excuse me. My mistake. With your machete."

"It wasn't mine. It belonged to Clarence!"

"So you do know him. We think you know some of these other people too." He handed me a small stack of photos. Gordon. Country Bob. The guy who handed me a joint during the concert. I had no frigging idea who he was.

"Yeah, I know these people," I said. "I know a lot of people. You won't believe this, but I do have friends." Then he handed me a picture of a beautiful young woman in a halter top with a guy that looked a lot like me, grabbing at her elbow, behind the stage at the concert.

"How about this woman? Something tells me you know her." This was the last thing in the world I needed right now.

"Yeah. That's the girl who sang at the concert—a Dylan song. A lot of people are interested in her. I tried to ask her for a date; she told me go pound sand."

"I can believe that," said Agent Dick Head. *Stick it up your ass, you fat slob*, I thought. I almost said it out loud. I should have.

"I know some other people in these photos," I said. "See that older guy standing next to me in the LIFE cover? That's my *father*. His name is Captain Louis Vitelli, U.S. Army, retired. Too bad he's not wearing his medals from World War Two. You guys might want to talk to him. He has to be a big subversive. Maybe he's a commie spy. He'd love to talk to you guys."

"Your father, huh? He must be very proud of you. What do you think, Tom? You think his old man is proud of him?" asked Agent Lard-Ass.

"Oh, ab-so-fucking-lutely," said Agent Dick Head. I hardly ever wanted to take a swing at someone; but I wanted to knock these assholes into the cinder block wall. Blood rushed to my face and I rolled my hands into fists before I could stop myself.

"He *is* proud of me, as a matter of fact," I said. Was that a lie? Maybe not. "So are you going to arrest me? Take me away in cuffs?"

"Whoa, whoa. Calm down. No one said anything about arresting anyone, Tony. Not yet, anyway. If you haven't done anything, you have nothing to worry about. We just want to talk to you."

"About what?"

"We hope you can help us find your old roommate."

"We're not friends. I don't know where he lives."

"Maybe you can find out. Your life will be easier if you cooperate with us. We hope you'll come downtown and talk to us. No hurry. Tomorrow will be fine. That's not so hard, is it?"

"Downtown? You guys have an office in Ithaca? Why?"

"Of course we have an office here. Do you realize that one of the biggest communist cells in the country operates out of this university?"

"Who? Where?" I had no idea what he was talking about.

The other guy, Agent Dick Head, said "It's called…The Students for a Democratic Society." He pointed to the signs that ran the entire perimeter of the room, the ones that said *SDS…SDS…SDS*. "Those guys. Ever hear of them?"

Chapter 68

"That was great!" said Steve. "The way you said you couldn't meet with them tomorrow because you had an appointment with your archaeopteryx. That's that giant prehistoric bird thing, right? That was brilliant. How'd you think of that?"

"I used to tell the wrestling coach that when I missed practice."

"I don't believe it."

"No, I really said that. Coach was so dumb—"

"No, I believe you said it, I just don't believe you were a wrestler. Anyway, my heart is broken. They weren't looking for me. I'm not dangerous enough, I guess. I've devoted my life to subversion and they don't care. So what did Clarence do to bring down the wrath of the U.S. Government?"

"You know as much as I do. I guess I'll find out when I meet with them on Tuesday."

"Are you actually going to go there? Tony, people go meet with the FBI and they never come back. They get sent to some secret POW camp someplace in the swamps of Florida where they get tortured into confessing to everything that ever happened. The bastards attach jumper cables to their balls and make them sit on ant hills in the desert and the ants crawl up their butt hole and lay their eggs in there. They drive bamboo splinters under their fingernails. They…"

"Do me a favor and shut up, would you? This isn't helping. Besides, I don't know anything, so they'll waste their time."

"That won't stop them from using the jumper cables." For emphasis he threw his arm down as if closing a giant knife switch, then he opened his mouth and eyes in a horrific silent scream, shaking every part of his body. I watched the show until it ended, which took longer than it needed to. Finally, he stopped shaking and said, "Besides, they think you know where Clarence and Melissa live. Don't go, Tony! Flee! We'll go together. Mexico! We'll go to Mexico! Tequila! Senoritas! Think about it!"

"Have you ever been to Mexico?"

"No, but I used to watch *The Cisco Kid* on Saturday mornings. What more do we need?"

I wasn't going anywhere—not Mexico, and absolutely not downtown to the FBI office—until I had talked to Melissa. That was supposed to happen any minute. Clarence promised me he would arrange it. He didn't exactly promise; what he said was, "If she wants to talk to you she will let you know. Give me your phone number." That was the best I could get from him. I gave him the dorm phone number, but now we were moving. Even if she called, I might never get the message. What a mess.

There were only a few kids left in the dorm, and they seemed to spend all their time on the phone. I was running out of time. If Melissa didn't call by tomorrow noon I'd miss her...the campus pigs were coming to make sure that we had moved, along with all of our stuff. Every time someone used the dorm phone I ran into the hall with a sign: *Please hurry, I'm waiting for an important phone call.* Most of the time the guys just ignored me or waved me away. A few guys gave me the finger.

Melissa didn't call. Gordon came back with Bob's truck to haul another load of crap, and I was pressed into service as a Sherpa. I couldn't hang around the phone any longer. I added another line to my important phone call sign: *If a girl calls for me, get her number and you win a free bottle of wine!* I taped it to the wall over the phone. Then I taped a pencil to the sign so anyone who answered the phone could write down her number. I couldn't hang around any longer.

We took one more load over to the apartment. That would make a total of three loads in Bob's truck, one each for me, Gordon and Bob. Steve brought his stuff rolled up in his frayed, old, army blanket sleeping bag which contained everything he owned, or needed, in the world. He traveled light. With one more trip to go, we celebrated our new pad by smoking a joint that Steve provided from his bottomless stash. Then it was time to eat. We immediately appreciated the convenience of living over a bar which made pizza.

"Excellent idea!" said Gordon. "When do we get to meet her sister? I got dibs!" Steve was doing his Cheshire Cat face, nodding up and down like the doll in the back window of the car ahead of you.

Country Bob just slowly shook his head at me. "Hey, Tony, did you ever hear the term *glutton for punishment?* I didn't think so. Look it up in the dictionary. There will be a picture of you."

"You're wrong, Bob, you're wrong. This is gonna be great. I can feel it."

"Well, just remember what we say on the farm—"

I immediately stuck my fingers in my ears and whistled *Somewhere Over the Rainbow* as loud as I could, stopping only to yell, "I'm not listening!" Bob waved me away as if I was an irritating mosquito. Steve said something I couldn't hear, but it might have been, "He *never* listens."

Chapter 69

The hardest part was figuring out what to wear. Which Melissa would meet me? The elegant sophisticated woman with the fur coat and the tailored jeans? Nah, it was too warm for a fur coat. Maybe the hippie in the embroidered peasant blouse and the sailor pants. Ah, those sailor pants. What I wouldn't give to see them again. Or possibly the militant protester in faded blue jeans and denim shirt, a soldier's green cap atop her thick braids. Or the folksinger, with the dazzling halter top and the cut-off shorts.

What should I wear, what did I have that would work with all of those Melissas, anyone of which might show up at the Ox? My entire wardrobe would fit comfortably in the small trash can I carried to the laundromat. My choices were limited. For colors, I could pick between black, dark blue, and something with the name of a rock band on it. Back in January, I could fit into a snug medium T-shirt…and now I wore a large or even an extra-large size. I hoped she wouldn't notice. I had long ago purged my closet of the pseudo-intellectual stuff I brought to school with me. But I did have the black sport coat, a black T-shirt, and reasonably clean blue jeans. Black went with everything. A black T-shirt and jacket would work great with either the artist, the hippie or even the radical look. I found the shirt and jacket deep in the pile in the middle of my room in the new apartment. It took me at least a half hour trying to locate them in the giant mess that you get when four people move in a big hurry.

I got to the Unmuzzled Ox a good half hour early. I had just enough time to pick up a bottle of Mateus from Collegetown Liquors with three of the five dollars Gordon had lent me. But he wouldn't budge on lending his guitar. If Melissa brought her Gibson, I'd just listen to her. She probably didn't want to hear me play anyway. The bottle of wine resided peacefully in a paper bag on the chair next to me, the corkscrew in the pocket of my black jacket. I'd uncork it at just the right time. It was all I could do to not drink it while I waited for her.

I couldn't stand the suspense.

I looked down at my stomach. With the jacket unbuttoned, it bulged like I had eaten a whole cantaloupe. I sucked it in. That looked better, but I couldn't hold it for long. I could button the jacket, but that looked stupid. I moved the candle farther from my chair, where the light was too dim to see my cantaloupe.

The Ox was pretty empty with just a few occupied tables close to the little stage where Melissa used to sing on open mic nights. I had gotten a table as far from everyone else as I could find, in an area of the church basement lit only by a few candles. Still, I had made it even more private. I moved the other nearby tables farther away, crowding them together, clearing a ten foot space between our table and the nearest other chair. Then I sat and waited.

I needed a cigarette. I had a pack in my pocket with a few Camels that Bob had given me, along with his usual sermon to "Either quit smoking or admit it and buy your own. You can't smoke OPCs your whole life." But I didn't dare light up. A few kids were smoking but the air smelled mostly of coffee and sandalwood incense. Melissa hated cigarettes. I knew she would smell it immediately, and would completely freak out when I kissed her. But if I had a secret cigarette that couldn't be detected I'd smoke it into ashes as fast as I could.

I thought about buying a cup of coffee or espresso, but decided against it. I didn't want her to think she had kept me waiting. I wanted it to look like I had arrived seconds before her, that my timing was perfect, and we could get coffee together. Even better, we'd skip the coffee and open the wine. I'd even buy a little plate of cheese, crackers and apple slices, which cost a buck. Melissa loved that. It was too bad they didn't have wine glasses at the Ox, but they'd give me two clean coffee mugs. I could go get the cheese plate and the mugs right now. No, that's not such a good idea… I might eat some of it before she got here. I'd wait.

Every time the door opened and new people came in I looked up to check them out. No Melissa. The place was filling up with kids. Couples mostly. A few carried guitar cases and brown bags with wine bottles in them. The soft roar of the espresso machine and frothing milk mixed with the Joni Mitchell on the record player. Then the music stopped and a short girl in bell bottom jeans tied with a scarf, stepped onto the tiny platform and read a poem she had written. I have no idea what it was about. I paid no attention, but I clapped politely, even though I knew no one could hear me way in the back. They could barely see me by the light of the single candle, in my black shirt and sport coat. I moved the candle closer to my face to make it easier for Melissa to pick me out. That made my stomach more obvious. As soon as I saw her, I'd suck it in. Yeah, that might work.

I didn't bring a watch and there was no clock. It must be way past nine. I remembered her note, "I'm late." Ha. Melissa was always late. Like now.

Where was she? Did she change her mind? Maybe the note under the door was a cruel joke. Maybe the guys had put there. They knew I was waiting for her to call me. But we were together the whole time. Why would they do something so crappy? The guys in the dorm! They had seen my sign! They could have done it.

Had she come in and left already? Did I miss her somehow? She told me to get a dark table. What the hell time was it? *Okay, I have to find out what time it is. I can't sit here all night.* I pushed my chair away from the table.

At the other end of the basement, the door opened again, letting in the noise of traffic and car radios. There in the doorway, lit from behind by the cars looking for a place to park on the narrow street, stood Melissa.

Chapter 70

Melissa seemed more intent on buying a cup of coffee than finding me. I knew right away that we would not be playing guitar and drinking wine together. I knew I didn't need Bob's room and that the boys wouldn't be meeting her imaginary sister. I also could have smoked a carton of cigarettes. We wouldn't be doing any kissing. I stood up and called to her. The girl reading the poem stopped and gave me the stink-eye. Melissa glanced at me and managed a smile so fleeting I wasn't really sure it was there at all. She wouldn't look directly at me. She wouldn't meet my eyes. She glided across the room like a ghost. Even as I held her chair for her, she wouldn't look at me.

None of the Melissas I had been waiting for had arrived. Instead I saw an entirely new one. She looked better than ever, and different from every other girl on campus, and I examined every detail as she approached. She seemed a foot taller than I remembered. It must have been the high heeled sandals. A billowy linen shirt in a dozen bright splotches of color like one of Clarence's dashikis disguised her perfect figure. Was it possible she had lost weight? Why? Her hair was piled on top of her head—the first time I saw her wear it like that—and held in place with a giant barrette, carved from a piece of some shiny black wood. Her fingernails were long and painted red. How can you play guitar with such long fingernails? Somehow, someway, she seemed older and even more sophisticated. I barely got out the words "I'm so glad you could..." when she cut me off and she began to speak.

"I'm sorry about the other day." The other day? The day I told her I would marry her? That's it; she's sorry? "You surprised me," she continued. "I couldn't believe you were serious. I didn't mean to...insult you."

"I *was* serious," I said. Now was the time to rephrase that "I'm going to marry you" thing.

She didn't give me the chance.

"I was serious too. You're a sweet, sweet guy, Tony. I mean that. But what we had, we..." I could feel whole room—the whole night—everything, suddenly sag. I put my hand on hers. She pulled it away.

"Melissa, can you look at me, please?" It sounded like I was begging her. Even I could hear that. "Just look at me, okay?" I wish I had added one more request—"smile"—because she looked up at me with an expression that told me I had just made another mistake.

"Let me finish. Please. What we had, Tony..." she paused. The seconds seem to drag into minutes, then hours, as I waited for her to finish the sentence. What did we have? What? She seemed to search her brain for just the right words. I could see from her eyes that my participation in this conversation would not be needed. I waited for the worst. Then she delivered it to me on a silver platter. Bigger than that: like a plate of greasy hash slung at me in a cheap diner. Here you go, Tony. Open wide.

"...it really wasn't that great."

The five words hit me right across the jaw. But not a fist. A frigging freight train.

"It wasn't that great?" I repeated, my voice breaking. "You're wrong! It *was* great. It was unbelievable. I've never been with anyone...Melissa, it was wonderful, don't you know that?"

"For you. Maybe it was all those things for you. For me, it was different. It was fun. Okay, yes, it was fun. But that's not enough."

"What else did you want?"

"More. Something more than just fun. A connection."

"A connection to what?"

"I don't know, Tony. A connection that we never made. I don't know how to explain it."

"You said that you liked me because I was different, because I really liked you. Not like the other guys. You said I made you laugh. What happened—"

"I did. Okay, I said that. But that's not *enough*. After a while I realized...it wasn't enough. I needed more."

233

"Like what? What did you need?"

She dropped her beautiful head to one side and suddenly look exhausted. "I didn't want to have that conversation then and I don't want to have it now. People change, Tony. It's not that big a deal. It was months ago. It's old news. It's bad news, I guess, but it's old news. What else do you want to know?"

"Everything." I felt like I had gone swimming, and now I had been swept out to sea, farther than I could swim. And each wave hit me in the face. "I want to know everything. It doesn't make sense. Something else is going on. I thought you loved me." She didn't reply. "We did…all of that…stuff and you didn't love me?"

"Maybe I did. Maybe. For a while. Things change. Like I said."

"When did they change? When did you know?"

"About halfway through the winter break. We were living on two different planets. You were living in your imagination. I was living in the real world. You saw one thing, I saw another. Reality and fantasy aren't the same thing."

"Why didn't you say something?"

"What good would that have done? I didn't think you'd understand. I didn't understand myself. I was a freshman. You were the first guy I met at Cornell. I was a kid."

"A kid? It was like seven frigging months ago…"

"And I was a kid seven months ago. So were you. Things change, Tony. Can't you understand that?" She looked around for the clock they didn't have.

"No. I can't. You knew right away that we couldn't be together, and you never said a word. You just let me fall crazy in love with you. Then all of a sudden you date some other guy—my roommate—and then, that same night, *the same night*, you leave me a note that says *Help!* Then you just disappear. You vanish off the face of the earth. Then you show up months later. You never call me, nothing, *and you're surprised that I don't understand?* Who could understand *any* of that? It doesn't make any sense!" My voice had gradually gotten louder and I felt something new welling up in me, an emotion that I had never associated with her. Anger.

"It makes plenty of sense. To *me*, Tony. You're right. Some of the stuff I did…if I could do it over again I'd do it some other way. But I've been through a lot, Tony, more than you know. Too much, I think. I wasn't just thinking about *you*, okay? Give me a break, I had to think about *me*. You don't know what I've been through."

"Like what? Tell me. What happened? Are you pregnant? What did I do wrong? Where did you go? Can you answer ANY of these questions?"

"I can answer all of them. If you really want to know. But one at a time. And I don't think you really *do* want to know. I don't see how it will help."

"Please…"

"Okay. Fasten your seat belt."

Chapter 71

The word "please' was almost the last thing I got to say. Melissa came out swinging. She must have said "Let me finish!" at least fifty times. She worked me over bad. When I finally stumbled out of the Unmuzzled Ox, I felt like I had crawled under the ropes, barely escaping from a prize fight which didn't go my way. I watched Melissa turn left when she reached College Ave, toward downtown. I turned right, toward campus. I was exhausted. I had been pounded senseless. I was also a moron. A tried and convicted frigging moron.

Everything I thought I knew for absolute sure had been wrong. To me, Melissa was the Earth and stars. To Melissa, I was the little patch of high ground, which gave her a better view. The conversation rang back and forth in my head like the clapper of the bell in the clock tower. It wasn't so much an argument as some kind of last judgment just before she tossed me into the fires of hell.

"Why did you hurt me?" I had asked her. "Because I couldn't keep up the act any longer. I did you a favor." Favors! Why do the people who are chopping off my legs at the frigging knees say they're doing me a favor? A favor is when you do something NICE for someone, not when you stick a knife in his chest.

"Why did you hang around so long?" I asked. "Because you ADORED me. And you made me laugh." I made her laugh. That's it. She kept me around because I made her laugh. Frigging hysterical. Let's all laugh. Ha ha.

There was more. Lots more. Somehow, the entire dialogue was

"What about the notes?" I had asked Melissa. "The note in the room—the second one—the one that said you were late—was that for me or for Clarence?"

"It was for Clarence. You didn't even live there then. Clarence had moved out too. I didn't know how to reach either of you. I knew I was pregnant as soon as I missed my period. I found out right after I got back to Ithaca. That's when I wrote the note. I didn't know the room was empty. I didn't know he had moved. I hadn't talked to anyone for a month. He didn't even know I was back."

"Why did you want to tell Clarence? Why not…"

"Because Clarence is my *friend*. Why is that so hard for you to believe? But I couldn't find him. He had withdrawn from school to work for the movement. That was something he really cared about…he was passionate about. It was more important to him than school. It was bigger than he was. That's what I mean, Tony. That's what he's like."

"But why not me?"

"Because you were my lover. Remember? You weren't really my friend. They're not the same thing." *What?* I started to breathe like I had just run the mile. Is this one of those "lessons?"

"What happened to the baby? Did you get a…an…"

"Abortion? You can say it. I've heard that word a lot lately. Yes. I got an abortion. Father Dan arranged it. My father paid for it."

"Father Dan? The Catholic priest? But you're a Catholic too! Abortion is a mortal sin!"

"Yeah, well, Father Dan thinks that abducting, drugging someone and then sexually assaulting her while she's unconscious is a 'mortaler' sin. And he'd appreciate if you don't run around telling everybody about it. That's how I found Clarence again."

"Through Father Dan?" She stared straight ahead and nodded.

"Clarence works in his office. Father Dan works for the movement. He's the spiritual leader, Tony."

And then I said something that ranks way up there on the stupid meter. Something someone would say if they paid absolutely no attention to anything, if they didn't read the papers, something maybe a deaf, dumb and blind guy with an IQ of ten would say. I opened my mouth and this came out: "The spiritual leader of the Black Muslims is a white Catholic priest?"

Melissa leaned back in her chair as if I was emitting some kind of deadly gas. "What are you talking about? You're not making any sense."

"Clarence told me that the both of you work for the movement. He's a Black Muslim, so I thought…"

"Clarence is not a Black Muslim, Tony. Who told you that?"

"He's black and he's a Muslim, so, um…" She took a few seconds before she spoke again. She frowned and stared at me like I was changing colors or growing another eye.

"He's not a Black Muslim. He's black and he's a Muslim. The *movement* is the *anti-war* movement. Remember that one? The thing I was so passionate about? The Paci-Fest was organized by that movement, Tony. Clarence and I worked on it. Father Dan worked on it. It was his *idea*. Nobody is a Black Muslim. But if they were that would be okay. Do you understand now?"

"I thought Father Dan was hiding out from the FBI because he vandalized a draft board."

She waited a few seconds before she looked away and said, "He is."

"Was Clarence involved in that? Is that why the FBI came looking for him?"

"Gee, Tony! *It's possible!* Is this starting to make sense?"

"They are looking for you too," I said. "Why?"

"I don't know, Tony. Maybe you should figure this stuff out for yourself."

"But you and Clarence aren't, you know, romantically involved?" She looked away. I think she rolled her eyes but I couldn't be sure.

"Why is that important? Why do I have to answer that? What does that even mean, 'romantically involved?'"

"You know. Sleeping together."

"That's none of your business."

"Just tell me. You owe me that. Please answer me."

"I don't owe you anything, Tony." I looked away. I had just received my answer. She hissed out a long sigh. "Okay, Tony. Here it is. Are you listening? Yes, I love Clarence. And he loves me. And no, we're not sleeping together. Okay?"

"But why…"

"Because I'm not black." She turned away to look at something on the wall.

I pushed my chair away from the table right about then and held my head in my hands. I said, "What we had was perfect."

"You imagined that, Tony. That's not the way it was. Some stuff is real. Some stuff is make believe. You didn't know the difference." With that, she stood up, and walked out.

Chapter 72

I stood on the corner of College Avenue and watched Melissa walk briskly in the direction of downtown Ithaca as if she couldn't get there fast enough. There was only one thought in my head, still throbbing from the whooping it had just received. *Now what?*

What do you do when you find out that everything you know is wrong? How do you get up the next day and keep on plugging when everything you have is suddenly worthless and you learn that everything you want you can't have? When all the stuff you want so badly to happen will never happen. It doesn't matter how badly you want it.

What would my mom say about this? She'd tell me, "Stop feeling sorry for yourself." How the hell do I do that? On any other night I'd find a bench someplace and settle down with the bottle of Mateus. I'd pull out the cork and…what do they call it? Drown my sorrows. Or, I could walk over to the old man's bar and see if Lorraine was there. She'd probably be perched on a stool, chain smoking Kools, draining glasses of Chablis. Maybe she could enlighten me. She'd probably know something about that.

I turned in the direction of the bleak tavern, the paper bag with the bottle tucked under my arm, and stopped. What was I doing? Was I going to sit in the alley and drink a whole bottle of wine by myself? Or flop on a barstool and suck up Saturday night specials till I ran out of money? What good would that do? All my problems would be there tomorrow. I'd still be the same, stupid, moronic block head, only then I'd have a hangover.

I'd be spending the evening alone after all. I began to walk, slowly, in the direction of campus. I had no particular destination, but my feet seemed to have thoughts of their own. Classes were over and the dark campus was nearly deserted. In another week it would be bustling with kids again, as summer session began. Those poor kids. How many of them will get clobbered like this? Why go to classes when everything you learn is useless?

I crossed the nearly empty Arts Quad. The street lights and the stars gave the library a spooky, Gothic appearance, like a gigantic haunted house. The clock in McGraw Tower read fifteen minutes to midnight. I had wasted a half hour just walking the few blocks from Collegetown, carrying the damn bottle of wine. Why the hell was I carrying it around? To remind me of how my night had crashed and burned? Maybe I should just say the hell with it and pull the cork. But then I'd have to drink from the bottle, stuffed inside the paper bag. That's what winos do. You always see winos chugging from bottles inside paper bags all the time, as if they had maybe a bottle of milk in there. But no one's fooled by that crap. A wino is a wino. Maybe that's me. Maybe I'm nothing more than a nineteen-year- old wino. Soon it will be my twentieth birthday. Then I'll be a twenty-year-old wino. Big deal.

I snorted, laughing through my nose, at something that wasn't the least bit funny. What would Melissa want me to do? *It doesn't matter, does it? She wouldn't tell me, even if she was here, because… I'm not "worthy" of her. Screw it. It doesn't matter anyway. I never learn.*

The bell in the McGraw clock tower rang twelve times, each dong bouncing off the stone buildings on the opposite side of the Arts Quad. When you listen to them one at a time, the beginning, the middle and the end…twelve dongs feels like forever. It was now officially midnight. That's as late, or early, as it ever gets. That meant it was the end of one day and the beginning of another. If there was ever a day that needed to end, it was the one I had just been dragged through. Each heavy dong of the bell felt like a wrecking ball, demolishing my life—everything I had done, and hoped for, since I had arrived in Ithaca. By the time the echo faded my life was a pile of rubble.

Three guys approached me out of the shadows. They were all skinny, but not muscular. They had somehow escaped the "freshman fifteen" pudge that most of us guys suffered from, especially me. They looked more like high school kids. They wore shorts and T-shirts like nearly everyone else on campus in early June, but their clothes looked brand new. The tallest one carried a bottle of Night Train Express, holding it by the neck like a club. Each of them was cultivating a beard. One guy was farther along than the other two, who just looked like they needed to scrub their faces. He held his hand out to catch my attention.

"Hey, man," he said. "Dig it. Do you go here?"

I stopped myself from answering him with a snotty, "Do I look like a high school kid?" I sure didn't feel like one. Instead I said, "Yeah. What do you need?"

"Can you tell us where we might find some ladies tonight? We're looking to meet some chicks."

"More than just meet them," giggled another guy. He wore glasses and looked like he might be smart enough to not wash out his first week. But he giggled like a ninth grader.

"Where are you guys from?" I asked.

"We're the class of 1973 from Brentwood, Long Island."

"Yeah," said the tall guy. "The 'elite' class."

"Can you help us out? Can you hook us up, amigo?" asked Glasses.

Great, I thought. Just what the world needs. More dorks from 'Lawn Guyland.' More dorks like me. I guess there is a never-ending supply of us. I scanned their faces. "Are you guys eighteen?"

"What do you care?" asked Shorty.

"Because they check proof on guys who look like you. And they'll take your bottle away. I'm trying to help you." Then I added one more line. "I'm doing you a favor." Everyone was always doing me favors. Now it was my turn.

"Screw it," said the tall one. "Never mind. Thanks for nothing. Let's keep moving."

What the hell did I care? Someone should have some fun tonight. "Wait a minute," I called after them. I pointed back toward Collegetown. "Walk that way. Cross the big stone bridge. Make the first left. There's a coffee house in the church basement. You can bring a bottle in there. No one will give a damn. They stay open till three. Any girls you find in there after midnight will be desperate. Do any of you guys know any poetry?"

"Mary had a little lamb!" said the tall one.

"You'll be fine." I said. All three punched each other the shoulders. The tall guy nearly knocked the short guy on his ass. Then they took off in the direction of Collegetown as if the Land of Oz lay at the end of the yellow brick road. "Knock 'em dead!" I yelled after them. I had done my good deed for the night. What a bunch of idiots. Did I ever look—and act—like that? Oh, yeah. Boy, did I ever. And so would every guy who came after me.

"You'll be fine." That's what my mom had told me. But I wasn't fine. I had made every mistake in the book. I knew *nothing* about women. But I had learned something important about love.

Here's what I had learned: *Love fucks you up*. The harder you love, the more fucked up you get. Being in love is like…I searched my brain for some experience that was comparable—it was like snorting speed. But it's worse. When you come down from speed you feel okay after a few days. But this…you go up like a rocket, then crash and burn like the Hindenburg. That's what I had learned.

That pissed me off. I should have known better. It shouldn't have been a surprise. The signs were all around me. You couldn't avoid them. Every novel, story, play, poem, and most of the movies…they are all about how great and wonderful and super-duper love is and how awful it is when it ends. But they didn't get it right. Not even Shakespeare got it right.

If love in the books and songs and movies is a campfire, real love is a frigging atomic bomb. It blows up in a blinding, ferocious explosion and it's all over in a fraction of a second. It destroys everything for miles around. How had I missed that?

A single streetlight stood before an arch of thick trees. This was the entrance to the path to the suspension bridge. Why had I come here? It was as if my feet knew where they were going. Of course. This was the way to Melissa's old dorm.

I had walked out onto the suspension bridge at night many times, but never on a night this dark. A sliver of moon threw a washed out pale yellow light, just barely enough to avoid tripping on the rocky path. I tramped along the narrow trail. Gravel crunched beneath my feet; I could hear the roar of the waterfall long before I could see it. The air smelled of moss and was wet on my skin. As I rounded the path and the bridge came into view, the air suddenly felt as if I had stepped into a walk-in cooler.

The suspension bridge was narrow, barely wide enough for the book-laden students and bicyclists wearing knapsacks to pass each other. But tonight I was alone. It spanned a wide and deep section of the Fall Creek. The suspension bridge was almost as well known in Ithaca as the McGraw clock tower. During the day, with the sun falling directly down on the deep gorge, it was a postcard photographer's dream. Craggy shale walls dropped to a roaring waterfall. The sign at the beginning of the trail said it was a hundred twenty five feet to the stone ledge below. On either side of the waterfall moss covered rocks dripped with white foam. Every surface was slippery with dew.

I walked out on the narrow bridge. The path hung from hundreds of steel cables and bounced with each step. On windy days the whole bridge would sway back and forth. Some kids wouldn't even walk on the thing. A chain link fence, six feet high, bordered each side of the bridge, and made it impossible to look directly down, unless you were about seven feet tall.

The wine bottle suddenly felt heavy and useless. What should I do with it? I didn't feel like drinking it. That was the last thing I needed. Maybe I should smash it on the rocks below. The wine bottle and I...we had a lot in common. We were both here because of someone else's money. We were both filled with promise and potential and we both would most likely be wasted. A lot of effort had gone into the wine and no one would ever drink it. A lot of effort had gone into...

I looked through the chain link fence at the waterfall and saw that something was different. Something had been added. The university had installed a spotlight in the side of the canyon wall, focused on the broken rock directly under the bridge. Why? What was it lighting up? I put the paper bag with the wine bottle between my legs and used both hands to pull myself up on the chain link fence so that I could look directly down. Only when I had both feet off the ground could I see what the spotlight was illuminating.

Someone had spray painted a crude drawing of a lifeless human form on the shale bed below, as if the police had traced the crumpled body of a jumper splattered on the rocks. One arm was twisted at an angle over the head, one leg turned in the opposite direction. The artist didn't have much talent, but the point was clear. The university had thought enough of the image to light it up at night. In large letters it said "When you're DEAD, you're DEAD."

They called this place Suicide Gorge. Three kids had thrown

themselves off the bridge since the beginning of the year. What did that feel like? To climb up on the fence and balance there while you prepared to lean forward, take off your glasses, take one last big breath of the cold damp air? Could you see anything on the way down? Could you feel the air rushing past your face? And when you hit...

Something tapped me on the shoulder. I froze. I didn't turn around.

"So, Mr. Vitelli," a female voice said, "Are you going to follow up your triumph in Cubist sculpture with a piece of messy performance art? I hope not." I knew that voice.

I carefully lowered myself down from the fence, keeping my knees together to not drop the wine bottle. When my toes touched the concrete of the bridge I turned to face my visitor.

Barbara Powell looked down at my awkward burden. "Ah," she said. "Is that a bottle of wine or are you just glad to see me?"

Chapter 73

It was a night of regrets.

I regretted that I had insisted on meeting Melissa. I regretted that she agreed to it. That I couldn't think of one damn thing to say in my own defense, that I had misread every clue. That I was, in the end, simply unworthy.

And right then I regretted that I wasn't a bat, one of the many that darted back and forth in the darkness. I'm sure I'd find it difficult to keep up the ultrasonic squeal that kept me from flying into the walls of the Fall Creek Gorge in the darkness. If I had been a bat, I would be laughing my furry little bat ass off at the poor guy—me—standing on tip toes, holding a wine bottle between his legs. Seconds before, that guy had been caught climbing the chain link fence high above a spray-painted drawing of a splattered suicide victim, brightly and officially illuminated by a powerful spotlight. If I were a bat, watching the show, I would be especially interested in how the guy answered the beautiful woman who had asked, "Is that a bottle of wine or are you just glad to see me?" A bat would simply land on the gentle curve of the woman's shoulder, snuggle up to her long, flawless neck, and wait for the clever response.

"Yes," I said.

I looked down at my feet and my shorts and my shirt to make sure I was wearing clothes. I felt buck naked. It was as if someone had just caught me smoking—no, they had caught me in the bathroom with a dirty magazine.

"And may I ask, just what are you doing climbing the fence above Suicide Gorge? Haven't you heard that can be hazardous to your health?"

"I'm fine. I'm not about to kill myself." I looked away, down, at the waterfall, anyplace but into her eyes.

"I'm very glad to hear that, Tony. I'd really miss you. Really."

"I was just walking across the bridge."

"Do you always climb up the fence above the waterfall to cross the bridge?"

"I'm not trying to kill myself. I'm fine." Wait. Didn't I just say that?

"Come on." She took my free hand and led me off the bridge path. "Give me the bottle. I'll carry it. You talk. Remember you invited me to go for coffee? Tonight's a good night for it. Let's go."

"It's really late for coffee..." I stammered.

"That's why God invented Sanka."

"Anything but Sanka."

"Then you can have chocolate milk."

"I'm not a kid."

She stopped at the end of the path and turned to face me. She wore short denim overalls, a white T-shirt, and sandals. Everything was splattered with paint. She took both my hands and looked into my eyes.

"I know you're not a kid, Tony. What happened tonight?"

"Nothing. I'm fine. I was just trying to see what was written on the rocks."

"You can see it tomorrow. You can see it from the both sides of the trail. Let's go someplace and talk."

"Where did you come from? Why are you covered with paint? What are you doing up so late?"

"I flew in with my guardian angel wings. My mommy said I can stay up late tonight." I'm sure she smiled when she said that, which I would have seen if I had looked at her face. She turned and pointed back down the path at a white building silhouetted by a street lamp. "That's my studio. I was working...painting. I'm finishing my MFA. I'm on my way home. Come on, it's my treat."

"I thought you couldn't date your students."

"This isn't a date, Tony. If this was a date you'd have flowers."

"I have a bottle of wine. Doesn't that make it a date?"

"Okay. Two points for the wine."

"You said I wasn't old enough. To date you."

"This isn't a date. Remember? Not a real one. We're going for coffee. Besides, that was a while ago. You're a lot older now...for some reason. We need to talk."

"Why am I so much older all of a sudden?"

"I don't know. That's what we need to talk about. I can see it in your eyes."

"What do you see?" All I could manage was short sentences.

"I'm a good judge of people, Tony. After all, I teach Art Appreciation."

"People aren't works of art," I said, like that gave me some sort of protection, some shield, against her x-ray vision that was looking right through me as easily as if I was a sheet of Saran Wrap. She smiled and shook her head, as if I had just said something really dumb.

"That's where you're wrong. Everyone is a work of art, an unfinished one. Some are more complete than others. For instance, you still need a lot of work. But when you're done, maybe they'll hang you in the Louvre."

"Probably they'll just hang me."

She tilted her head to one side and smiled again, but nothing felt funny. "I think the artist who's working on you has put down his palette—the one with the yellows and reds and greens—and picked up one with the browns and blacks and purples."

"So now I look like an Easter egg?" She stopped again and looked into my eyes. I turned my face away and looked down at my hands.

"No, Tony, you don't look like an Easter egg. If you were an Easter egg you'd be yellow and pink and smell like vinegar." She tried a smile on me but it didn't work. Then she frowned. I really, really didn't like to see her do that. "But if you jumped from the bridge you'd look just like Humpty Dumpty. You'd be sprayed all over those rocks down there. Why don't we stop with the metaphors? Let's just talk like normal people. What were you doing on the fence, Tony?" I could see a boatload of worry in her eyes, behind the sarcasm. It scared the shit out of me.

I shrugged. "Just wanted to see what was down there."

"Should I believe you?" I shrugged again and nodded. I didn't look up. I felt like a little kid, and I was tired of that. "So you're okay?" she asked again.

"Yes, I'm fine." I was about to add something like, "Really, no problem. Honest," or some other crap, but instead I said something very different.

"I'm really glad you're here, Barbara."

It took a few seconds for her to respond. She studied my face. She examined me as if I was an oil painting she had found at a garage sale. Was I a worthless piece of trash? An undiscovered treasure by an old master? I had no idea what I looked like. What expression should I have? What would the painter be doing with my jaw, my eyes, my mouth right now? What colors would he use? I couldn't even guess. Was I smiling? Was I about to cry?

"Let's go someplace where they have electricity," she said. "There are still a few places open. Where would you like to go?" She took my hand and we began to walk back up the path to the street.

"Any place," I said. "Any place but the Unmuzzled Ox."

"Ah. The Ox. The place where couples go to break up."

"I never heard that. Is it really?"

"I've been in Ithaca for six years. I, myself, have ended at least four relationships there."

"Where did you sit?" I asked. "I mean, when you broke up. Which table?" But I knew the answer.

"At the very back. Always, at the very back. Forget the Unmuzzled Ox. I know the perfect place. Bud's Diner."

Chapter 74

The only lights still burning were at Bud's Diner. The joint looked like a railroad dining car about to pull out of the station. We could see it glowing in the middle of the end of a long dark block bordered on one side by a junk yard and a used car lot on the other. Bud's Diner was where you went at two in the morning and you needed a break from an all-nighter and you were hopped-up on No-Doz or white crosses and you knew you needed to eat something even if the speed had crushed your appetite. I suspected that it had yet to serve its first cup of decaf coffee. We walked hand in hand, like high school sweethearts. After a few blocks, I had to ask.

"Why are you holding my hand?"

"That kind of a question makes me think maybe there *is* a big difference in our ages. Here's why. I'm not afraid to tell you that I like you and I'm worried about you. I don't want you to run in front of a bus."

"Buses don't run this time of night," I said.

"Was it a girl, Tony?"

"Was what a girl?"

"Whatever put you on the fence."

"I told you I wasn't going to kill myself."

"No, of course you weren't. My mistake. So it wasn't a girl, then?"

"No. It wasn't a girl."

"What was her name?"

"Melissa." There wasn't much point in arguing with her. I waited for what I knew was coming, then said, "Aren't you going to tell me she's not worth it?"

"You already know that. Nobody's worth it. Not even me."

———◆———

The little diner was just a few hundred feet in front of us when Barbara Powell stopped alongside a beat-up hippie van painted with swirling paisleys and flowers and giant lady bugs. The artist had used his happy palette—the one with the yellows and oranges and reds and greens. Nearly every inch of the rusting metal had been covered with paint. A row of narrow windows ran along the roof line. A peace symbol—my dad called it the footprint of the American chicken—was glued just under the windshield. A dozen antiwar stickers hung off the bumpers, each one glued to another. She cupped her hands against the passenger window and peered in. A bed, littered with blankets and an army duffel bag, took up most of the room in the tiny van. A small sink and camping stove took up the rest.

"I love these things," she said. "I went across the country to California in one of these in the summer between high school and college. It was old even then. I lost my virginity in a bus that looked a lot like this one."

I smiled for the first time that evening. "It's pretty handy having a bed with you wherever you go, huh?"

"Oh, not on the bed. Right across the sink."

Someone had just kicked me in the ass and yelled, "Cheer up!"

"Marry me!" I said. It came out of nowhere, and I laughed out loud. I followed it with an equally ridiculous, "I think I just fell in love with you." I hadn't heard the sound of my own laughter for days. It felt frigging great to laugh.

"I never get married on the first date," she said.

"It's not a real date, remember?"

"I still won't marry you. Not tonight, anyway."

"Damn," I said. Then I added, "Everyone tells me that."

"Don't worry, Tony, you'll feel better after you get something to eat. You've had a rough day."

"I had a rough *yesterday*." I said. "Today is shaping up pretty good so far."

Chapter 75

It was tough sleeping on the flattened cardboard boxes. It was my first night in the new apartment. I guess I thought it would be furnished. It wasn't. I woke up early and I had gone to bed late, alone, despite my best efforts. The bottle of Mateus, unopened and still in its paper bag, stood on the floor near my makeshift bed. I hadn't smoked a thing or had a drop to drink, but I still had a throbbing headache. What a frigging night.

I had planned to wake up with Melissa...although there was no way in hell she would have consented to the brutal accommodations. I must have thought she'd take me to her place. Hell, I didn't know what I was thinking. Or even if was thinking at all. I'm surprised I even survived our 'heart to heart' meeting. I never suspected I was such a brain-dead moron.

And then, out of nowhere, Barbara had appeared. She wouldn't come home with me either. Maybe I did have cholera.

Melissa tossed me into the garbage and I came on to my art teacher like I was the best looking sailor in port. That didn't make her feel particularly special. But at least she smiled when she pointed me in the direction of the Royal Palm and said good night. *If I could have had either one, who would I choose? Oh, what the hell is wrong with me? Why am I torturing myself? I can't have either one. I'm lucky I made it home in one piece.*

I pulled myself off the floor and stood, my joints cracking like I was sixty years old. If every day was like yesterday, I'd be dead before the weekend. I'd dig the grave myself and then jump in. It would be a relief.

I found my toothbrush and headed for the bathroom. I had no idea where I had packed the toothpaste. Good, there's a tube of Stripe. It's probably Gordon's. He buys weird crap like that. I had to come up with a story. The guys expected a good one. I couldn't use too many details of what had actually happened. They didn't need to know that stuff. *The truth was no excuse*—that's what you learn in writing class. Make stuff up. The guys would be all over me. It would be a barrage of, "Where is Melissa? What happened?" But what could I tell them? I'd simply invent a story. That's just who I was.

I stretched and yawned and climbed into the beat-up shower. The apartment bathroom was already in need of cleaning. There were hand prints and a spray of water spots on the cracked mirror and standing water in the sink. Clogged. Day two and the sink was already clogged. There was almost no hot water. Then, the shower head blew off the pipe—it had been stuck on with masking tape. Classy. I'd just deal with it.

I had to figure out my story before I walked into the kitchen. The guys would hang on to every word. I'd tell them how I broke it off with Melissa and how I had found Barbara weeping on a park bench. I pushed the toothbrush, loaded with a thick bead of Stripe, into my mouth. I had never used that toothpaste and I wasn't ready for the intense kick. On what planet does Stripe taste like cinnamon?

Bang! I was awake. In front of me was the face of someone who looked like hell…a guy who had a lot of work to do. Me. Two days before my twentieth birthday, I had some big unfinished business to take care of.

I had messed up. Gigantically. It wasn't Clarence's fault. He had won Melissa fair and square. Melissa wasn't a car. He didn't tow her away, she wasn't stolen off the street. She took off all by herself. She was gone and it was nobody's fault but my own. I wouldn't be getting her back. If this had been a poker game, I'd be homeless.

What now? How can I make this right? Do I apologize? Send a card? Send flowers? Maybe I should just keep my mouth shut. Maybe I've caused enough damage. What do I do? I *frigging hate the guy*, and that's not going to change. The FBI is going to pluck him off the street like a ripe apple, and I can't wait. It serves him right.

Someone banged on the door.

"*Get out of the damned bathroom!* There are three other guys who live here, remember? And we all have to pee!"

"Not me!" yelled Steve, "I used the sink in the kitchen."

"Meet us in front in ten minutes!" yelled Bob through the door. "You, me and Gordon have a date with a couch. It's out in front of Beta Theta Pi. I can't get it in the truck myself. It's not going to last, so we have to get moving. You hear me? Ten minutes. And get out of the bathroom before I piss on your cardboard carton."

I took one more long look at the face in the dirty mirror. I knew that guy. I knew what he would do. *He'd do the wrong thing.* But there was still time. Why not do the right thing, for once? Just this one time?

Chapter 76

Bob pointed the truck back up the hill to Collegetown and our new apartment. The couch, bouncing around in the back, was a Japanese contraption called a futon. You could sit on it or you could unfold it and maybe sleep on it. If you were really exhausted. It looked only a little more comfortable than the flattened cardboard boxes, and it smelled like cigarettes and beer, like everything else in Collegetown. I sat jammed up against the passenger door and Gordon was squished between us.

If I didn't speak up pretty soon, I'd have to walk all the way downtown again. "Turn around," I said. "I need to go back to the Afro co-op. I have to talk to Clarence. It can't wait."

"After everything you've just gone through you want to make nice with Clarence?" asked Gordon.

"I'm not trying to make nice with him. I just need to tell him something."

"Like what?"

"That the FBI is after him. I have to clue him in."

"Why, exactly, do you need to tell him anything but 'Adios, muchacho?'"

"Because of what Melissa said. I had a lot of stuff wrong. Everything, actually. He's still an asshole, but he shouldn't go to jail because I kept my mouth shut. Come on, please. Turn around."

"Tony, you can't go anywhere near there," said Bob. "They might be watching the house." Bob had a special ability to see into the future.

It was like he had a frigging crystal ball. Everyone seemed to have one of those. I must have been absent the day they passed them out.

"He's gotta get out of there. The sooner the better."

"Did you ever think that if he leaves town he'll take Melissa with him?"

"Yeah. Over and over. And that's exactly what's going to happen, Bob."

"Are you ready for that?"

"I'll never be ready for that. But that's what *has* to happen."

"Is this about those guys who trashed the draft board?" asked Gordon. "It is, right? I knew it. That's heavy, Tony. You don't want to be anywhere near them when that goes down. Is Melissa mixed up in that too?"

"I don't know. I don't want to know. But if she is, I hope she gets out of town with Clarence. She's in love with him."

"He's shacked up with your girlfriend and you want to *help* him? Am I hearing this right?" asked Bob.

"They're not shacked up."

"Oh no. Certainly not. How silly. And you believe that?" asked Gordon. "What are you smokin' Tony?"

"Melissa says he doesn't like white chicks. As in, he doesn't sleep with them."

"Now I've heard everything. The dude is crazy," said Gordon.

"Yeah, maybe he is. He's a jerk. I got that. But that's the deal. Turn around, Bob."

"Tony, listen to me. You can't go there. Look, let me do it. I'll break the news to Clarence. The Feds don't know me. I can do it; he's a friend of mine. I can—"

"Turn around, Bob," I said.

"Okay, I got it. Now I understand," he said. "This is the last chance you'll get to see Melissa. Is that it? You're going to risk everything just to see a *girl* one last time? You're nuts. Don't do this. I'll tell him. What do you want me to say to him? You have a message for Melissa?"

I thought for a few seconds. What could I say to her? What should I have said to her last night? What could possibly make any difference now? In Melissa's life I amounted to no more than a fly on the wall. What would she want to be the last thing she heard from me?

"Tell her I love her." As soon as the words left my mouth, they sounded strange. Like sour notes on a piano. My mouth tasted like I had been sucking on nickels and pennies.

"Oh, give it up, Tony," groaned Gordon. Bob just shook his head.

"Turn around, Bob," I said, but I knew that wasn't going to happen. No way was Bob going to take me back there. The next time the car stopped it would be back at the apartment above the Royal Palm. I put my hand on the door handle, as Bob slowed down for a right turn on State Street.

I hit the pavement running and sprinted back in the direction of the co-op where Clarence and Melissa lived. I didn't turn around or slow down, I just ran like hell while Bob yelled from the car window.

Chapter 77

I didn't expect to see Clarence out in the open where God and the FBI could see him, but there he was, packing his suitcase into an old blue Chevy Impala. He turned when he heard me jogging up the driveway, huffing and puffing, like a guy who didn't do a lot of running unless someone was chasing him. He frowned when he recognized me. He straightened up, folded his arms and walked in my direction, meeting me at the end of the driveway. He stood between me and the car.

"What are you doing here? I thought we had concluded our business."

"Where is Melissa?" I demanded. I had intended to sound friendlier than it came out. There was no way I could call Clarence a friend. Even though he stood a head taller than me, I made eye contact and held it. He glared back. Neither of us even blinked. Then he spoke.

"As I said, I believe we have nothing further to say to each other. I don't have time for a chat."

"Maybe it's my turn to do *you* a favor." The hell with trying to be friendly. Clarence didn't understand friendly.

"I very much doubt that. I don't require any favors from you."

"The FBI is looking for you, Clarence."

Unless you count sarcasm, Clarence had no reaction to this information. "Really?" he said. "What a surprise. The FBI has been looking for me since January. This is not news. What business is that of yours?"

"Where is Melissa?"

"Every time I see you, you ask me that. You sound like a parrot in a pet shop. Why do you think I know that? She doesn't belong to me. I am not in charge of her. I have told you that before."

"Is that your car? Where are you going?"

"I assume you understand that you are the last person I would tell that to. Or are you that brain dead?"

"You know what?" I spat this out as if I had bitten into a dog turd. "Forget that. I don't want to know. I don't really care where you're going. The only reason I'm here is to tell you that the FBI is looking for you. They want me to go to their office and answer questions about you."

"And what will you tell them?"

"I don't know. I don't know what the hell you did and it's none of my business. If they want you that badly they can find you themselves. I want nothing to do with this. I just came here to tell you they're looking for you. Okay, I've done that. That's it. I'm finished."

"This is interesting. Now why the big change of heart? Why would you suddenly have concern for my welfare, pray tell?"

I stopped staring into his eyes and looked away. But just for a second. "I talked to Melissa. I had some stuff wrong..."

"And you just realized that? Amazing. Your mental prowess is breathtaking. Do you think this will square us up?" He threw his big head back and barked out a laugh. Once again I wanted to throw my feeble little fist into his big strong jaw, but I knew how that would end.

"I just want one thing from you. Where is Melissa?" He didn't answer me. "If you won't tell me where she is, give her a message for me. Just tell her..." I couldn't say it. I wouldn't be able to look at the smirk on his face. "Tell her goodbye."

"I am not your message boy. Tell her yourself." He turned toward the blue car with the Illinois license plate. "Melissa!" he commanded.

I looked through the rear window of the Impala as someone sat upright in the passenger seat, a mass of chestnut hair. There she was. She had been hiding from me. A shiver passed over me. *She had been hiding from me.*

I walked to the door. She didn't open it, or even look at me. Her expression was as rigid as if carved from granite. Each second that passed ripped away memories like a roaring chainsaw. I delivered my message, but it had changed. Maybe I said, "You have no idea how much you meant to me." Or maybe I just thought that, I can't remember. Maybe I said nothing. The details of those few seconds are pretty murky. My eyes burned. I remember that much.

Clarence closed the trunk of the old Chevy then climbed into the driver's seat and pulled the door shut. But there was one more thing I had to tell him—something important. "Hey, Clarence," I yelled. "What happened to that crap about how your woman will always be a soul sister? Did you forget that?"

He turned to me and smiled. "I changed my mind."

My stomach contracted as if I had just been shot. I whipped my head around so they couldn't see me throw up. Then I just stood there, wiping my mouth as Clarence drove away as slowly and carefully as if he was taking his frigging driver's test.

Chapter 78

Poof, they were gone. Both of them. Both at once. What just happened?

I had spent the whole year building an enormous mansion of bricks and stones and wood, had carried each piece by myself and nailed it into place until a huge building stood on a massive hillside, all of my own making. A building that I had worked on every day, all day long. Then, in one quick moment, an earthquake had swept it off the cliff, turning it into a pile of broken rubble, tumbling it into the ocean where it was washed away by a single wave. That's what it felt like. The vast mansion that was Melissa Kolaski was now a vacant lot. Barely a trace remained. A few bricks, some shingles. That was it.

I should have been devastated. I wanted to stop and sit down and just cry. Like a crybaby. I didn't care, no one could see me. I tried to do just that. But nothing happened. I couldn't cry.

Why not? Just a few minutes before, I had wanted to—maybe I even did—now, when nobody was looking, when I could just let it rip, I couldn't do it. Something had changed. Something big was missing, and in its place, something had been added. I knew what that was because I had felt it before. Anger. There was more than that. I had been *betrayed*. Melissa was hiding from me. I couldn't believe it. I could hear the blood pulsing in my ears. I could not remember another time when I was this furious.

Had I really spent...not spent, *wasted!* my whole first year at college searching for her—as if she alone possessed the secret to my happiness? Yes. How do you recover from that? This was big, big enough to take me down. I couldn't allow that. What would my father think of this? He'd kick my ass. He'd point to my crotch and shrug. "Whatever happened to the cogliones?"

◆

I jammed my hands into my pockets and began the long stomp up the hill to Collegetown. My pockets were stuffed with pieces of paper, Reminders of unfinished business, souvenirs of my long journey from September to June, a trip I wouldn't wish on anybody.

I found the crumpled business card from Agent William McKelvey. Oh, yeah. That asshole. I couldn't wait to talk to him. "Hey, Agent McKelvey," I said aloud to no one, "Guess what? My memory came back! Yeah, I'm as shocked as you are. Anyway. Mr. Clarence lives at the Afro American Co-op on Cayuga Avenue. Yeah. Pay him a visit. See if you can find any trace of him other than a can of Mountain Dew and a shirt with a red fist stenciled on the back. The extra, extra large one. Good luck."

The next piece of paper was another I-O-U, for $20, which I had promised to sign and return to Bob. Bob collected IOUs from me like I collected cigarettes from him. Twenty bucks was exactly how much I expected to receive tomorrow, in the mail, from my mom. Tomorrow would be my birthday. Oh, yeah. Big deal. Happy frigging birthday, Tony. Ain't it great to grow up?

And the third paper was, what? I couldn't remember. I fished it out and looked at it. It was neatly folded, and in a graceful handwriting read, "Tony. Open in case of emergency." Oh my God! *It was Barbara Powell's phone number.* She had given it to me at Bud's diner last night, when I got back from the bathroom. I had forgotten about it. Now I finally had a chance to read it. "Barbara's Rescue Service, Open 24 hours." Had I needed rescuing? That seemed so long ago, and it was just yesterday. Maybe I should call her. Was this another emergency? Hell, yeah, it was.

By the time I climbed the rickety stairs to the crappy apartment over the Royal Palm, I had crashed. A dozen cups of coffee had fueled me through an all-nighter boxing match—with me as the main attraction. Me versus an endless tag team of big, ugly dudes who hit like jackhammers. Each guy had stepped into the ring, pounded the snot out of me then slipped away before I could deliver my famous right hook, or whatever secret weapon had kept me alive this long.

Steve let me in. I hadn't even had a chance to get a key. There, on the little table we had made from a cinder block and Bob's Animal Husbandry textbook sat something I hadn't seen since I left home. A black telephone. Not a cursed *pay* phone, but a real phone you could just pick up and dial without scrounging for coins. This was a phone like my parents had!

"The telephone guy just left," said Steve. "Pretty neat, huh? I ordered it just before we moved. It works! We have a phone number and everything. Now we can order pizza delivery! We don't have to walk all the way downstairs!"

"*You* ordered a phone? Whose name is on the bill?"

"Yours, of course. And Bob's and Gordon's. I don't exist, remember?"

We had a phone! I didn't have to wait in line for the pay phone, didn't have to ransack my pockets for enough change! A telephone was the height of luxury. I had missed it for the whole first school year and now I had my own phone to use whenever I wanted. I didn't know if I should yell at Steve or kiss him. No, definitely not kiss him. I should call someone!

There was, in fact, a call I had to make. I pulled out the piece of paper with Barbara's number on it, picked up the brand-new telephone receiver and dialed my very first phone call on it. I got so excited I couldn't make my fingers stab the right holes on the dial. It took two tries before the call went through. I waited...after four rings an unfamiliar voice picked up... probably a student intern, answering her phone. "Miss Powell isn't here right now," she said, as if her next act was to fall into a deep and dreamless sleep. "But I can take a message."

I wasn't ready with a message and I was nervous enough already. I stammered through, "Yeah, uh, tell her, um, 'hi'...And also, I just wanted to say...thanks, I guess...I had a rough morning, that's why I sound like this." I waited for a response, but heard nothing. Maybe the girl on the other end had passed out from boredom. "No, don't write that down," I rambled on, "just tell her that I had to go downtown. I had to see Clarence. Did I tell you about Clarence? I mean Barbara, not you...anyway..."

"Hold on," came the voice. "I can't write that fast. How do you spell 'Clarence?'

"C...L...A"

"Did you say C or Z? Wait, let me read that back to you. Who is this, anyway, She's gonna ask me."

"Never mind. Just tell her Tony called. That's T...O—"

"I know how to spell Tony."

Of course you do. After all, *you go to Cornell, right?* I read the number off the little round piece of cardboard in the middle of the dial and hung up. Then I fell in a heap on my pile of cardboard, in the middle of the afternoon, and zoned out.

I remember my dream. I was about to eat a charcoal broiled porterhouse steak. Even as I slept, I knew it was a dream. I hadn't seen or eaten or even smelled a piece of steak since I had arrived at Ithaca. The cafeteria's version of steak resembled hamburger, but tougher, with a thick gravy that can only be described as "brown." I gradually opened my eyes. Sleeping on a piece of cardboard is like being squashed into the pavement by a steamroller. But I could smell an actual piece of beef being cooked. I had to search for a childhood memory to confirm the smell. It had been that long since I had eaten a real steak.

I had been asleep for just a few hours. Here's my advice to anyone looking for a good night's sleep: one, don't drink a dozen cups of coffee, and two, don't snuggle up on a pile of flat cardboard boxes. They are nowhere near as comfy as they look.

How much of yesterday had really happened? Please God, not all of it. I dragged myself off the cardboard and used my only piece of furniture—a chair left behind by the previous tenants—to hoist myself up to a standing position. Everything ached. I followed the aroma to its source, the small wooden porch off the kitchen, above the street.

Gordon, Steve and Country Bob stood on the porch tending a tiny Japanese hibachi grill, about the size of my despised *First Year French* book. A one inch thick piece of chuck steak, slightly bigger than the grill, sizzled over the coals. Four baked potatoes, wrapped in foil, lay on a plate, covered with a towel, and the smell of burned potato skin mixed with the smell of char-broiled beef. It was just about the best smell ever.

"Please," I begged, "tell me some of that is for me."

"It's Sleeping Beauty!" said Gordon, waving a barbecue fork like a magic wand. "Yes! You get a piece of steak! You also get a beer! You also get a bill for twenty bucks for your share of the food and the barbecue grill and the beer and everything else we bought! I hope your mom doesn't forget your birthday is tomorrow, Tony, because that's when you run out of credit! Now you owe both Bob and me a twenty."

"And me, don't forget," said Steve the Freak, "Your insurance company denied the claim."

"We also got you a mattress, my boy," said Bob. "A brand new, gently used, mattress that the frat house where I work threw out. I got four of them. We decided to let you sleep—You look like hell, incidentally. They're a little stained. Also, a little aromatic."

"Yeah," Steve said. "Just a little."

"Yours is down there." Bob pointed down to the sidewalk. A narrow and steep stairway separated me from my very own mattress. "All you have to do is bring it upstairs. Such a deal."

"So, Tony," said Gordon. "What happened? Did you see Clarence? Was Melissa there? Tell us!" That stuff all felt like it happened a thousand years ago.

"Yeah. They were there. I saw them."

"Well, tell us what happened!" yelled Bob.

I would not be dragged through this again. Storytime was over. I'd just tell them the truth. But not now. Now, I would eat my steak, drink a beer, call Barbara again, and then I would pull my very own mattress up the stairs, throw myself on it, and sleep like a dead man until my birthday money arrived.

Chapter 79

"Happy birthday, Tony. Get up." I yawned, forced my eyes open and stared up at Bob. I sat up on my new, used mattress. It was lumpy and smelled like it had been pulled out of the lion cage at the zoo, but it was a big improvement over the flattened boxes. A cat. They must have had a cat. Maybe twenty cats. I used to *like* cats. I already longed for the luxury of McFadden Hall.

"So where's the dough? Did your mom stiff you or did you spend the money already?"

"What time does the mail come?"

"Ten o'clock."

"So maybe by ten o'clock I'll be twenty dollars richer."

"And maybe by five after ten you'll be flat broke again."

If my mom had been in charge of the card and the twenty bucks, I would have gotten it a week before my birthday; she didn't like to put stuff off. But today was my actual, for-real birthday, and I had not gotten the card and the twenty yet. That could only mean one thing. My dad was taking care of it. He did things in a precise way, and to my dad, birthday cards are supposed to arrive on your birthday.

The whole idea of hearing from my dad made me nervous. He had not called or written since the LIFE magazine came out. He had seen my dorm room with the radical posters and the Mr. Natural comics and all the commie pinko faggot signs. He'd even seen Steve, an actual real-life commie pinko faggot! What could he possibly think of me? Had he seen the bong? The whole room had smelled of pot. He had to know. I had no idea of where I stood, only that he had gone out of his way to avoid me.

The birthday card arrived right on schedule. The square envelope, addressed in my dad's careful and precise handwriting, could only be a birthday card. It was the first piece of mail any of us had received. I had made real sure my parents had my new address so I wouldn't miss it. I didn't want a card with cash money sitting in the Ithaca dead letter office. I ignored the sappy sentiment on the face of the greeting card and flipped it open, expecting to see a twenty dollar bill and a line or two of some irrelevant message. He'd be good for "Happy birthday," or something just as eloquent and sentimental.

But there wasn't a twenty. Inside were three folded bills. They looked like play money; they were blue and not that beautiful green I knew and loved. Then I saw the extra zeros. He had sent three, one hundred dollar American Express Travelers checks. This was a small fortune.

Had my father lost his mind? I pulled them from the card and saw what he had written—in pencil, always in pencil—under them. Two words. Not "Happy birthday," but "Call me."

Suddenly I had a quick blast of panic. Was he trying to pay me off? Clear his conscience about not ever seeing me again? Didn't my mom have any say in this? Did she beg him to give me another chance? Should I take the money and run, or call him and hear about all the things I did to disappoint him? I stared at the contents of the card and then, without saying a word, I held the bills out to show Steve.

He whistled softly. "Take the money and run, Tony."

Chapter 80

If my father was about to toss me out of family, I wanted to know right away. Whatever happened, I would be okay. If I could survive the clobbering I had taken the last few days I could live through anything. And now I had a phone; I might as well use it. I dialed the 516 area code and watched the dial spin back to the starting point with each stroke, clicking all the way. I hated calling my father. I could never predict his mood. Happy, sad, angry, furious, I never had any idea of what awaited me. But my mother answered the phone, which I didn't expect. She never picked up if my dad was home. She sounded nervous and worried.

"Mom, what's wrong? Dad asked me to call him."

"He won't come to the phone right now, Tony. He doesn't...feel well. He asked me to talk to you." I knew that a call from me wasn't always the highlight of her week—or month—but she usually sounded at least happy to hear from me. But not now.

"What's wrong, Mom? I can hear it in your voice. Why doesn't Dad want to talk to me? He can't even say, "Happy birthday?" This could mean only one thing. I was getting the boot. I'd be on my own. No family, no money, no way to pay for school. It would be a bitch, but I would make it.

Then my mother said, "He hasn't spoken to anyone for the last two weeks, Tony."

"Is he sick? What happened?"

"Do you remember your friend Jerry Harrison from high school?"

271

"Sure. Dad told me he was in communications school in the army. They were going to make him a non-com, whatever that is."

"That's right. Jerry's father worked with Lou at the Can Company. They've been friends for years. Well..." she paused for what felt like a half hour. Her voice was shaking when she started again. "Jerry didn't make it."

Maybe he didn't make it through the training. Maybe she meant something, anything, other than what I knew she meant. "Like, what didn't he make? What does that mean, Mom?"

"Just what you think it does, Tony. He didn't make it. He was killed in Vietnam. Jerry's dead."

My mind emptied of everything I wanted to say. I took a long breath and tried to think of a better reply than, "Shit." I knew this would happen eventually. Tens of thousands of kids had been killed. I knew that sooner or later one of them would be a friend of mine. It hit me hard and out of nowhere, like a rattlesnake.

"They were supposed to give him a desk job!" I shouted it, as if I had just remembered an injustice that could be righted, and this whole thing could be instantly reversed if only someone knew that. "That's why he enlisted! He wasn't supposed to be in combat!"

"Well, he was, Tony. He wasn't there a week. Your father took it very badly, as if Jerry had been his own son. Now he's terrified of what could happen to you. He wants you to come home. Dad has changed, Tony. When he came back from his trip to Ithaca, when he got hosed and tear gassed...and then he talked to your roommates all night...now this. He's a different man. I'm very worried about him. I tried to get him to talk to Father Nelson, but he won't go. He won't talk to anyone. I've never seen him like this. I wasn't aware that he even knew Jerry that well."

"How are Jerry's mom and dad?" It was all I could think of saying.

"Not good. Bad. They're in bad shape. Dad wants you to come home."

"I can't come home. I'm still a student. I didn't flunk out, Mom. I've got to go to classes in the fall. I have to finish college. That's what Dad wants. Tell him not to worry."

"Just come for a visit. He wants to tell you something. He said he wants to tell you he loves you." I heard what she said, but my breathing was shallow and fast. It took me a few seconds before I could reply.

"He doesn't have to tell me that. I know that... I know he loves me, Mom."

"He's not sure that you do. He wants to tell you to your face...to make sure you understand that. He can't remember...ever... telling you that. He asked me to tell you something about the money he sent you."

"That was a fortune. He shouldn't have done that."

"He took early retirement from the Can Company. He begged them. He started talking about retiring as soon as he got back from Ithaca, Tony. He said he was sick of the whole thing...sick of working, sick of...pretty much everything. This all happened so quickly. I don't know what I'm going to do with him. He just stares at the TV all day."

"What did he want to tell me about the money, Mom?"

"Your roommates told him about what happened to your guitar. He said to tell you to go buy another one. Buy a good one this time, Tony. Get something you can tune."

Chapter 81

Back in the dorm, Steve had always eavesdropped on my phone calls. But he quietly crept out of the room as soon as he heard the sound of my voice, saw the look on my face. I sat and stared at the telephone long after I hung up.

Jerry Harrison was dead. This was the first of my friends—people who I knew well, whose face and voice and jokes I could see and hear in my mind—the first to die, the first kid I knew I would never see again. For some reason I felt guilty, as if I had gotten all the breaks and Jerry had just gotten a frigging bullet in his head. I was sick of people saying stupid shit like "Who said life was fair?"

Okay. Life isn't fair, I got that. But why did I grow up thinking that it was?

Jerry was the kid who was always up for a game of army. We played it in the sand lot at the end of the block. He had an old Daisy BB gun for a rifle. I used my dad's M-1. It was a real rifle but my dad kept the bullets and the firing pin locked away. Chunks of dirt were our hand grenades. We called them dirt bombs. We fought on the honor system. We yelled *POW!* with each imaginary shot, and "Got you!" whenever our opponent was caught in the cross hairs. Jerry never cheated. When you shot him, fair and square, he fell. Then he got up and did it again. But not this time.

Next to the black telephone were the three blue travelers checks. I stared at them until my eyes watered. I finally picked them up and walked to the bank. I hadn't had a drink, and it was only ten thirty in the morning, but my stomach was twisting and churning like I had just been thrown out of all the bars in Collegetown.

Maybe it was all his own fault. He *wanted* to be in the army. But what happened to his desk job? Did they *lie* to him? Would they do that? I knew Jerry's mom and dad. No one was as proud of their kid as Mr. and Mrs. Harrison. He was like a god to them. Will I have to stand there and watch his mom and dad bury him? Maybe the funeral was over and done with. I hoped so. I wasn't sure I had the cogliones for it. How many other friends are dead or wounded that I don't know about? Why am I the lucky one? What did I do to deserve that? Nothing.

It took me over an hour to carry the travelers checks to the bank, which was only a few hundred yards away. I made a detour through the tiny park that overlooked Cascadilla Gorge and sat on the concrete park bench. I stared at the water rushing though the creek. A ton of memories rolled through my brain, flashing on all the stupid stuff Jerry and I did together. Seventh grade, eighth grade. The junior class trip to the City, the shirts and skins basketball games in gym class, stealing cigarettes from his sister. The stink bombs we made in chemistry. And catching Jerry in the sight of my dad's M-1 as his head popped out of the bushes, and me yelling POW! And Jerry falling, yelling "You got me!" That one I couldn't get out of my head.

Finally I stood up. My back ached and I felt stiff all over. I dragged myself out of the park, with my hand jammed into my pocket, touching the three travelers checks—probably more money than Jerry had ever seen in one place. I had to get to the bank before it closed. What time was it? Banks closed at noon on Saturday in Ithaca. I had no idea what time it was. It could have been any time at all.

Chapter 82

But it was my birthday. I was still in school. I had a place to live. I had money for the first time in a year. I had the number for Barbara's Rescue Service, which was as good as a *Get out of jail free* card. Probably better. And I had an instruction from my father to do something I was actually able to carry out. The scale wasn't balanced, but I had to keep going. My mom and dad would want me to do that. Jerry would have wanted me to do that.

❖

For the first time, my wallet felt healthy and well fed and ready for the workout I was about to give it. The boys hit me hard. It turned out that Bob and Gordon had kept careful records of all my IOUs for beer and cigarettes and all the times I was supposed to chip in for gas. They hit me up for a quick sixty bucks. Even Steve expected payment for my doctor visit, which I had the good sense to ignore. Hell, all doctors have to do free clinic work, right? If he ever hit the lottery, the three of us were going to attack him like a school of starving piranha.

Bob drove me to the Cayuga Beverage Center to pick up a quarter keg. I had to buy the beer for my own birthday party. Things could be worse; at least I could afford it. In fact, I was loaded, at least for the time being. Genny Cream Ale, the cheapest they had, cost fourteen bucks for a quarter keg, plus a twelve dollar deposit on the keg. That added up to a quick eighty six bucks that vanished in just a few minutes.

If I didn't buy a new guitar pretty damn soon I'd wind up with another Stella.

The guy who ran the Ithaca Guitar Works, just around the corner from the apartment, had Martin and Gibson and Harmony guitars and a few I hadn't heard of. I got lock jaw just looking at the price of the Martin twelve-string. Three hundred bucks wouldn't touch it. You had to already be famous to afford a guitar like that. Famous guys already had good guitars. I'd have to set my sights a little lower.

Eric was the name of the guy who ran the store. He knew me well. I had come in every few days, for weeks, ever since I stepped on the guitar my parents gave me. I'd spend a half hour farting around with all the instruments, starting with the most expensive, picking them up, playing the first few bars of *Blackbird*. That tune is a bitch; and my version of it was what you might call 'free form.' The only person who knew I was playing an actual song was me. Then I'd set the guitar back in the stand and pick up another. I never even bought a pick (three for a quarter) because I no longer had a guitar of my own. My guess was that Eric was pretty sick of seeing me.

"What's the best guitar for about a hundred bucks?" I called to him from across the store.

"If I tell you, what are the chances of you actually buying something for once?" I was waiting for this. I pulled the remaining wad of bills from my pocket.

"Depends," I said, waving the roll around in the air as if I was hailing a cab, something which I had never actually done, but I had seen plenty of other people do. "Are you ready to deal?"

A half hour later I carefully hoisted my brand new Yamaha FG-180 series, dreadnought style, six string acoustic guitar with real Grover tuners and a two piece back, a pearl inlaid neck and light gauge bronze steel strings. The case was real wood—not cardboard, and covered with some kind of fake alligator hide. The inside was plush red velvet. The Japanese guitar was a dead ringer for a Martin D-35, the guitar of my dreams. Then I gathered up a capo, a pack of picks, a harmonica-looking thing that made six notes, one at a time, so you could tune, and a bottle of guitar polish. I set my booty on the counter while Eric tallied up my bill on a piece of paper. The whole thing cost a hundred thirty-five bucks, which I peeled off my roll, one bill at a time, snapping each of them like I spent that kind of dough every day. Eric tuned it for me—perfectly, on the first try—and it stayed that way. It sounded like heaven.

"I kind of wanted a twelve-string," I said as I packed up to leave.

"Nah," said Eric, "You don't want a twelve-string. You won't be able to tune it."

Chapter 83

I carried my purchases back to the apartment, lost in space and time. It didn't make sense: Jerry was dead and I had a new guitar. I didn't play well enough to deserve it. Maybe I would never be able to play it well enough. It might be a long time before I played it.

These thoughts ran round and round in my brain until Steve said, "Your girlfriend called." The odd arrangement of the three words, "your," "girlfriend" and "called" kicked me in the head. As far as I could remember, no one had ever said those words to me, in that order, ever before. This was all new. Especially the word "girlfriend."

"I have a girlfriend? Who was it? What's her name?"

"Barbara. Isn't that your girlfriend?"

"Did she say she was my girlfriend?" Steve stuck out his lower lip and shrugged, which meant either "I wasn't paying attention" or "I'm making all this up."

I went on. "I guess my message got through. I had some problems with the phone."

"Yeah. I know what you mean. Phones are really complicated and hard to work. Anyway, she's coming to your birthday party. I invited her."

"Does she know all we're going to do is drink beer and sit on the porch?"

"Yeah. But she thinks we ought to bring the keg down to the bottom of Fall Creek Gorge and go skinny dipping. Me and Gordon and Bob think that's a much better idea. We voted and now it's a plan.

Also, since you're the birthday boy, you get to carry the keg."

Steve was wrong on both counts. I wouldn't be carrying a full quarter keg of beer down into the gorge and then haul the empty barrel back up. In fact, I had refused to even carry it up the stairs to the porch. I had used the time honored excuse that everyone understood: I paid for it. Steve carried it because he never paid for anything. I thought it was going to kill him. I wasn't getting naked for this group either, even though I seriously wanted to see Barbara dressed for skinny dipping. But I didn't want to share the view with the guys. I had seen as much of their bare asses as I cared to, and it wasn't pretty. As for Barbara, I was saving myself for a date, as unlikely as that was.

"What a load of crap," I told him.

"Well, yeah. But part of what I said is true."

"Which part?"

"Barbara's coming to your party. I think you're supposed to be happy about that."

I did the honors precisely at six PM, which is what the invitations would have said if we had them. The boys clapped as soon as the fresh keg made that wonderful hissing sound. Foam belched from the tap and filled four big red plastic cups before good, clean, life-restoring beer flowed. Bob, Gordon and Steve crowded me, holding out their cups, waving them back and forth like a nest of baby birds with big red beaks, wide open. Bob's stereo speakers competed with the jukebox downstairs, and *Born to be Wild* shook the rickety porch.

There would be no gut-wrenching Dylan songs tonight. Not on my damned birthday. I thought of the bell in the clock tower. I was now as old as I had ever been, and as young as I'll ever be. We would not play sad songs on my birthday.

"So what does she look like?" asked Bob.

"You'll see her, if she actually shows up. And, no, she doesn't have a sister."

"She'd better hurry," said Steve, "if she wants a beer. This won't take long. It's only a quarter keg. You cheapskate."

"Melissa's a tough act to follow," said Bob.

"Melissa who?" I asked, practicing. This was going to be tough. I watched my red party cup fill up with beer and said to myself, *Melissa's not here. Melissa's not coming. Melissa is gone.*

A voice called up from the street. "Is this the residence of the famous birthday boy?" Bob, Gordon and Steve stared at the newcomer, already heading up the porch stairs.

"Holy crap," said Bob. "Is that Barbara? She'll *do*, Tony. Very *nice*."

She had no trouble finding the place. Bob could have told one of the foreign students, a fresh arrival from a country with an unpronounceable name, a stranger who didn't speak any language that had vowels in it, that we lived over the Royal Palm bar and that guy would have found us instantly.

She pranced up the stairs for all the world to see. She looked so different from Melissa I had to remind myself they were the same genus and species. Tall, blond, slender, with the biggest smile in all of Ithaca, she looked like she was on her way to a party—mine. In her hands was a small wrapped package, tied with a bow. A birthday present, I guessed. What else could it be? How did she have time to get me a birthday present?

Chapter 84

What would we have done without her? What a bleak group we would have made. If I had lit up a box of sparklers and Roman candles, I could not have kick-started the party like she did the instant her high-heeled sandals, laced all the way up her long legs, touched the last step. Her white cut-offs stopped above her knee…way, way above. A picture of Mona Lisa was silk- screened across the front of her spotless white shirt. Not a stray drop of paint anywhere. The shirt fell off her left shoulder as if the neck hole was too big and the shirt didn't quite fit, which was just fine with me. Her left shoulder was bare. I didn't see a bra strap. But why Mona Lisa? Of course. Barbara was an artist.

Old Mona's famous smile looked unconvincing sitting right below Barbara's own. There was nothing enigmatic about the expression on my guest's face. She was happy. No question about it. She blazed like a lighthouse, and the guys scrambled to be included in the beam. The party of four had became a party of five. It felt like five hundred.

"If she doesn't work out," Gordon said into my ear, "give me her phone number, okay?"

Three other guys we didn't know, guys who hung out at the Palm, had watched us tap the keg. I thought they'd crash the party, helping themselves to the beer, but they kept walking. When they saw Barbara, they were back in a flash, up the stairs, and instantly became my best friends. Everybody talked and laughed and joked—almost exclusively with my radiant guest; I could have left anytime and would not have been missed.

The party had six people too many. Maybe if the six guys were pushed together on the edge of the balcony, that whole side of the rickety old porch would collapse into the street, leaving me, Barbara and the keg. Would that work? But they were all clustered around her. I'd have to somehow separate her from the crowd...but then they'd follow her...and maybe the whole damn porch would collapse along with the two of us. Maybe I could poison the potato chips? No, they'd notice the taste. How could I get rid of these guys and still keep Barbara? There was no practical solution that wouldn't involve a jail sentence. The words to a Calypso song came to me: *If you want to be happy for the rest of your life, never make a pretty woman your wife...*

Steve saved my ass and prevented a sixtuple homicide. He called out that one infamous word...the word that was universally feared and dreaded at beer parties everywhere. Good old Freak.

"Foam," he announced as the keg sputtered and farted the last few drops into his cup.

He might as well have said, "Everyone get out of here! There's a bomb in the barbecue grill!" The six guys instantly looked at me and assessed my plans for the evening, then everyone turned and beat feet down the stairs with barely a "Thanks and good bye." The three guys we didn't know were at least polite, and said "Happy birthday," each calling me by a different name.

The last remnants of the sunny afternoon were disappearing behind the buildings across the street. Eight people had finished a quarter keg of beer in just under an hour, which was probably a record. If Barbara hadn't been there to slow us down, I'd have guessed maybe ten or twelve minutes.

I carried a half-melted, thick candle in a pickle jar lid from the kitchen table and set it down on the milk crate we had been using for a table.

"Happy birthday, Tony," Barbara said. She looked around as if searching for missing people, then stuck out her lower lip and made a sad face. "Aw, gee. It's too bad all your guests had to leave, huh? I was looking forward to talking to them all night." She grinned. Then she picked up the wrapped package and, holding it with two hands, presented it to me. "Happy Birthday," she said. "Congratulations. Our age difference is now officially insignificant. That makes me fair game...just so you know."

"You didn't have to buy me a present," I said, which was what my mom had told me to say whenever anyone gave me a present.

"I didn't buy it. I made it. Open it up."

I tore the paper off the package. Inside was a wooden picture frame which still had the tag from Woolworth's on the back. I think I had the same expression as she did when she shredded the paper covering my Cubist guitar—anticipation, curiosity, delight. Then I saw the drawing. I didn't know whether to laugh or cry. But a big belt of some emotion—one of those—rushed through me as I stared, stunned, at the drawing.

The suspension bridge, high over the waterfall. It looked just like the one in my memory, the image I will never get out of my skull. Balanced on the very top of the fence was Humpty Dumpty, holding onto one of the cables. He had a big smile on his face, which was most of him. The whole drawing was done in black charcoal pencil, except for Humpty. He had bold stripes in colored paint—purple, brown, maroon—across his shell. He had black, curly hair and glasses. He looked just like me, if I had been born a big colored Easter egg with bad vision.

"I want you to hang it in your bedroom and look at it every day. I don't want you to ever forget that. Can you do that?"

"Absolutely," I said quietly.

"Do you like it?"

"I do," I said, remembering her precise words when she saw the guitar. "I love it."

"Do I get an A?"

"Absolutely. Boy, do you get an A."

Then she hugged me and kissed me on the cheek. The hug lasted just a little longer than I thought it would. She was warm and taut and her perfume was just barely perceptible, like riding a bike past a flower garden.

Chapter 85

The keg was dry but the party hadn't ended. Barbara settled into one of the lawn chairs and made a long exaggerated sigh, as if she was settling in, maybe for the evening. Could the party just be getting started?

Could it be this easy? Nothing was ever this easy for me. I hardly knew her! I dated Melissa for months…and still I screwed it up.

"Did you get anything except a keg of beer for your birthday?" she asked when her sigh had finally faded.

"And the painting? I got a beautiful original painting too, don't forget."

"Yes, you did. Is that it?"

"My parents sent me some money. I bought a new guitar."

"Do you play?" Doesn't she know what a lousy musician I am? I felt like I had known her a long time, that she was an old friend. But we had barely talked enough to get even this far. She knew next to nothing about me. I guess that was a good thing. She doesn't know what a jerk I could be. I could start fresh. What an opportunity! But how should I answer that? How do I play?

"Badly," I said.

"Do you sing too?"

"Worse."

"Are you being modest?"

"Honest."

"I'd love to hear you. Play me a song?" This was a surprise. Almost no one ever asked me to play. People who had no idea whether I was a klutz or another Eric Clapton somehow instinctively knew: *Beware. This guy sucks.* But I wasn't in the mood. There were bad memories hiding in that guitar. I had just gotten it and I already knew I might never play it. Playing guitar might be something that I *used* to do but didn't do anymore, like playing army or drinking Saturday night specials at the old man's bar.

"Maybe later," I said. *Maybe never.* "Let's talk. Besides, all the songs I know are sad. I don't want to be sad tonight."

"I don't want to be sad any night," she said.

"Tonight's different. I don't want to get any sadder than I already am. I got some bad news today. A friend of mine got killed in Vietnam." I hadn't mentioned this to anyone. Not even the guys.

The shock and sorrow on her face were genuine. She stepped toward me and picked up my hand in both of hers and squeezed it. "Oh my God. I am so sorry. That's horrible. This world is insane. Are you okay?"

Was I? Everything was so damned complicated. I could feel the heat from her body. Her eyes were wide and blue. In the evening light the pupils were huge and dark, and I stared into them. "Playing sad songs will just make me sadder. I'm okay, really."

"No bridge tonight?"

"No bridge. Ever. I have a painting. That's all the bridge I need." She sat back in the lawn chair.

"Some of my paintings are sad," she said. "I go through a lot of purple and brown and maroon paint. I'm not exactly over my own last trip to the Unmuzzled Ox."

"Is that the one where you sat in the very back?"

"That's the one. I still have a touch of the flu from that one."

"What was his name?"

"Paul. He's gone. I don't mean gone, gone. He's just not in my life anymore. He dropped out of school and just took off. He did plenty of damage on the way out. This was two years ago."

"What was he like?"

"What was he like...hmm. Good old Paul...I guess you could say he's practically perfect in every way. Tall, dark and handsome. An Adonis. Perfect body. Unbelievable in bed. Funny. Sensitive. Rich. Every woman's dream."

"A lot like me, then."

"Not even a little like you." She grinned. "That's not even a little like him either. I made that up. Oh, he wasn't bad looking. Not great, but good enough for us po' folk. That was never the problem. He was an artist. Another painter. A brilliant one. He has a short list of stuff that's wonderful about him and a long list of stuff that's not."

"Sounds like a normal guy. That sounds like every guy I know."

"When I was with him I thought I could get away with anything. I could think or feel or do anything at all and it would be okay. I felt free around him. Artists love people like that. We swarm around them like bugs. It doesn't matter what kind of artist, either. Painters, writers, actors, musicians; we all love someone who is bright and shiny and unusual. We want to pick those guys up like loose change before anybody else can get to them. The brighter and shinier they are, the more issues they have. Paul had more issues than the *New York Times.*"

"Like what?"

"He had a big problem with telling the truth. And cheating. He'd cheat on me with girls that most guys wouldn't cross the street for. He treated it like some sort of competitive sport. I wasted a year on him."

"But you still love him?"

"I hope not. Maybe I do. God knows why. But here's the scary thing. If he walked in here right now I'd figure out a way to go home with him. Screwed up, right? He has some kind of mysterious, horrible power over me. Do you know what that's like? When someone else has that kind of power over you?"

I knew just what that felt like.

"Maybe we could set him up with Melissa. Maybe we could sit back and watch them break each other's hearts." We both smiled, but I took no pleasure in seeing Melissa's heart broken by anyone, for any reason. I never wanted that, not even now.

"After he took off I had three more boyfriends, one right after the other. All catastrophes."

"Why were they catastrophes?" I had never heard of a relationship or a boyfriend referred to as a catastrophe. But that was a great word. I could see how that was a perfect description.

"Because...because Paul was gone but he had never really left. Every new guy who tried to get close to me...I'd just compare each one to good old Paul...I couldn't help it. And each guy, one by one, they figured that out, got tired of it and pretty soon we were having coffee in the back of the Unmuzzled Ox . Then I'd walk home alone again."

It was dark now; the only light came from the big neon palm tree above the bar downstairs. No moon. The porch light didn't work; no surprise there. I found Bob's matches and lit the big candle and sat back down. The little porch glowed with the warm, flickering light. Our voices became softer also, as if we didn't want anyone to listen in. The record player had shut itself off. The street noises below us made us sit very close to each other so we could hear. Now it was my turn.

Chapter 86

"Country Bob once said that I had to get the old cow out of the barn door before I can get a new one into the stall. Or something like that. Actually, I think it was me who said that. Anyway, it was about cows."

"I love the image. My old boyfriend as a cow. I can just see him. A brown cow or a black and white one?"

"A black and white one. It works better if you think of a black and white one." It was an odd thing to say, but it was true. In my mind, the cow was always black and white.

"So did you?" she asked. "Did you get old Bessie out of the doorway?"

"I'm still working on that, I think. She's a big one, old Bessie. Do you agree with that? Someone can't make room for a new person in their life until the old one is gone? Do you think that's how it works?"

She answered right away. "No. Because if that were true, that would mean that you can only love one person at a time. I know for a fact that's not how it works. But here's the thing. It all depends on the cow. Not just any cow can get into the barn." I laughed at the direction this was headed. "Okay, forget the cow. Let's use people. Not just any *person* can squeeze their way into your life and replace the old one. He has to be special," she paused. "*She* has to be special. Sometimes you have to wait. And then you make room for that person. Even if you thought there wasn't any room, you find some. You make a place." She waited for me to speak.

But I didn't say anything. This was a subject that she thought a lot about, wrestled with, over and over. I had just now been tossed into the ring for the first time. I didn't have an answer all ready to go. I had to think...about something I had tried hard *not* to think about.

She said, "I don't want it to be like that, do you? That's not very romantic."

"I wouldn't know," I said. "I'm not very romantic myself." Barbara surprised me by laughing out loud.

"Tony, you are, too, romantic. Most definitely. Don't you know that?"

"Oh, yeah, right. That's me." What the hell was she talking about?

"So what do you think," she pressed me. "Can someone just love only one person at a time?" She waited. Had I? Ever loved more than one person at a time? Not my family...someone else? Did I now? She wanted an answer.

"Sure. I mean, I...God, I hope so. My life is going to be a lonely mess if that's true...No, that can't be true." I stopped to think before I spoke again. *What was I doing?* I had never talked to anyone about stuff like this. Certainly never with Melissa. The beer made my face warm. *Don't say anything stupid. Think.*

What the hell? Go for it. "Some people say that you never run out of love," I began. "That it's a box that can never be filled up. And it can never be emptied. Or, maybe it's not a box. But it's something like that. All we do is just keep putting love in the box and taking it out and giving it away. You never run out. There's always some left or room for more." I looked at her expression to see if that was as stupid as it had sounded. But she nodded for me to go on.

"There are a million sayings about love. Poetry is full of them. Do you read a lot of poetry?" She shook her head. "Well, I do. They make me. Here's the thing. Most poetry is about love. You can find a saying for however you feel. Whatever it is, good or bad, you can find it. Someone wrote a poem about it."

"I've got one for you," she said. "How about this? Anyone can have anyone they want if they only love them enough. What do you think of that?"

"Who said that? Is that really a saying or did you make that up?"

"Both. It's a real saying that I just made up. Do you believe it? Can a person get the one they want if they just love them enough?"

I would have taken a long sip of beer to get some time to think, but my red cup was empty. "I'm not sure. It didn't work for me. But it worked for Melissa. She got the guy she wanted. It took a while but she got him. So I don't know. The rules are pretty confusing."

"There aren't any rules, Tony. All's fair, and all that."

"That's not true. There is absolutely one big rule. One person gets to love. One person gets *to be loved*. That's how it works."

"I hope not. That's too sad. I think *both* people get to be loved. That's the whole point. That's what's so wonderful about it. That's why people do the crazy stuff they do to get it. I think it happens all the time. Like loving more than one person. That happens all the time, too."

"How do you know that someone can love more than one person at a time?" I asked. It was her turn to think before replying. The way she spoke told me she wasn't sure she wanted to talk so much.

"Well...I think maybe I still love Paul...I shouldn't. But maybe I do. But that's okay. I shouldn't have to stop loving him before I can love someone else..." she stopped in midsentence.

"Someone else?" I asked.

"Like you. Maybe I love you, Tony."

Chapter 87

The guy with the black hood had just thrown the switch on the electric chair...the one I was sitting in. But instead of killing me, it sent a giant bolt of *life* through my spine. So that's what that sounds like! I had waited all year for those words and now I was hearing them from a girl—a woman—who I barely knew. For a few seconds nothing made sense, as if the map in front of me had suddenly switched from downtown Ithaca to Tokyo. I felt like someone had written my next lines for me but I hadn't had time to study them. So instead I just said, "Wow."

"I think you weren't ready for that."

"I've been ready for that for a long time."

"But not from me. I guess I blew your mind. Maybe you should just forget I said that."

"That's the best thing anyone has said to me all year. How can I forget that?" *Don't even try to un-ring that bell.* I wanted to jump on the rope and wake up the whole town with it.

"But you're not quite ready. There's still a cow in the doorway, isn't there, Tony? I can't move her. You're right. She's a big one. I can help, but you're going to have to do that yourself."

I could deny it, but why? She'd know, she'd figure it out. She had experience with this exact problem. "How will I know when she's gone, Barbara?"

"Don't worry. You'll know."

She stood up and reached for her book bag. She was getting away!

"Wait, are you leaving? You don't have to leave..."

"Sure I do. Don't panic. I won't be far away. You can't get rid of me that easily. But this is as far as we're going with this right now. Don't lose my number." She leaned over and kissed me on the forehead. That made twice. Once on the forehead, once on the cheek. Then she turned and walked down the narrow stairway as gracefully and quietly as a Siamese cat. Halfway down she stopped and looked up at me.

"Keep me in your pocket. I'll put you in mine. You know, in case something happens. Let's be ready so we don't waste any time. Let's stay close, like in each other's pocket. Things change quickly around here, Tony. You wouldn't believe. Stuff happens just like *that*."

Chapter 88

I didn't see her for a whole week. I called her at her office, I even practiced it this time, something like "Hi! I sure would like to see you again. Maybe we could get together for a glass of wine or I could play you a song." But her office intern answered the phone again and that got shortened to "Call me...it's Tony." But could I? Play her a song? I hadn't picked up the guitar since I had gotten it.

I didn't feel like there was a big urgent deadline to seeing her again. I wasn't really worried about it for some reason. Whatever this was, it didn't feel delicate and frail, it felt solid and strong. This was a new experience. It made me think...*Is this how it's supposed to be? Do people really live their lives like this? Incredible. If I had only known. You'd think they'd teach that in college, but no, you get to figure out all the really important stuff all by yourself.*

I got used to the shabby apartment but not my lumpy mattress. Leaving the window open didn't help. I blew some of what was left of my birthday money on an almost perfect mattress from the Collegetown Thrift Shop. I had a feeling it would come in handy. Little by little the guys and I accumulated cast-off furniture and filled the cupboards with cans of Campbell's soup and boxes of rice and fake macaroni and cheese. I even got the summer job, in the language lab, the easiest job anyone ever had. Every day as I walked across the bridge to campus—instead of climbing that infernal hill—I would see a girl that I thought I knew. But these girls were tall and slender and had blonde hair. I was looking for Barbara. Not out of desperation, I knew I would see her again.

But what would happen when I did? Would I screw it up? I had had enough pain for one lifetime. She said I'd know when I was ready. I knew what I wanted to happen…who wouldn't? But was I ready? That I didn't know.

There was one thing that I had not attempted, I had deliberately avoided. I had to see what would happen, how I would feel. I needed to know. Until I did, my life was stuck, somewhere between 'ready, set" and the word "go" which never came.

———◆———

Today was the day. It was a beautiful Saturday, just like my birthday, when I had received a most valuable and unexpected gift from a girl I barely knew. A day like that.

My new guitar had spent the week in its case, barely touched. Gordon had played it for a minute and pronounced it "far out." I couldn't trust myself to play it. I had been in no hurry to find out of what would happen if I did. But I couldn't put it off any longer. This was something I had to do in private, in a very particular place. I picked up the case by the handle and headed for the door.

Gordon was working on his fifth cup of instant coffee. "Where are you headed?" His pupils were tiny and his hand shook. It would take us weeks to recover from finals.

"Out," I said, as if my mother had asked that question.

"With your guitar? Are you really going to play it?" He could see the determination in my eyes. "Good luck, Tony. You can do it, buddy. We're rooting for you."

The Echo Chamber in Anabel Taylor Hall was just a few blocks away. I almost never went there alone, and I hadn't been there, at all, for months. Melissa and I had sat and played and sang together there so many times…until she tired of me and vanished without a word. The handle on the guitar case felt warm, like the hand of a beautiful girl. Would this one break my heart too?

I pushed on the wrought iron handle and the big oak door creaked as it swung back on its hinges, just like it did when Melissa had found me sitting on the floor playing *Visions of Johanna* on my sixty dollar twelve-string. As soon as I heard the creak I looked around for her. It was a reflex action; I was ready for it. I didn't need to tell myself, "Melissa's not here." The smell of the coffeehouse down the hall hit me with aromas of cinnamon and espresso and chocolate, and swept me away like a time machine, carrying me back to that October night. But I was not here for coffee.

I sat down on the cold floor and unsnapped the case on my Yamaha six string, a guitar with the lines and the sound of a Martin D-35, which no kid my age could afford. I lifted the maple and rosewood creation from the deep, velvet lined case. There wasn't a scratch on it, not even on the pick guard. The strings, light gauge bronze Martins, still sparkled; they had yet to vibrate in song themselves. Today was their day too.

I was alone in the marble and granite hall, where every sound echoed and made good players sound fantastic and players like me sound almost good. I hadn't played in months. The calluses on my fingertips were gone, but the strings rang cleanly, without a trace of a buzz. There were no muffled notes, not even the pinky ones. My fingers didn't hurt even after all the time off. I began to play the G chord so softly I wasn't sure I was playing at all. Then louder, the sweet sounds reverberating off the walls. I can get through this, I told myself. Just start singing.

"Ain't it just like the night to play tricks, when you're trying to be so quiet?" My voice cracked, way off key. I grabbed it by the hair and dragged it uphill, into the melody I remembered. I didn't use the songbook. I remembered the words. I don't think I could ever forget them. But then I stopped.

I knew the experiment would fail. Somehow, some part of Melissa was tangled up in some part of me, like tree roots around a chain link fence. Maybe I would never be free. I had my answer. I would put the guitar back in the case and carry it back to the apartment. It might be a long time before I played it again.

Chapter 89

I heard the door creak and I looked up just as I snapped the case shut. I took a short breath when I saw who it was. Barbara walked in. If a bulldozer had just plowed through the front of the building, it wouldn't have let in as much light. "Your roommate told me where to find you," she said. I moved over on the step to make room for her and she sat down. "He told me to come here."

"How did he know? I didn't tell him where I was going."

"He said you took your new guitar, so there was only one place you would be. The Echo Chamber."

"Yeah...well, I'm supposed to be romantic."

"So do you come here often?" A pickup line, the oldest one there is. I grinned.

"I used to. This was where, uh, what's-her-name and I used to come to sing."

"You're out of excuses, you know. I expect a song, Tony. Gordon even told me which one."

"Are you going to sing with me?"

"I'm not much of a singer. I'm a painter. Come on, Tony, I want to hear you play your guitar. Please?"

"So tell me, as if I didn't already know, what song am I supposed to play?" I unsnapped the case and settled the guitar on my right knee. I wasn't through being tortured.

"Gordon says you know some Dylan songs. Do you know *Visions of Johanna?*"

"You want to hear that one? Out of maybe a million Dylan songs you want to hear that one, huh? What a coincidence."

"He said I shouldn't leave until you play it. He said it used to be your favorite song and now you won't play it anymore. That maybe you'd play it I asked you to."

"Yeah, that sounds like something he'd say. Did he tell you *why* I don't play it?"

"He didn't have to. I think I know. Do you want to tell me?"

"It's something I have to figure out by myself."

"Maybe it's something you have to figure out with *me*. I'm just as interested in this as you are. I have a hand in this game, Tony. And I'm all in."

Holy crap! This was a hand I could win! Finally! "If I sing then we both sing. Is that fair?" I didn't care what the answer was.

"Let's do it. But don't laugh." I plucked a few strings, pretending to tune an instrument that I knew was at pitch, perfectly tuned, warmed up, motor purring, my foot over the gas pedal, ready to go. I watched her sort through the pages of chords and lyrics until she found the song.

I stared at her, memorizing the color of her hair, the curve of her neck, the shape of her chin. What a gorgeous creature. Why was she even here? What can she see in me? She actually liked me. I was sure of it. Then I realized something—all at once—like that damn light bulb people always talked about. But this one was brighter than that, it was sudden and blinding like the flashbulb in a reporter's big camera, and I was staring right at it when it went off.

If I let this one get away, I am truly, for damn sure, the dumbest motherfucker on the planet.

I had forgotten about the experiment. I had forgotten why I had even come to the Echo Chamber. The only thing that mattered was this: My purpose in life was clear: God had put me on this Earth to sing with this beautiful woman.

"Okay, I found it," she said. "No laughing. Remember, I'm not exactly known for my vocal talent." I began to play, first the intro, and then the chords to the first verse.

"Ain't it just like the night?" I sang, and Barbara joined in at exactly the point where Melissa had, back in October. But instead of singing like God's personal angel, *she sang worse than I did!* I stopped and laughed.

"Well, you suck too," she said. That was as far as she got before her own laughter. "You're worse than I am."

"Am not!" I laughed. "You're the worst."

"I guess we won't be doing a lot of singing, huh?"

I put down the pick, reached over and took up her hand. I waited a few seconds before I said, "I'm not worried. I'm sure we'll find *something* to do." Her eyes opened wide and her eyebrows shot up. Somewhere, from some unknown place, I had just gotten my very own crystal ball. I knew exactly what the future held and what I had to do.

Now. I pulled her into me and kissed her with all I had. She kissed back like an Olympic competitor going for the gold. Like we had money on it, like we were starving and we were the midnight buffet.

I had to get the damn guitar back in the case before the tuning pegs perforated my chest. I slammed the lid, and took the opportunity to take a deep breath. Barbara watched me, thinking of something appropriate to say. I knew it would be good.

"So tell me, Tony, how's that cow doing? Is she still stuck in the doorway?"

"Cow? What cow?"

She took a deep breath and let it out slowly. She arched her head back and stretched her neck. Then she squeezed her hands together and spoke.

"What happens now?"

Good question, and one that I could answer. She hadn't moved away, she hadn't stood up, and she held her mouth in a certain way, half open, in case I needed it, which I did. It was time to leave the Echo Chamber. It was time for all kinds of stuff.

"We could go back to my apartment," I said. "If you want. It's not too far..." My face was flushed and my hands shook. I closed the latches on the case.

"I've been there. You didn't have a bed."

"I do now." I took the guitar in one hand and Barbara's hand with the other. We pulled open the oak door and headed toward the bridge to Collegetown.

"Tony? I just need to know one thing. It's important," she said.

"Yes?"

"Is *this* a real date?"

"Yes. Absolutely. This is as real as a date can get."

The End

About the author

GINO B. BARDI lives in Hudson, Florida with his wife Patricia, five parakeets and three cockatiels. They have three beautiful daughters. A 1972 graduate of Cornell, he was present and accounted for in every scene in *The Cow in the Doorway*. He swears he made it all up. After forty-four years writing almost everything but fiction, this is his debut novel. He encourages readers to contact him with comments at ginobardi.author@gmail.com. Be nice.

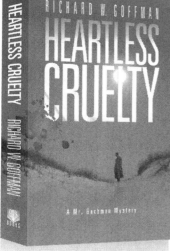

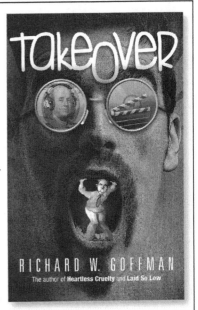

Made in the USA
Middletown, DE
19 April 2016